After the
Cold War

After the Cold War

Essays on the Emerging World Order

Edited by
Keith Philip Lepor

University of Texas Press
Austin

Copyright © 1997 by the University of Texas Press
All rights reserved
Printed in the United States of America
First University of Texas Press edition, 1997

Requests for permission to reproduce
material from this work should be sent to
Permissions, University of Texas Press,
Box 7819, Austin, TX 78713-7819.

⊗ The paper used in this publication meets the
minimum requirements of American National
Standard for Information Sciences — Permanence
of Paper for Printed Library Materials,
ANSI Z39.48-1984.

Library of Congress
Cataloging-in-Publication Data

After the Cold War : essays on the emerging
    world order / edited by Keith Philip Lepor.
        p.   cm.
    Includes bibliographical references.
    ISBN 0-292-74693-8 (cloth : alk. paper)
    1. International relations.   2. World
    politics — 1989–   I. Lepor, Keith
    Philip, 1961–   .
    JX1391.A44   1997
    327 — dc20   96-23670

In memory of

my father Captain Jack Lepor,
my sister Beth Anne, and
my friend and confidant at
Oxford University, Albert Hourani

P76641

Contents

His Excellency

Mikhail Sergeyevich Gorbachev

Former President of the
Union of Soviet Socialist Republics

Foreword

The ongoing discussion of the new situation with which the world has been faced is acquiring fresh urgency. This should not be surprising, for the problems that we inherited from the past have been compounded by the profound changes that have occurred over the past few years. What is more, we are still far from having found, or even sketched out, realistic solutions to those old and new problems. Failure to find such solutions should be of increasing concern, as we watch new developments and fresh problems — often troubling and sometimes of tragic proportions.

This book is a capsule reflection of those daunting problems. It contains thoughts, assessments, and proposals for action coming from persons whose credibility, experience, and record of achievement have made them known throughout the world. For that reason alone, this book deserves close attention and thoughtful reading.

It is not my intention here to characterize or evaluate the various ideas and suggestions contained in the contributions that follow. That, after all, is up to the readers. But there is one point that must be made. This book reflects both the inherent unity and the great and growing diversity of the world community, which is faced with common problems and processes. Hence both the striking similarity in many aspects of the broad view of the past and the future and the equally evident differences in the solutions that are being proposed.

I see nothing tragic in those differences. They are rooted in objective realities. The task, as I see it, is to find a common denominator for the interests that they reflect. If we are to find a way out of the current situation, we must address this task together.

I am convinced that in searching for a way out of the current state of world affairs we should first of all take due account of the lessons of the recent past, when collective efforts put an end to the Cold War. The Cold War ended primarily because of the realization, on both sides of the wall dividing the East and the West, that its continuation would spell death for all. This realization — that change is vitally necessary — played an important and in many ways defining role.

Another essential factor was political will. It, too, was shown by both sides, leading to specific and resolute steps. Even those steps, however, would not have had the desired effect if they had proceeded from the assumptions of a "zero-sum game," with both sides believing that what is good for one of them is thereby bad for the other. A very different approach, one based on a search for a balance of legitimate interests, helped to resolve many issues that seemed beyond solution if viewed from the perspective of the old confrontational mentality.

All this, taken together, made possible — perhaps not always but in most cases — genuinely collective action by the international community, focusing its energies on constructive efforts to come to grips with the most intricate problems of world politics.

This led to effective and mutually acceptable decisions, with a necessary element of compromise, that have changed the world. And, however critical the approach that we may take in analyzing the recent past, a number of positive shifts cannot be denied:

- An end has been put to the confrontation between military alliances.

- International relations have become more democratic and more homogeneous.

- The arms buildup, particularly the nuclear arms race, has been halted and partly reversed.

- The few remaining totalitarian, militaristic regimes are declining.

- A number of regional conflicts have been settled.

The world is not the same as before. International relations have objectively reached a new dimension. Mankind has a new window of opportunity—a new chance for survival. But have we achieved all that we sought? We have not. Indeed, in place of old problems and difficulties we see new, unexpected ones. What we have today can hardly be called a New World Order. So far, it is rather a "world disorder."

Why have things turned out this way? I think that on top of objective difficulties arising from the end of confrontation and the removal of Cold War constraints from problems that were left unsolved for years and even decades, other factors have also played a role.

One of them deserves particular mention here. It is that the international community and the many nations that play an important political role have in effect retreated from the principles that guided their joint efforts to end the Cold War. The lessons of recent history have been largely forgotten.

The instantaneous and large-scale growth of freedom of choice in the post-confrontational period was used, in many cases, not for focusing all efforts on a search for collective solutions but for asserting and demonstrating ethnic and national ambitions, often unrelated to real and legitimate interests. The principle of painstaking search for a balance of interests is, more and more frequently, being forgotten, making fruitful collective efforts impossible.

The future hinges largely on whether new global politics becomes a reality in time to respond to the new challenges of the approaching new millennium. However different and difficult may be the tasks faced today by individual nations, new global policies can be developed—but only if there is agreement on certain essential priorities.

We need to respond to these global challenges:

- the challenge of interdependence;

- the challenge of the nuclear danger;

- the challenge of the environmental crisis;

- the challenge of society's moral decline.

No one will be able to avoid these challenges. But are we capable of responding to them effectively?

The current state of world affairs, and the state of the Earth we inhabit, give no cause for optimism. Our civilization, which has evolved over centuries, is exhausting its vitality. Crises are developing everywhere. The demons of the past and the perils of the future haunt the lives of nations and of the world community.

Nevertheless, I see no reason to lose hope. The lessons of ending the Cold War are proof positive that, today too, the world community can cope with the problems confronting it.

We face, above all else, the challenge of interdependence. How shall we respond to it?

It is obvious to me, as I believe to many others here, that we need international interaction in order to curb spontaneous processes and establish a certain degree of control over the course of events.

The question, however, is this: can we hope to have global interaction if we fail to prevent new global divisions?

We have to speak about this because, while the politico-military confrontation has become a thing of the past, we see, even in Europe, symptoms of a new kind of divisions — economic, political, and even religious. They manifested themselves again last December at the Conference on Security and Cooperation in Europe (CSCE) summit in Budapest.

Contrary to the concept of a united Europe from Vancouver to Vladivostok, which was adopted by all parties to the CSCE process, we are being presented with ideas implying two or three Europes, which would have different rights and different roles, among other things, in the security area. This, however, would condemn us to relive the past, albeit in modified form.

Furthermore, no genuinely collective action by the world community is possible unless new relations are built between North and South, bridging the confrontational divide between these two vast parts of the globe. Already, a "theoretical" rationalization of this division is being put forth — that is, the idea that the clash of civilizations is inevitably coming to replace the conflict of ideologies.

It is true that mankind's universal civilization incorporates various regional or national civilizations that have always existed and will continue to exist. But globalization must manifest itself in an intense interaction of all nations, with each one retaining its own identity. Anything else would condemn the world to countless cataclysms and endless confrontation.

Careful attention should be given to the regional, national, and civilizational specificities of the South. Having broken with its colonial past and grown disillusioned with attempts to emulate models from the West or from the East, the South is now looking for its own ways to the future. The results have been mixed: among other things, we have seen extremism, various kinds of fundamentalism, and other negative and even tragic phenomena.

Overall, however, the South has ventured on a search that is historically quite positive, and it would be disastrous if the West responded to it with a fundamentalism or intolerance of its own. What is needed is understanding, solidarity, sensitivity, and, of course, effective support—and where necessary direct assistance of a kind that helps each nation to exercise its free choice, as is its right.

Furthermore, if we are to act in full awareness of the world's interdependence and diversity and gradually learn to control global processes, attempts at hegemony of any kind must absolutely be excluded. This requires a psychological and political breakthrough similar to the one that occurred at the ending of the Cold War. As international relations are being reshaped, no nation or group of nations may claim the right to "be in command" or, even less, to impose their will on other countries.

A real and important requirement of our time is to enhance the role of the United Nations. As I see it, the underlying principles of this unique world organization remain generally valid. But let us not forget that they were formulated half a century ago. Since then the world has changed beyond recognition, and I therefore feel that there is a need today for certain amendments to the U.N. Charter that would make it fully consistent with the challenges of the future.

Moreover, the United Nations needs a concept of action or, if you will, a comprehensive strategy of global partnership. The Agenda for Peace put forward by the U.N. secretary-general is an important step toward the development of such a strategy, but to complete this task the United Nations would probably need the help of some kind of Council of Sages — eminent persons not beholden to any authority who could offer a systematic and realistic vision of what the organization needs.

As an important component, the concept of global partnership should include a carefully devised set of procedures making it possible to predict conflicts and stop them at an early stage — before they develop into a tragedy.

I want to repeat what I have said before: the United Nations can be effective only if it succeeds in combining its own global efforts with those of regional organizations that promote security and cooperation, including, of course, those in Europe. This must become a rule everywhere.

Finally, over the past decades public movements and organizations have been playing an increasingly active role, virtually becoming new subjects of world politics. I feel that the time is ripe for the United Nations to develop a closer working relationship with those forces and organizations, with the world of science and culture, which represents a vast and potentially inexhaustible resource.

The awesome challenge of the nuclear danger is a dreadful and continuing threat to our future. It is a direct consequence and essential manifestation of a centuries-old cult of force. But in a world of interdependence, interaction, and cooperation, the use of force, and particularly of nuclear weapons, must be ruled out as a matter of principle.

This point bears repetition, for although the Cold War has been relegated to the past, confrontational political thinking and methods of force in domestic and international politics have not. What is even worse, the past few months have provided new evidence of the persistence of power politics, when weapons were used readily and often without any justification — and, I would add, with no result whatsoever.

Overcoming confrontational, power-politic mentality is essential if we are to have a peaceful future. Above all else, mankind must do everything possible — even what seems impossible — to enter the twenty-first century on a steady course toward a nuclear-free world. I therefore call for the following vitally needed steps:

- further real cuts in nuclear weapons, leading ultimately to their complete elimination;

- as a first step toward that goal, immediate and complete cessation of nuclear testing;

- substantial strengthening of the nuclear nonproliferation regime, including tough sanctions against its violators;

- the establishment, under the aegis of the United Nations and with full participation by the International Atomic Energy Agency, of an effective global system of ground, air, and space inspection that would rule out any attempt to prepare for using the energy of the atom for the purposes of war.

After the nuclear challenge, the challenge of the environment is the most dangerous reality of our time.

Nature is already punishing us severely for our arrogant and domineering attitude to its existence, laws, and needs. New technologies that would reduce the damage inflicted on nature are therefore clearly necessary. But technology, in and of itself, cannot provide a solution, for the problem lies primarily with the modern concept of production and consumption or, speaking more broadly, of man's existence as a whole. Hence a radical improvement requires a dramatic change in that concept, in our traditions and in the way we live. We need to ecologize global production and a certain self-restraint on the part of people in rich countries, putting an end to the prevailing cult of excess.

Finally, it is vital to develop a conscious collective policy of the solidarity of world community. Market economics, with its newly acquired global reach, should form the basis for an ecological and social economy, an economy of solidarity. There has been a growing recognition of the need for this, but so far, mostly on the theoretical level. We must begin to put it into practice.

To that end, mankind needs a Global Environmental Charter or, even better, a universally binding United Nations Environmental Code.

Furthermore, science and education at all levels and in all regions should be dedicated to the mastering and consistent application of moral principles in relations between man and the rest of nature. This is all the more necessary since the increasingly urgent problem of global population is ultimately one of general culture, education, and upbringing, which must be reoriented toward a civilized utilization of man's potential.

In the final analysis, the key to the problem lies in man's ability to rethink his relationship with the rest of nature. The current crisis of the environment stems, psychologically and politically, from the idea that "man is the king of nature," inherited by the present generations from the Age of

Enlightenment. We need a new paradigm that would bring us back to reality. In other words, we must recognize that man is but a part of nature, that his own destiny and that of planet Earth, depends on his attitude to the world around us.

The challenges of the coming millennium discussed here therefore impose a profound change in the mentality and psychology of humankind, a genuine revolution in the minds of men — a spiritual revolution.

One question, however, may be legitimately asked: when did man live in accordance with the spiritual values truly reflecting his better nature?

Indeed, man has never behaved in full accord with those values. What is worse, today we witness everywhere acts of utter contempt for even the most elementary moral and ethical norms that have evolved over many centuries, contempt for human life, for compassion and tolerance, solidarity and mutual respect, honesty and decency.

As for the so-called new values imposed by the current way of life and instilled in millions of people by the mass media, many of those are in fact the antithesis of genuine values. They inspire selfishness, greed, cruelty, and contempt for one's fellow man. They engender indifference to the suffering of others and to the fate of future generations, even that of our own children.

Affirming genuine universal values means to work everywhere against whatever runs counter to them. It means to act everywhere against all that demeans and damages the individual dignity of man and to assert true respect for the individual in deeds and not just in speeches from the high rostrum.

The reader may ask whether I have perhaps set my sights too high and whether the global challenges described here really have much to do with solutions to the problems so painfully felt by many people and nations. To this question, the answer can only be positive.

In this day and age, when the world is becoming increasingly interdependent, global challenges have a direct and immediate bearing on solving even the most specific problems. Again and again we have to recognize the truth of the old maxim: if we fail to sort out matters of general principle, we will be helpless in confronting problems even on an apparently smaller scale.

So it is quite appropriate that each of the articles contained in this volume explores in some way or degree those major issues of our time, examining the more specific tasks through that perspective. I wanted to call readers' attention to this valuable feature of the book and also to share with them my own views, based both on my practical experience and on the analysis of the unfolding process of change — one that is full of contradictions but, ultimately, profoundly rejuvenating.

Preface

From the fall of 1992 through the spring of 1993 I gave considerable thought to the feasibility of writing a book addressing substantive geopolitical concerns in the post–Cold War era. I was first prompted to do so by what I perceived as a misplaced euphoria that appeared to sweep the West in the aftermath of the collapse of the Soviet Union. The perception that the world had suddenly become a safer place, devoid of significant international conflicts, seemed not only ludicrous but dangerous since it led some individuals in the American "establishment" to lean toward isolationism.

My motivation in writing this type of book was tempered by the realization that few would be interested in what my thoughts on this subject might be. For this reason, I concluded that a more effective way in which to project my ideas, and to focus a debate on this subject, would be to manifest them in the context of a forum. Within this forum the world's most eminent statesmen and stateswomen would be invited to articulate their respective visions of the future in an unedited fashion and to address specific questions based upon their individual experiences.

In the spring of 1993 I began to formally develop relationships within the diplomatic community, where I was perceived, and accurately so, as someone with no institutional biases or hidden agendas. The access I was given at the highest levels of government and throughout the diplomatic establishment afforded me an opportunity to convince the principals concerned about the merits of my proposed book. The most difficult aspect of this project was having these distinguished participants follow through with their commitment in a set time frame and to deliver a substantive text based upon my specific questions. Attempting to direct, mediate, and lobby over two dozen heads of state, while at the same time being sensitive not only to conflicting ideologies and national egos, but also to considerable cross-border tension and animosity, has been a great learning exercise for developing both diplomatic and negotiating skills. This project presented me with one of my greatest logistical challenges while simultaneously establishing lasting friendships with policymakers and leaders throughout the world.

Many leaders prepared these essays at a time when they were experiencing significant domestic challenges that took much of their time. Several leaders who had agreed to participate, such as Prime Minister Chuan Leekpai of Thailand and Foreign Minister Mohamed Salah Dembri of Algeria, were forced to abandon their commitments due to domestic political considerations.

From the commencement of this undertaking, I have adhered to several firm guidelines as the editor of the volume. Participants were identified and invited to contribute on the basis of their international significance and the perceived value of their contribution, regardless of their political views, some of which do not reflect my own beliefs. Similarly, any editing of the contributed texts has been undertaken so that it will in no way modify or truncate their basic views, irrespective of my own. Finally, as editor, I absorbed all expenses incurred in this project. I have neither solicited nor accepted remuneration in any form from any outside source.

A variety of distinguished individuals who were approached directly or through their respective capitals or diplomatic missions and asked to participate, but chose not to, included Israeli, Japanese, and European statesmen and stateswomen. The lack of interest, particularly of European leaders, despite multiple invitations to a spectrum of current and former leaders as well as the efforts of many in the foreign diplomatic community in Washington, D.C., and New York, leads me to ponder what this implies about their concerns for the future of Europe. Does this mean that they are uninterested or does it mean that it is simply not as important as they say it is?

Those formally invited included, in part, Jacques Delors, president of the European Union, and its commissioner for external political affairs, Hans Van den Broek; President François Mitterrand of France, Foreign Minister Alain Juppe, and former Paris mayor Jacques Chirac; Chancellor Helmut Kohl of Germany, Foreign Minister Klaus Kinkel, and Hans-Dietrich Genscher, former foreign minister and deputy chancellor and current member of the German parliament; Prime Minister Silvio Berlusconi of Italy; Prime Minister Ruud Lubbers of the Netherlands; Prime Minister Felipe González of Spain and Foreign Minister Javier Solana Madariaga; Prime Minister John Major of Great Britain, Baroness Margaret Thatcher, and Peter Lord Carrington, M.P.; the late Manfred Worner, secretary-general of NATO; President Lech Walesa of Poland, Prime Minister Waldemar Pawlak, and Tadeus Mazowiecki, former prime minister of Poland and current member of the Polish parliament; and President Václav Havel of the Czech Republic.

There are many people to thank for the success of this undertaking. However, first I must thank those world leaders who believed in me and were willing to put their international reputations on the line for me by carrying through on their promises of contributing to my book. I wish to thank them all for their gracious and invaluable support, assistance, and confidence. Nonetheless, I owe a special thanks to former Soviet president Mikhail Sergeyevich Gorbachev, South African president Nelson Mandela, Brazilian president Fernando Henrique Cardoso, and Indonesian foreign minister Ali Alatas for their unwavering belief in me and confidence in my ability to succeed with this undertaking.

The unique nature of this book required significant global logistics, which in turn necessitated considerable financial resources. For that I am particularly in the debt of my brother Scott, who has been a source of great support and encouragement over the years. My good friends Andres Branger and Cheri Dorondo provided me with encouragement, support, and their valuable time when needed. I wish also to take this opportunity to give a special thanks to my friend Vitaly Korotich for his enthusiastic support and confidence in the success and merits of this book in the early stages when

success was anything but assured. Others who were particularly supportive include my friend and advisor from Christ Church, Oxford University,
Peter Oppenheimer, Professor David Dorondo, Richard Pinsky, Mark
Gunthier, Vafa Akhavan, Mike and Nancy Froman, Robert Tomkin, Russel
and Andi Jacobs, Gene and Charlanne Van Beveren, Professor Tom
Edwards, Jack Haggerman, and Tim and Katherine Nash. I would also like
to thank Professor Edouard Bustin for his suggestions on Africa and Professor David Scott Palmer for his suggestions on Latin America; and my
thanks also go to an old friend from Cairo for his advice on the People's Republic of China, Nicholas Kristof, former Beijing bureau chief of the *New
York Times*. Other friends who offered me advice and assistance include
Ted Van Dyk, Sheryl Cashin, Jin Park, Jonathan Kessler, and Luis Martin.

I am also very thankful to my editor at the University of Texas Press,
Dr. Ali Hossaini Jr., for having the foresight to believe in the merits of this
project and to provide me with the backing of the University of Texas
Press at a time when other publishers dismissed it as an impossibility. One
of the great benefits of having worked on this book has been how virtual
strangers have befriended me and bent over backwards to assist. One such
individual was my editor's father, Dr. Ali Hossaini Sr., and for that I will
always be grateful.

The contributions from both Prince Sadruddin Aga Khan of Iran and
Aleksandr Yakovlev of Russia, long identified as "the godfather of *glasnost*,"
were greatly appreciated, although I was unfortunately unable to use them.
I wish also to thank Nathan Gardels, editor of *Global Viewpoint*, for syndi-
cating segments from two of my essays from President Nelson Mandela,
which was in fact the first articulation of South African foreign policy by
his administration, and also from Russian foreign minister Andrei Kozyrev
through the Los Angeles Times Syndicate. This provided my book in its infant stage with great international exposure and momentum by exposing it
to a worldwide readership of 30 million in fifteen languages through 250 of
the world's most prestigious newspapers.

Literally hundreds of foreign diplomats were of assistance to me in this
project. Unfortunately, space limitations preclude me from listing them
all. However, I would like to list some of those who were of particular support and assistance. They include Dmitro Markov, press secretary, Ukrainian Embassy; Counsellor Almaz N. Khamzaev, Embassy of Kazakhstan, and
Konstantine Zhigalov, director of the International Department, Office of

President, Alma-Ata; Vladimir I. Derbenev, Russian Embassy; Minister Counselor Antonino Mena Goncalves, Brazilian Embassy, and Sergio Danese, political advisor to Brazil's foreign minister; Counsellor Amir H. Zamaninia, Iranian Mission to the United Nations; Nizar Hamdoon, Iraqi ambassador to the United Nations, and Majeed A. Khalaf; Mohamed A. Azwai, Libyan ambassador to the United Nations, and Deputy Representative Ali Sunni Muntasser; Ambassador Fayez A. Tarawneh, Jordanian Embassy, Washington, D.C.; Themba Vilakazi, Fund for a Free South Africa, and Beryl Baker, private secretary to President Mandela, Johannesburg; Jean-Claude Aime, chief of staff for the Office of the U.N. Secretary-General, New York; and Ferjani Said, Office of Renaissance in Tunisia, London; Siddhartha Shankar Ray, Indian ambassador, and First Secretary Vikas Swarup, Embassy of India; Minister Shireen Safdar, Pakistani Embassy, and Ambassador Maleeha Lodhi; Counsellor Hupudio Supardi, Embassy of Indonesia, Ambassador Arifin M. Siregar, and Nana S. Sutresna, executive assistant to the Chairman of the Nonaligned Movement, Jakarta; Ambassador Raul Rabe, Embassy of the Philippines, and J. Apolinario L. Lozada Jr., presidential assistant for foreign affairs, Manila; Ambassador M. L. Birabhongse Kasemsri, Embassy of Thailand; Christian Pauls, political counselor, German Embassy; Ambassador Ricardo Luna, Embassy of Peru, Third Secretary Jose M. Boza, Embassy of Peru, Mariela Guerinoni Romero, secretary-general of the presidency, and Walter Negreiros, director of foreign policy, Lima; Ambassadors Patricio Silva and John Biehl, Embassy of Chile, Mathias Francke, third secretary, Christian Tolosa, foreign policy assistant to the president, Santiago; Søren Sondergaard, European Commission; Baron Willem O. Bentinck, Royal Netherlands Embassy; Jan Zelenka, Embassy of the Czech Republic; Pavel Palazchenko, International Foundation for Social, Economic, and Political Research, Moscow; Chargé d'Affaires Maciej Kozlowski, Embassy of Poland; Counsellor Carlos Robles Fraga, Embassy of Spain; Minister-Counsellor Keng-Yong Ong, Embassy of Singapore; Counselor Wang Qiliang, Embassy of the People's Republic of China, and Ma Zhen Gang, director of the Department of America and Oceana Affairs, Ministry of Foreign Affairs, Beijing; Ambassador Ahmed Suliman, Embassy of Sudan; Ayodele Aderinwale, Africa Leadership Forum, Abeokuta, Ogun State, Nigeria; Arturo Sarukhan, executive assistant, Office of the Ambassador, Embassy of Mexico; Minister Jose L. Vignolo, Embassy of Argentina; Chargé d'Affaires

Massoud Maalouf, Embassy of Lebanon; Ambassador Walid Al-Moualem, Embassy of Syria; Jose Ponce, press secretary, Cuban Interests Section; and Robert Jongeryck, chief of staff, Embassy of France.

Finally, I wish to thank Martha, my sister Beth, and my mother for always being there for me over the years and helping make whatever accomplishments I succeed in possible.

—Spring 1996

Keith Philip Lepor

The dramatic images of the destruction of the Berlin Wall in November 1989 had a profound psychological effect on viewers around the world. The wall had come to symbolize the physical, philosophical, economic, and political division between East and West, and its fall now symbolized a new era. Few observers could have foreseen the upheaval across Eastern Europe that led to this collapse of communism in the German Democratic Republic, Czechoslovakia, Rumania, Bulgaria, Hungary, and Poland. Still fewer observers could imagine what this collapse would bring to Moscow some twenty-one months later: the August 1991 aborted coup and the subsequent rapid dissolution of the Soviet Empire; President Mikhail Gorbachev's resignation in December 1991 as the eighth and final leader of the Soviet Union; and Boris Yeltsin's democratic victory as president of the Russian Federation in June 1991 and his assumption of leadership of a new Russian Federation to replace the Soviet Union.

Perhaps nowhere outside the former Soviet borders did this transformation have as significant a psychological impact as among military and political strategists in the United States. Since the end of World War II, there had been two competing superpowers, and with the collapse of communism, foreign policy analysts in Washington and throughout the world have been scrambling to understand the ramifications of this collapse and to anticipate future implications. The Bush administration attempted to come to terms with what it called the New World Order, but President Bush could not seem to define that order clearly enough for the American people, nor could he make them grasp its potential effect on domestic politics. More important, he lacked domestic political and economic focus and consequently lost his bid for the presidency to Bill Clinton, who was elected to the White House in 1992 on a mandate for domestic economic revitalization. This mandate soon became a preoccupation at the expense of foreign policy, however.

Clinton believed that he had only to "jump start" the American economy and the world would take care of itself. This misguided belief would not have been so troubling had American foreign policy been passed to exceptionally competent architects and administrators, skilled at translating American domestic policy benefits into foreign ones. But the administration's diplomatic team soon displayed a lack of strategic and geopolitical vision and experience when it came to articulating that American foreign policy. This was a critical shortfall as the United States sought to negotiate the new minefields unearthed by the dramatic changes accompanying the end of the Cold War.

The post–Cold War euphoria over "a new era of opportunity" seems, in this light, particularly optimistic, for while the Cold War may be over between the United States and the Russian Federation, as the successor state to the former Soviet Union, the world in many ways has become a much more dangerous and unpredictable place. It is this fact which the following collection of essays attempts to address. The book aspires to present a highly informative look at the post–Cold War world through the eyes of twenty of its most provocative and influential leaders, men and women who have either played a significant role in or are currently shaping events during an extremely mutable period in international politics. Their contributions confront specific questions on the challenges that await the community of nations in the post–Cold War world. These essays should facilitate more informed discussions, even reassessments of American foreign policy, a policy struggling to adjust not only to dramatic geopolitical changes but also to America's own reduced economic and political resources. Perhaps ultimately these essays may help counter what appears to be growing isolationism in the United States, a movement that threatens to disengage it from the international community at a time when its involvement is crucial.

New World Definitions

The "post–Cold War world," the "New World Order," "fragmented multipolarity," the "new interventionism"—what do all of these terms mean? Although they attempt to simplify the dramatic global strategic transformation currently under way, they remain "think tank" argot that does not enhance our understanding of *current* international relations much less future ones.

What is happening to the international system as we approach the twenty-first century? On the one hand, with the technology and telecommunications revolution, the world is increasingly characterized by a growing cosmopolitan world culture and made more accessible by air travel. But the world is also undergoing widespread denuding of rural environments, massive migration into urban slums, growth in bitter ethnic disputes, and an intensified urgency to deal with a variety of ecological and demographic problems, all of which paradoxically create economic and political schisms between "East" and "West" certainly, but more profoundly between "North" and "South." Without the imposed superpower order, there is a risk that nations with diverse ethnic populations will continue to disintegrate into warring factions with no recognizable sovereign borders and that this disintegration will worsen, fomented by technological advances like television and facsimile machines, which lead to a more informed but disaffected underclass. Finally, the end of external support for these regimes comes amid advanced decay and a faltering governance within many states.

What will be the fate of those failing nations and how will the international community respond? Are we beginning to witness the breakdown of the international system entirely? Has the nation-state outlived its usefulness? These questions seem much more useful in helping define our evolving world order than does short-lived political jargon, and the following essays should provide valuable insights relevant to answering these questions. However, it is important to note that there are issues which transcend a purely regional importance and will affect global stability and the new notions of international security into the future: these include the environment, nonproliferation, terrorism, global finance, international crime, and narcotics. What follows is a brief global survey and conceptual framework from which each essay might be viewed.

East Asia

The success of newly industrialized countries like the Republic of Korea, Taiwan, Singapore, and Hong Kong; China's dramatic growth; and the success of the "new tigers" of Malaysia, Thailand, and Indonesia are all examples of what is commonly called the Asian economic miracle. Asia's export growth has turned the region into one of the most important economic engines of the global community. Yet Asia can by no means be considered a "Pacific Community" for a number of reasons, including intra- and extraregional political and security concerns, uncertainties resulting from democratization, intraregional economic factors, and other international undercurrents and tensions. The post–Cold War order, specifically the end of the U.S.-Soviet rivalry, has had a significant impact on the region's strategic and security concerns, particularly in that it has given rise to two new regional superpowers — China and Japan.

The fundamental economic growth and change that have occurred in China since 1979 suggests to many that China may surpass the United States as the largest world economy in the coming century. This growth cannot continue, however, until the political future of China becomes clearer. The assumption of power by Deng Xiaoping's chosen successor, Jiang Zemin, the Chinese president and general secretary of the Communist Party, seems improbable. In his place some sort of a collective leadership appears more likely. Should this transition be disorderly, internal political instability would reverse the great successes of the Chinese economy, and China would prove an immediate threat to its neighbors, particularly Vietnam and India, with whom China may resume border disputes. Despite the security a modernized and nuclear arsenal brings, China also remains particularly anxious about Japan and the Russian Federation. It has responded through increased military spending, despite the fact that China is more "secure" than it has been since 1949. It seems more likely that China sees the reduction of both U.S. and Russian influences in the region as an opportunity for its own projection, both on the Asian continent and in the South China Sea.

Japan is *currently* the main economic engine in East Asia. The strength of the yen has led to a migration of Japanese manufacturers throughout Asia, and as Japanese economic and business interests shift increasingly toward Asia, it is only natural that Japanese diplomacy should do the same. These diplomatic shifts, however, will increase the risk of confrontation with the interests of the West in general and the United States in particular. Japan has become an increasingly independent actor, seeking to solidify itself in both global and regional institutions. Given the potential for instability throughout the region, Japan will at least in the short-term wish to continue to benefit from U.S. security guarantees, but in time a more confident and adventurous Japan will seek a higher profile and a broader international role, with less or little reliance on U.S. security assistance. Sino-Japanese relations have improved through economic dealings between the two countries, but should the American presence in the region diminish without a significant multilateral security arrangement, it is possible that historical tensions between China and Japan could resurface, particularly if Japan attempts to use its regional economic leverage to counter any of Beijing's strategic regional moves. Japan has a massive military budget, and if the political will develops, it could conceivably convert its civilian nuclear-processing program into a formidable nuclear arsenal.

The Korean Peninsula is home not only to one of the world's most dynamic and successful economic development stories, but also to one of its most potentially deadly conflicts. A formidable military exists in the North under the new and as yet unsolidified leadership of Kim Jong II. On the Korean Peninsula, the end of the Cold War has had little effect on the arms race. Pyongyang's long-term nuclear weapons program must be looked at in the context of the question of Korean unification. Given the deterioration in U.S.-Japanese relations as well as the U.S. military reduction in South Korea, Seoul may feel it necessary to keep a nuclear option open.

Although East Asia is poised for considerable economic growth into the next century, Sino-Japanese and Korean security and stability must be vigilantly pursued by all powers involved. Other issues, however, are equally difficult, and their resolutions equally crucial if economic growth is to continue: Chinese impatience with Taiwan over Beijing's desire for unification with the mainland; threats to critically important shipping lanes like the straits of both Malacca and Singapore in the South China Sea; Russo-Japanese dispute over the Kuril Islands, seized by the Russians at the end of World War II; and potential instability in the Russian Federation, possibly affecting the resumption of Sino-Russian border disputes along the Amur and Ussuri rivers. These concerns will grow as U.S. regional economic and military, particularly maritime, power is perceived to diminish; stability and peace in Asia will be maintained not through bilateral agreements with the United States but by a balance of power regionally. There are in fact numerous territorial disputes affecting the region; the Spratley Islands in the South China Sea, for example, are currently claimed by Vietnam, China, the Philippines, Malaysia, Taiwan, and Brunei.

Interregionally, Northeast Asia — specifically the People's Republic of China, the Korean Peninsula, and Japan — is of the greatest strategic importance to the West. Since the end of the Korean War, the Chinese, Soviets, and Americans have all sought to ensure stability in the region, for any hostilities would ultimately involve them all. One multilateral arrangement, the Asia Pacific Economic Cooperation forum (APEC), has met with some success in stabilizing the region. It encompasses numerous extraregional powers, including the United States and Canada, and seeks to promote cooperation among the region's economies through regional trade and investment liberalization by the year 2020. Likewise the Association of Southeast Asian Nations (ASEAN), comprised of the most dynamic countries of Southeast Asia, creates a stabilizing influence by providing a forum for nations such as Indonesia, Malaysia, Thailand, Singapore, Brunei, and the Philippines to consider strategies for economic productivity. While Indochina has considerable economic distance to travel, it also seems well situated to join in the region's prosperity particularly as Vietnam has recently joined ASEAN.

South Asia

South Asia was the site of one of the last Cold War confrontations, namely in Afghanistan, but it faces a far more deadly conflict today: South Asia is the most dangerous nuclear flash point in the world. India, now a South Asian superpower, has even more to contend with than its internal security challenges, most notably communal rivalries among and between Hindus, Muslims, and Sikhs. India's detonation of its first nuclear weapon in 1974, while aimed at enhancing its own security vis-à-vis China, initiated an arms race in South Asia with Pakistan, which sought to develop its own nuclear deterrent in response. To the great concern and frustration of the West, India has been unwilling to sign the Nuclear Nonproliferation Treaty (NPT), protesting that it is "inherently discriminatory." India perceives the NPT as a mechanism that blocks the proliferation of nuclear

weapons to nonnuclear nations while simultaneously providing inadequate guarantees of security. Another objection is that the NPT does not
get rid of existing stockpiles in weapon states.

Pakistan is also an important NPT nonsignatory state, and considerable
debate goes on within the intelligence community over Pakistan's nuclear
program. Pakistan also faces serious internal problems from Islamic fundamentalists, which may increasingly work to destabilize Islamabad and per-
niciously affect its relationship with India, particularly regarding Kashmir.

Another major potential security threat to India exists in the form of the
People's Republic of China. While New Delhi and Beijing have pursued
closer relations in recent years, sidestepping their territorial disputes along
the Himalayan border and deciding to expand relations, India will not forget the 1962 border war with China nor can she ignore China's current military strength. Presently, efforts by the West to pressure India into conformity over issues such as nuclear nonproliferation and human rights have
made it more attractive for New Delhi to nurture its relationship with Beijing. However, their volatile strategic rivalry will ultimately resume.

Despite China's improved relationship with New Delhi, it cultivates
good relations with Pakistan, a strategic maneuver clearly indicating that it
considers Islamabad a significant tool for Chinese foreign policy in South
Asia. The Indians have little to fear unless Pakistan is able to work together
militarily with the Chinese. An undertaking of this nature would leave India with a confrontation on two fronts. Consequently, India maintained
close relations with the Soviet Union as a balance to Chinese ambitions,
but with the dissolution of the Soviet Union India now seeks stability
through an evolving relationship with both China and the United States.

Middle East

The Middle East is not only a region steeped in intractable conflict, Islamic fundamentalism, and dominant oil resources, but it is also a geographic region rich in history and culture. Its diverse collection of states,
spanning two continents, confront a variety of challenges in the post–
Cold War world.

Since its founding in 1948, Israel has been seen by the Arab world as
one of the principal threats to regional order. To the contrary, however, Israel appears to have helped "unify" Arabs — that is, until the late President
Anwar Sadat made his historic trip to Israel in 1977. Following that trip

came a peace treaty between Israel and Egypt. After many lost opportunities a new era in dialogue commenced with the October 1991 Madrid Conference. This was eventually followed by the August 1993 Oslo accord and consequent PLO-Israeli accord in September 1993. The dialogue between the Israeli government and the Palestine Liberation Organization (PLO) under Chairman Yasser Arafat led to an interim agreement over Gaza and Jericho. Jordan then followed Egypt's example in July 1994 with its own peace treaty.

Considerable work remains in stabilizing the region, however, not only in helping Palestinians realize their national aspirations diplomatically but in resolving legitimate Israeli security issues. These efforts must all be pursued rapidly but warily, as the fundamentalist Hammas threatens to undermine the PLO's hold over the territories. Syria also remains a serious threat to regional stability, but without the backing of his former Soviet patron, President Hafez al-Assad is unlikely to attempt direct military confrontation unless he can achieve strategic parity with Israel. The status of the Golan Heights is the key to the resolution of this conflict, and the security concerns for Israel here are immense. As such, lasting peace will be impossible without international guarantees and involvement.

Countries throughout the region face a host of problems both economic and political. Some of these are external as the West, for instance, attempts to isolate Libya in view of accusations against Colonel Muammar El-Qadhafi for supporting international terrorism. One must admit a certain inconsistency here, however, considering the West's continued courtship of other "terrorist nations." Syria's terrorist status, for example, was suspended in exchange for its support during the Gulf War against Iraq in 1990. In return, Lebanese sovereignty was sacrificed.

With the collapse of communism and the former Soviet Union, the West has identified what it views as a new sinister threat emanating from the Muslim world in the form of Islamic fundamentalism. This threat affects such countries as Egypt, and while authorities there have serious problems with Islamic insurgents and the Muslim Brotherhood, this confrontation is far less serious than the civil war currently tearing away at Algeria. The cancellation of Algeria's first democratic elections in January 1992 led to the current crisis with the Islamic Salvation Front. Should Algeria not succeed in coming to terms with this challenge, the military-backed regime will be replaced by an Islamic government that may adversely affect the stability of Algeria's neighbors, notably Tunisia and Morocco.

In yet another region of the Middle East vital to western strategic interests, Iran and Iraq actively antagonize the West while pursuing their own antithetical ambitions. Nuclear nonproliferation issues are particularly worrisome here, for without superpower rivalry, it is more difficult to keep these states in check. Now that Iraq is under United Nations sanctions in the aftermath of the 1991 Gulf War, Iran has emerged as the main threat to future western interests in the Persian Gulf.

The eight states bordering the Persian Gulf possess much of the world's largest oil reserves and are the greatest source of world oil exports: Iran, Iraq, Kuwait, Saudi Arabia, Bahrain, Qatar, the United Arab Emirates (UAE), and Oman. Since 1981, Kuwait, Saudi Arabia, Bahrain, Qatar, UAE, and Oman have formally come together in a security and economic group known as the Gulf Cooperation Council (GCC), but the GCC offers little hope of regional policing and enforcement without extraregional cooperation and support.

The instability in the Gulf region has it roots in the historical rivalry between Persians and Arabs on opposite sides of the Gulf. There are many border and territorial disputes throughout the region: the islands of Warbah and Bubiyan are the subject of a dispute between Iraq and Kuwait; Bahrain and Qatar argue over the Huwar Islands; Iran has territorial claims on the island of Bahrain and currently occupies three islands in the Strait of Hormuz—Abu Musa and the Greater and Lesser Tumbs—sovereignty over which is claimed by two of the emirates in the UAE, Ras al Khaimah and Sharjah. The strategic value of the islands is defined by the flow of Arab crude oil to the West and Asia, which dramatically enhances this region's importance.

There are also internal threats to the stability of Saudi Arabia and Kuwait, two of the most important countries on the Arabian Peninsula. Both are dominated by regimes ruled by single powerful families—the al-Sa'ud and the al-Sabah families, respectively. The time is rapidly approaching when these ruling elites will not be able to buy the political allegiance of their own people, particularly as financial resources are reduced. Contrary to a belief that prevailed for a time in the 1970s, the Organization of Petroleum Exporting Countries (OPEC) is not able to exercise a decisive influence over the world market price of petroleum. Conflict may also result within the Saudi ruling family as the line for monarchical succession begins to blur. Finally, an increasingly frustrated and educated middle class threatens to rebel against what it perceives to be a corrupt and illegitimate leadership. These factors in conjunction with rising Islamic fundamentalism throughout the region do not augur well for Arab countries that are not truly democratic and are unable appreciably to enhance the standard of living of their own peoples.

Europe

As both a beneficiary and a victim of the Cold War's end, Europe has been forced, more than any other region in the world, to confront the conundrums concerning post–Cold War relationships. Ironically, the very events that seemed to usher in a new period of security—the collapse of East-bloc communism, the reunification of Germany, and the withdrawal of Soviet/Russian troops and tactical nuclear weapons from Central Europe—have instead led to a resurgence in ethnic conflicts and nationalism and to doubts about the legitimacy of the "nation-state" itself. All of this in turn complicates European economic interdependence, political integrity, and security.

The December 1991 Maastricht treaty on European union, signed by the twelve-nation European Community, was to be part of the natural progression of both the 1958 creation of the Common Market and the 1987 Single European Act, which formed an integrated customs union. When the single market subsequently opened in January 1993, it coincided with the worst recession in sixty years. As regards economic and monetary union, the realization of a single European currency encountered an immediate obstacle in the form of Germany's high interest rates. At the same time, the common foreign and security policy, also put into effect by Maastricht, was quickly exposed as unworkable: the Yugoslav civil war demonstrated Europe's inability to act in unison when dealing with a crisis on its own doorstep. Other security crises still hover over Europe. Algeria and Islamic fundamentalism in the south threaten to disrupt North Africa and could lead to a massive refugee exodus affecting France, Spain, and Italy. Russian instability could likewise result in a mass migration of refugees. The collapse of the Soviet Union, the spread of democracy, and the resultant paradoxical disorder, even chaos, in Eastern Europe have prompted some former Warsaw Pact states (Poland, Hungary, and the Czech Republic, for example) to request membership not only in the European Union but also in NATO in order to attain a cheap security guarantee of their eastern frontiers against a possible Russian attack.

But even NATO's survival seems questionable, as perhaps the Bosnian crisis suggests. Although it has made halfhearted attempts to evolve into an organization as useful at present and in the future as it was in the past, its success has been marginal. The success of undertakings like the United Nations peacekeeping missions and involvement in the prevention of regional, often ethnic conflicts in conjunction with the Organization for Security and Cooperation in Europe (another multilateral security organization) will depend not only on the strength of its core members' political will. A new realism is required, given the absence of any major ideological obstacles to introducing peacekeeping troops, and a proper assessment of the situation is also required to see what role these troops can play.

Commonwealth of Independent States

The Commonwealth of Independent States (CIS), a group of sovereign nations previously belonging to the Soviet Union, consists of Azerbaijan, Armenia, Belarus, Georgia, Kazakhstan, Kyrgyzstan, Moldova, Russia, Tajikistan, Turkmenistan, Uzbekistan, and Ukraine. The Russian Federation, under the leadership of President Boris Yeltsin, is the dominant member of the CIS and successor state to the former Soviet Union. The relationship of the Russian Federation to the other CIS states is one of "first amongst equals," and one in which Moscow seeks to consolidate its own power and foreign policy goals through both subtle threats of force (and not so subtle, as in Chechnya) and through economic pressure.

The most formidable threat to the Russian Federation is the precarious state of the economy. After decades of state domination and the consequent mismanagement, corruption, and waste, Russian industry is in desperate shape. While Prime Minister Victor Chernomyrdin's economic reform policies have had a degree of success, supported by accompanying political changes, the economy still requires that some key issues be tackled, such as privatization, agricultural reform, and the breakup of the industrial empires that are the residue of the military industrial complex. These tasks will require further sacrifices from a population impatient with the speed and benefits of economic reform.

The Russian Federation also confronts a number of security concerns, either real or imagined. These include threats by minority groups within the Russian Federation (as in Chechnya) and its southern neighbors. Central Asia is of great concern, as civil strife could erupt in areas where either regional and ethnic splits exist or where there are power struggles between the old and new "elites." These ethnic conflicts range from antagonisms surrounding Islamic fundamentalism in Tajikistan to clashes between the local nation and the Russian minority in Moldova to a combination of political, communal (among Abkhazians), and geographic separatism in Georgia. Russia has deployed its forces to "reestablish order." Yet another concern for Russia is the civil war between Armenia and Azerbaijan over Nagorno-Karabakh. Finally, the federation worries about the prospects of an expanding NATO alliance, which may extend membership to Moscow's former Warsaw Pact allies. This development could certainly rekindle historic Russian insecurities about encirclement by hostile nations.

Russian reaction to these perceived threats — its invasion of Chechnya, for instance — has considerably increased the concern that democracy and economic reform may be derailed. Now there is growing concern over right-wingers like Vladimir Zhirinovsky, whose proposed aggressive policies of expansion and domination are reminiscent of the past. Yeltsin's inability or unwillingness to take the necessary and difficult measures required to deepen market reforms in the Russian economy increase the risk of the rise of the right and of military intervention in government.

In recent years, the United States and other advanced western nations have attempted to include the Russian Federation in their economic and military dealings: President Yeltsin was asked to participate in the last G-7 summit of leading industrial nations and Russia was invited to join NATO's Partnership for Peace. The West hoped in this way to have a favorable influence on Moscow's behavior. Russia has taken advantage of this dialogue, as well as Europe's possible interest in expanding NATO, by seeking the approval of the Organization for Security and Cooperation in Europe (OSCE) to police the unstable region south of the Russian Federation. Russia would like the OSCE to become the principal institution for conflict resolution in Europe. The CIS would then become an agent of the OSCE, and as such would give the federation the right to intervene through the CIS in its sphere of influence anywhere within the former Soviet borders. Russia's neighbors interpret these maneuvers as a reiteration of the old Soviet expansionist foreign policy.

Africa

Africa is undoubtedly the world's most troubled continent, racked not only with AIDS, tremendous poverty, corruption, and political unrest but also by ethnic and tribal conflict. The superpower rivalry that formerly imposed a type of organized chaos on Africa defined the continent's strategic importance mostly in ideological terms. With the dissolution of this face-off, however, Africa seems to have lost much of its strategic appeal. South African mineral reserves, Namibian uranium deposits, and Angolan and Libyan oil still dominate western involvement with the continent, but the end of the Cold War has brought with it an overall disjunctive strategic view of Africa. Only concerns about Islamic fundamentalism and mass migration to Europe seem to focus it.

While Africa's problems seem monumental, the most overwhelming challenge is economic development, and here Africa faces a classic paradox. In order to develop economically, Africa needs political stability, but to achieve stability, it needs economic development to enhance the general welfare of its people. Political freedom, in and of itself, does little to benefit economic development if the past serves as an indicator. The chaos usually following political reform only discourages foreign direct investment and hurts the rural poor. The Organization of African Unity (OAU), the continent's primary political gathering, may in time be able to deploy its own peacekeeping force to thwart such chaos — resulting mostly from tribal conflict — but currently the OAU is incapable of achieving this objective, and the disorder and economic impediments continue.

South Africa, one possible exception to this apparent rule, is the continent's most promising long-term hope for economic growth. Nelson Mandela's government could possibly energize not only the South African economy but those of the entire southern Africa region. Perhaps it will also prove that tribal differences can be set aside for general economic and political welfare. In any event, South Africa's importance for regional stability cannot be overstated.

Latin America

Latin America confronts two major issues: the need for political and economic liberalization and the need to improve social justice, which in part depends on maintaining government services. There is a degree of tension between these two objectives. Regionally, there are three economic organizations aimed at further developing Latin America. The first is NAFTA, which now affects only Mexico, although Chile has been invited to join. The second is the Mercosur free-trade area, which has been made possible by the political stability in the southern sphere of Latin America. This group will bring together Brazil, Argentina, Uruguay, and Paraguay into a customs union with a common external tariff. The third organization is a regional one reactivated in the 1990s and called the Andean Pact. It is comprised of Colombia, Ecuador, Peru, Bolivia, and Venezuela. At the Summit of the Americas in December 1994, the hemispheric leaders agreed to set up a Free Trade Area of the Americas by 2005, which would include all of these organizations and the countries of Central America and the Caribbean.

Not long ago a survey of Latin America would have included numerous military dictatorships. Today, democracy appears, at least for the present, to be taking hold in Latin America. The real test of democracy will come, however, when and if the region's economies do not grow at the speed required to meet the increasing expectations of their populations. As with other developing regions of the world, it is of critical importance that all countries pursue responsible and sustainable economic development.

There are also security concerns throughout the region. Guerilla insurgencies exist not only in Peru but also in Colombia, Guatemala, Ecuador, Bolivia, and even in our NAFTA partner, Mexico. Drugs and their associated corruption have had a pernicious effect on countries from Colombia and Bolivia to Panama and Mexico and threaten security as well. The potential for conflict exists not only between Chile and Argentina over the Beagle Channel, but elsewhere in Latin America too as nationalism, dormant but not dead, rears its head at the borders of countries like Peru and Ecuador. Cuba remains the only communist government in Latin America but poses no threat to the hemisphere. Cuba does, however, have tremendous potential as an economic miracle once the United States lifts its economic embargo and the Cuban government further liberalizes the country's economy. The principal defensive pact in the region is the Organization of American States (OAS).

As we prepare to enter the twenty-first century, ideological conflict no longer provides a frame of reference for either viewing or understanding East-West and North-South relations. New paradigms must be created in which members of the international community will have to come to terms not only with the new geopolitical reality but with the increasingly dangerous and serious challenges ahead. Furthermore, although the schism between North and South will continue to grow in the future, the identity of the Third World today, given the new emerging industrial countries, is far different from that of twenty years ago; as such, the simplistic rhetoric of the past will be inappropriate in understanding or anticipating the future.

Part 1

The Post–Cold War Order: Conceptual Foundation

His Excellency

Nelson Mandela

President of South Africa

Toward the Twenty-first Century

As the theme of these essays is of enduring importance, I want to commit the unforgivable sin of beginning this contribution on a personal note. I have lived for seventy-six of this century's ninety-five years. My life and my freedom have been bound by the abuse of power that has marked politics for the best part of the twentieth century.

With many across the world, I prayed for the ending of the stalemate in international relationships that was known as the Cold War. The crumbling of the Berlin Wall on November 11, 1989, marked the beginning of its end. The changes symbolized by this event have fundamentally altered the way in which we understand the human condition. As a result, all leadership is called to meet new challenges on this, the eve of the twenty-first century.

Understanding Global Change

In almost every corner of the world, in almost every aspect of our lives, stock explanations no longer offer solutions to penetrating new questions. These are times of great uncertainty during which change will be our constant, perhaps our only, companion.

This apprehension is intensified by the realization that the tools that we have used to understand the world have been found wanting. Since the sixteenth century, the nation-state has provided a ready guide to international politics. But these past six years have demonstrated how inadequately states are at coping with global transition.

Faced with the enormity of events, states appear too puny, too clumsy to deal with diverse issues — like trade wars and health care — which now touch the lives of ordinary people. Sovereignty, once one of the central organizing principles of our world, has been profoundly disturbed. It is no longer absolutely certain where countries end and people begin. This is why the tyranny of the mapmakers has become a common theme among those who try to understand why it is that states are failing in the 1990s. The sheer speed of events also defies comprehension.

But the nation-state still remains as the focus of loyalty for millions and is seen as the appropriate arena for the defense of people's interests.

Given the uncertainty of our times and the rapidity of change, it is not surprising that there is a deep disillusionment with politics in many parts of the world. Actually, what has happened is something far more rudimentary: democratic systems that were once considered adequate have collapsed and communities are probing new ways of conducting politics. In countries as geographically far apart as Italy and Mexico, accepted political processes have been shaken to their roots.

Economic developments have influenced these political maladies in profound ways, but economics alone offers few solutions to a plethora of post-industrial problems. The marketplace has not triumphed and the end of history has not arrived. The evidence is clear: income differentials in many capitalist countries have widened, not narrowed, and poverty and wealth levels between rich and poor countries have increased.

Deep-seated worries have survived the ending of the Cold War. Although the nuclear arms race should have ended, many profound questions about its future remain. Large quantities of fissile material and lethal equipment are seeping beyond the control of recognized international authorities. This is why the old question of who will eventually control the atom bomb remains one of the central security issues facing the planet.

Feeding upon these insecurities are a host of unknowns that offer challenges to governments and, because so many of them know no borders, to geographic regions. In southern Africa and other parts of the Third World, the arc of the killer diseases — tuberculosis, new strains of malaria, and AIDS — has been extended. Acting alone, governments appear to be powerless to deal with them, but joint action may only encourage further complications and even hamper long-term economic cooperation as individual countries try to fence themselves off.

As population growth rates show no signs of slowing, fears of diminished access to food loom large in Africa and elsewhere in the South. These concerns place new and often totally unmanageable constraints on governments. Add to these the specter of water shortages, and the conflict over the staff of life no longer seems to be in the realm of fiction.

As they witness these events, people and nations are increasingly anxious about their individual and collective futures. If governments respond to these insecurities with indecision and vacillation, the world will become a dangerous place in which the opportunism of the day will triumph over the necessity to make far-reaching choices. This is not the time for indecision. What governments do today will influence that future, but the key to action lies — as it has done across the ages — in an understanding of the past.

The processes of global transformation were under way long before East Germany collapsed. Indeed, even before the Reykjavik summit of April 1986, the event that many historians regard as the turning point of the Cold War, the international system was in the midst of deep structural change.

From the late-1960s, economic power was slipping from individual countries toward an entrepreneurial pool of skills that knew no national boundaries. A new agglomeration of power was fundamentally changing the nature of international economics. No longer was prosperity wedded to the domestic performance of individual countries — the fate of national economies was often being determined elsewhere. The oil crisis of the early 1970s is a very good example.

This trend toward apparent interdependence was speeded by the increasing impact of communications, a revolution associated, more than any other, with the miracle of the microchip. In turn, this rebounded in technological breakthroughs that allowed corporations to operate further and further offshore. Industrial production, which increasingly took advantage of competitive wage rates, was scattering across the planet: recognizable brand names became more global, less national. And invisible new services rechanneled the nature of economics, dragging it further from the national to the global.

As financial markets found renewed vigor beyond the nation-state, traditional forms of economic activity were re-ignited throughout the world. Operating around the clock, international capital markets had replaced the British Raj: they were the empire upon which the sun could never set.

In this, a world increasingly without borders, the old ideological enmity between East and West, between communist and capitalist, was losing its grip. The loss of national control on both sides of the divide provided the anvil upon which the events at Berlin's Brandenburg Gate that heady November evening in 1989 were forged. However, states still pursue interests that they perceive to be absolute national interests.

If there is a lesson to be learned from all this, it is that national freedom and economic fortune are indelibly etched within the human spirit. This makes it easy to understand why some countries will find it difficult to sustain the control they now insist on exercising over the political processes within their borders. These deserve some attention because they demonstrate that history, however differently we may think, is punctuated by evolution: it advances by fits and starts—a moment of release here, a tightening of pressure there.

Throughout the world, there appears to be a deep longing for participation and empowerment. Organs of civil society abound in their bewildering but welcome diversity, and even where there is great economic development, people demand political rights. The choice, they are saying, is not between bread and freedom. They want both bread and freedom. In developed and formally democratic countries, governments have become remote, fewer people vote in elections, and there is a feeling of crisis about institutions and their relevance.

Resistance to authoritarianism, of one kind or another, is a universal phenomenon and will continue as long as the spirit of dominance is perpetuated. This shows how resistance can endure, despite an apparent momentum toward transition. The point is simple: change and continuity are two sides of the same coin. Even the revolution that has accompanied the ending of the Cold War has not devalued the currency of this old axiom.

Other examples, like law, reinforce the point. Although the conventions that have governed international law appear to have been influenced by the breakup of countries, basic tenets are in place. In the popular mind, however, there seems to be an increasing distance between political rhetoric and the principle involved. The result—as the ongoing debate about intervention in the Balkans so graphically demonstrates—is a confusion of purpose and process, of proposal and policy, of philosophy and practice.

While under pressure to respond to a tragedy of monumental proportions, certain countries in the West, bewildered about change, are seemingly unable to decide where alliance obligations end and where declared humanitarian principles begin. This suggests that the cadence of international life and diplomatic practice has been profoundly affected by the changes of the past five-year period. And yet for all its purported newness, essential dilemmas will return to haunt the international community throughout this interregnum and beyond.

As the situation in the Balkans also demonstrates, long-dormant animosities have been unlocked by the ending of the Cold War. These now threaten the very borders of individual countries. Of immediate concern is the near uncontrollable violence that has accompanied the growth of narrow "nationalisms." The erosion of sovereignty has paradoxically been accompanied by an increase in the means to ensure its separateness: the right to differ has, tragically, become the fight to differ.

These entanglements offer some interesting insights into the theoretical debates of international politics. Much of the discussion about the self-styled New World Order has been about how parameters could be set outside the concept of collective security as determined by the United Nations. The Gulf War experience demonstrates how easy precedent can be established, and, with great tragedy, Somalia suggests how quickly international idealism can be questioned at home and abroad. So while establishing patterns of international behavior is important, these will probably remain impossible for years to come.

The World in South Africa

Nevertheless, we are — to use a famous phrase from another transition in history — present at the creation. Thus, there is a need to develop a sense of orderliness in the world. To do so a direct link needs to be established between responsible membership of the community of nations and global stability and progress. The converse holds that if countries want to enjoy the rights of community, they need to act responsibly.

Philosophers teach that the rights of citizenship follow from the sharing of values in the common cause. As we choose for the new century, each country needs to build upon a set of common properties that will aim to anchor within the ambit of a legitimate New World Order a world in which the timeless qualities of justice, stability, and emancipation are central.

Before turning to the contributions that South Africans can offer to this common international good, I have a few preliminary thoughts on a theme that will come to dominate this chapter — South Africa's international standing.

The test of South Africa's foreign policy will be found in the quality of its domestic politics. Attentive to the interests of its people, a democratic South Africa will have to create and recreate the high ideals to which its people aspire. Respectful of their rights, South Africa's government will want the country to be a symbol of a world in which diverse people can live in peace and harmony. The quality too of the government will be reflected in foreign policy.

For decades the country's international relations, like its domestic politics, were symbolized by the apartheid scourge. Although the Cold War was drawn into the national lexicon, the country largely escaped the ideological ravages of the post–World War II period. Given the deepening crisis in South Africa, the international community gradually came to recognize that the single most important issue facing the country was not the East-West conflict but the struggle for human dignity and racial equality. The world's people contributed to ending apartheid by boycotting and isolating the South African regime. The country's people rose in revolt and the political movement waged a struggle for liberation.

As the 1980s closed, white South Africa was the most isolated and embattled country in the world. But South Africa's people were never excluded from the international community. The country's contribution to the common properties will follow from this unique experience of isolation and the opposite, embrace. Its global destiny is linked to maintaining vigilance around the same precepts that united the world against apartheid, which were able to distinguish between principle and prejudice, which separated ethics from expedience, ingenuity from ineptitude.

Because the world is a more uncertain place, the international community dare not relinquish its commitment to human rights. Global change has, if anything, heightened the salience of the issue. The unfolding tragedies — whose images are the lifeblood of the influential electronic media — underpin the importance of respect for human rights in securing our common future.

While governments should be mindful of the high ideals of human rights, they should be conscious of a democratic realism that surrounds the issue, too. Given the potency of the changes in the world, the neglect of human rights is a certain recipe for internal and international disaster. The powerful secessionist movements which are found throughout the world are nurtured by neglect.

Given their experience of struggle and of transition, the ending of apartheid summons South Africans to service in the cause of human rights. The country is a signatory or will become one to all the conventions on human rights—not only those that are compulsory and those within the framework of the United Nations but also of the African Charter on Human and People's Rights.

As the century closes, new avenues through which to explore human rights have opened. South Africans are concerned that these should not be neglected in the confusion that has accompanied the ending of the Cold War.

Take the rights of women. Humankind will not meet the next century without the power, the compassion, the understanding, and the leadership of women. Emancipation is not confined simply to a single gender. Women will not be free until men free themselves. South Africans of all colors are increasingly united around this issue. We draw upon our experience to take forward this crusade at the forthcoming world conclaves on women.

In my address to the Nobel Institute in December 1993, I raised my concern for the plight of the world's children. Far more than ethnic groupings that can muster battalions or explode bombs, children are entitled to their own unique identity: a world in which childhood is more than a right, a world in which the right to be a child is sacrosanct. The agreements reached at the World Summit for Children in 1990 point the way. But to triumph, all humankind must recognize that the universality of children's rights are intimately linked to advances in democracy and sustainable development.

Changing times have also thrown into sharp relief new dimensions in the eternal quest for rights concerned with the human condition. Of central concern is the issue of the environment. South Africa's government is acutely aware of the challenge which the physical destruction of the planet holds for our children and grandchildren. We recognize that we dare not neglect the issue for a day longer. South Africa will therefore seek to become a signatory to and an enthusiastic advocate for the global conventions that deal with climate change and biodiversity. Even though South Africa was not formally integrated into the United Nations, it has been actively involved in the promotion of the international conference on desertification. In our region, South Africans can help ensure the sound management of resource endowments; cooperating in the development of environmentally friendly energy resources seems an obvious contribution.

Our position on these issues cannot be divorced from the centrality of development. With the 1987 Brundtland Report, we recognize that poor, weak societies — those at the margins of the global system — are closest to the most debilitating effects of environmental destruction. There are ways to break the cycle that links destitution to environmental destruction. Tackling the poverty that is the root cause of environmental degradation and establishing an equitable transfer of resources from the North to the South are two such examples.

Reconciling environmental concerns with developmental ones calls for a renewed and truly global effort to correct wasteful patterns of resource consumption. This will require a creative sharing of sovereignty: only international institutions with real capacity can save humankind from environmental disaster.

Although the record is mixed, the world has experienced a wave of democratization since the mid-1980s. In Central and South America, the process appears well under way despite human rights violations in a string of countries. In Eastern Europe and in Africa, things are less certain, although the passion for democracy is palpable on the streets. And in Asia the process is a mix of authoritarianism and guided democracy in economically buoyant countries. Despite this record, the cumulative outcome of all these energies are clear — there is a belief that only true democracy can guarantee political rights.

This is why the decision by South Africans in 1961 to take up arms to secure their rights was an essential step in the global march toward democracy, and why we South Africans enthusiastically embrace the international cry for democracy.

South Africa will be among those countries whose efforts are to promote and foster democratic systems of government. This is especially important in Africa, and our concerns will be fixed upon securing a spirit of tolerance and the ethos of sound governance throughout the continent. There cannot be one system for Africa and another for the world. If there is a single lesson to be drawn from Africa's post-colonial history, it is that accountable government is good government.

It is a mistake to interpret this as Afro-pessimism. South Africa cannot escape its continental destiny, nor does it wish to do so. If we do not devote our energies to Africa, we too could fall victim to the forces that have brought near ruin to its furthest corners.

Through the wonders of modern science we are all understanding more about the past. The "out of Africa" theory has firmly established that homo erectus migrated from this continent 1.8 million years ago. As a result, Africa's people are indelibly part of humankind's cradle; because of this, we have a duty to speak openly and honestly about our common concerns.

The international community has a notoriously short concentration span. Since the ending of the Cold War, attention has moved eastward, weakening Africa's economic position. There is less and less assistance from the outside world, and Africans have responded by transforming the continent's economic base. But the international community needs to examine the reasons why it has turned its back on Africa's people. It is clear, for example, that scientists in the former Soviet Union and in Eastern Europe enjoy greater resources from the West than do their peers in Africa. Is this, as many would have us believe, a new form of racism?

The violent breakup of states points to the horrors facing countries in Africa and elsewhere that are not prepared to accept diversity as integral to the human condition. These failed states will fall prey to greater internecine strife, sapping if not destroying the potential of their people. They will fall further and further behind the great technological advances that are being made elsewhere.

Many believe this fate beckons my own country. They are utterly wrong. Few people on earth have experienced intolerance as have South Africans: this has steeled our vigilance toward democracy and tolerance. Even in the darkest days of apartheid and the most tragic moments of our turbulent transition, South Africans of all colors and creeds have, with great personal courage, shown respect for difference. A central goal of South Africa's foreign policy, like its domestic politics, will be to promote institutions and forces which, through democracy, seek to make the world safe for diversity. This is our vision for the twenty-first century.

We recognize that this challenge is immense. South Africa is a nation of eleven major languages and many religions. The intricate negotiations over our transition have secured rights for all these groupings, however. The rich, diverse, and individual cultures of our people will feed the cauldron from which a new South Africanism will emerge. Unless a place under this sun can be found for all our people, our policies will have failed, our long struggle rendered meaningless by a failure to secure the human worth and individual dignity of each South African.

Because apartheid corroded the very essence of life, South Africa's leaders are charged to build a nation in which all people — irrespective of race, color, creed, religion, or sex — can assert fully their human worth; after apartheid, our people deserve nothing less than the rights enjoyed by democracies around the world.

Freedom and economic development are linked in bewildering ways. Unless the poor materially benefit from political change, the best constitution will be under siege from forces hostile to the historic settlement. Securing democracy in turbulent recessionary times is not easy, but it is a challenge to which leadership must respond.

In South Africa, we will have to create jobs in urban and rural areas, improve access to housing and basic services, and restructure social security programs for the very poor, the disabled, and the aged. We will do these things because they will buttress our democracy, yes. We must do them because they will help with our development, true. But we must especially do them because they are in the interests of our people. Only by looking toward the interests of a nation's people can the foundations of democracy endure.

South Africa and the World

Unresolved — perhaps irresolvable — tensions link the trend toward democracy, at the national level, with the pressures for globalism. This condition parallels a conflict between the weakening hold of governments over the actions of individual citizens and the strengthening international power of commerce, industry, and finance. No frameworks exist to resolve clashes of this kind without deepening the potential for further conflict. They represent, therefore, a formidable challenge to international law and statecraft.

The ending of the Cold War has released a tide of migrants and refugees across the world. Although the phenomenon predates the nation-state, an urgency has been added by the magnitude of the problem and the destruction that has been visited on national groups, like the Kurds.

These issues test the international system in profound ways. Migration defies notions of sovereignty; it tests a range of international legal authorities; it calls for new kinds of international organizations. But acknowledging all this only highlights one of the ironies of the international search for peace and security: although the force of worldwide migration threatens the nation-state, the long-term questions that it raises can only be answered by cooperation between states.

The United Nations — which has been freed from the straitjacket of the Cold War — is a helpful place to start thinking about clashes that lie beyond the immediate horizon. South Africa's experience teaches that the United Nations has a pivotal role to play in fostering security, order, and emancipation.

Multilateralism and collective action — especially in the field of threats to the international order — must be the route we choose to provide the response of the international community.

To succeed, however, serious attention must be paid to a restructuring of the organization. If the United Nations continues to be dominated by a single power or group of powers, its legitimacy will be called into question. Not only should we have democracy within countries, it must also be practiced between them.

With others, South Africa will explore the various proposals that have been put forward for the strengthening of the powers of the General Assembly. Again, with like-minded states, we believe that the Security Council needs to reflect the full tapestry of humankind rather than, as is presently the case, the sectional concerns of powers that helped create an international system which has run its course.

The other faces of the United Nations will need changing, too. An agenda will have to be determined in which economic, social, and ecological issues are raised in their mutual context. A promising start has been made following the acceptance of Agenda 21 at the United Nations Conference on the Environment and Development (UNCED) in Rio De Janeiro in May 1992. To be successful, however, the objectives and activities of Agenda 21 need to be revised in tandem with the much-needed debate over the reform of the entire United Nations structure. For instance, the effectiveness of ECOSOC needs to be weighed against the deepening poverty throughout the world. With these considerations, the healthy process of strengthening and restructuring of the Secretariat, including making it financially accountable, are important steps forward.

In addition to acceding to the major arms control regimes, South Africa will actively support the commitment of the United Nations to a general and complete disarmament under effective international control. It will not be easy to check the flow of weapons — both large and small.

Much of the blame for South Africa's unnecessarily violent transition lies in the proliferation of small arms throughout southern Africa. This experience has established a direct link between easy availability of small arms and the pace and direction of ethnic mobilization. Nevertheless, little of the blood spilled on our streets or our veld was caused by weapons made in our country. Tragically, South Africa's experience is not isolated: no single other issue challenges the United Nations with greater urgency than the need to create the means to stem the flow of small arms worldwide.

The established system of arms registries has been found wanting: the pressure to export weapons in a world starved of hard cash and filled with conflict appears to have been too tempting. The initiation of new control and registration devices needs to be linked to a renewed worldwide crusade against armaments. It was this same combination of transparency and public passion that helped to quell a tide of weapons after the atrocities of the First World War. There is every reason to believe that with the vast and pinpointed reach of modern communications, a similar strategy can be equally effective late in the twentieth century.

Multilateral organizations at the regional level also need strengthening. The Organization of African Unity will need to adjust to the changes at work throughout the world. A democratic, nonracial South Africa closes a chapter in the continent's long and arduous efforts to end colonialism and racism. But the book of continental unity and closer cooperation remains open. Many issues in Africa require attention: our televisions relay only the most obvious problems — wars, famine, the death of children. These images mask, however, a range of deep-seated problems on a continent that has been profoundly influenced by global change. They can be tackled only if all Africa's leaders are prepared to heed Ahmed Ben Bella's May 1963 call that helped create the Organization of African Unity: "We must all die a little so that African unity can become a reality."

Successful foreign policy in the post–Cold War era will be essentially conditioned by a state's geography and economic performance. Both these issues will require careful attention because they directly touch the lives of a people — South Africa's — long deprived of international contact. Both will also test the ingenuity of policymakers because success in both areas will stand in stark contrast to how for nearly five decades apartheid South Africa conducted its affairs.

South Africans have a special relationship with the peoples of southern Africa. We belong to each other. We are bound by deep historical and cultural ties that predate colonialism. Equally important, we are part of a regional economy that has existed since the mid-nineteenth century. In recent times, individual states — Tanzania, Angola, Zambia, and others — helped sustain our people during exile's dark days. We will craft our policies, therefore, in concert with the states about us, conscious of the fact that we, not they, are the younger of southern Africa's sons and daughters.

Economic patterns in southern Africa have been highly uneven and inequitable. The regional economy that emerged under colonialism entrenched the domination of one country — our own. Others were incorporated in subsidiary and dependent roles; they were labor reserves, markets for South African commodities, suppliers of certain services — such as transport — or providers of cheap and convenient resources — like water, electricity, and some raw materials. South Africa's visible exports to the rest of the region exceed imports by a factor of more than five. This reflects the productive base of the stronger and highlights the barriers that have kept regionally produced goods out of South Africa's market. This must change if the region is to grow.

Given our closeness, it is not surprising that all of southern Africa suffered under apartheid. While South Africans experienced discrimination and repression at home, southern Africa fell victim to apartheid's destabilization strategy, which left two million dead and inflicted a terrible toll on their economies. Apartheid's legacy can be addressed only within a regional context. This is why closer forms of cooperation and economic integration will yield benefits for the entire region.

In forging cooperative links, our people will draw on an African tradition to foster the cause of continental unity. The region should mirror efforts elsewhere in the world that prove greater regionalism enhances the prospects for wealth creation.

Southern Africa is delicately poised, however, and the joint regional endeavor needs to take account of the interests of the weaker states. Increasing South Africa's trade with the region should not be at the expense of industrial development in other countries, nor should it squeeze out trade opportunities between the other countries of the region. The same principle applies to the short-term interests of South African transport, water, and electricity utilities: these should not be promoted at the expense of development projects in the rest of the region. A cooperative stance within the region will be most conducive to long-term acceptance by our neighbors if we regard them as trade or project partners. The long-term interests of the South African economy will best be served by an approach to regional cooperation and integration that seeks to promote balanced growth and development. Trade opportunities will be much greater in an economically active southern Africa.

Similar considerations will govern the recasting of the migrant labor system. This practice is plainly detrimental to long-term development goals and human security. Nevertheless, a number of countries are critically dependent on migrant labor for employment and foreign exchange earnings. In these circumstances, South Africa cannot adopt a narrow approach to the issue, nor can it make unilateral changes to the system. A regional solution that takes into account the needs of the labor-supplying states is the only way out of a cruel, cruel dilemma.

South Africa's government is involved in consultations with the Southern African Development Community (SADC) and with the Eastern and Southern African Preferential Trade Area (PTA). These are important vehicles in establishing a regional identity, but the region cannot afford a duplication of integration efforts. Southern Africa must set its compass for the twenty-first century. As in other regions of the world, we will have to choose a single regional institution and support it through the troubled times. This means the region will have to plan its future steps. As the distinguished African statesman Julius Nyerere once put it, "To plan is to choose." There is no avoiding this issue any longer.

South Africa can prosper only if the principles of equity, mutual benefit, and peaceful cooperation are the tenets that inform its work. Reconstruction cannot be imposed on the region by external forces. Building southern Africa must be the collective enterprise of all its people.

In the region's future, militaristic approaches to security and cooperation have no place. Reconstruction should be rooted in peace-based and development-oriented approaches. With its neighbors, South Africa will promote the creation of regional structures for crisis prevention and management. These should be augmented by institutions that offer facilitation, mediation, and arbitration of interstate conflicts.

The growth prospects for neither the region nor South Africa can be divorced from the other conditioning factor of foreign policy, the pathology of international economics.

New economic conflicts and income divides are surfacing throughout the world. The chasm between the industrialized North and the underdeveloped South is deepening. If there is to be global harmony, the international community will have to engineer mechanisms to bridge these gaps. This will not be easy. As the near impasse over GATT graphically demonstrated, restructuring economic institutions in recessionary times is not a simple matter. Plausibly, South Africa can play some role in this because it is situated at a particular economic confluence. This is why a discussion of its economic recovery plan offers instructive insights into the plight of weaker countries.

Current orthodoxy suggests that only a holistic view of economic planning can possibly succeed. This draws the regional dimension closer to the broader objectives of international economic policy, whose primary goals place South Africa on the path of economic development. Slow growth, severe poverty, and extreme inequalities in living, income, and opportunity standards are three residual problems that need to be addressed. These problems are not uniquely South African; they describe conditions in a host of countries. Apartheid exacerbated South Africa's concerns, to be sure, but the country displays the symptoms of countless countries caught in the development squeeze of the late twentieth century.

With the exception of brief booms in the gold market, South Africa's economy has grown slowly since the early 1970s. The annual gross domestic product increased from almost 6 percent in the 1960s to less than 4 percent during the following decade to barely 1 percent during the 1980s. The economy contracted sharply during the recession-bound 1980s: in all but one of the past twelve years, per capita income has declined.

Endemic poverty is manifest in extremely high levels of unemployment. These are thought to be nearly 50 percent, and the social and economic indicators for the black population, particularly in rural areas, are very poor. These problems are compounded by apartheid's wanton legacy — all inequalities are entrenched along racial lines.

The World Bank has estimated that South Africa's whites have a personal per capita income level that is 9.5 times higher than that of Africans, 4.5 times higher than that of people classified by the apartheid system as colored, and 3 times than that of Asians. Patterns of inequality extend beyond these figures to the provision of services, access to education, employment opportunities, and wealth generation — all heavily favor the white population.

From the late 1980s, South Africa's faltering performance was compounded by a series of political questions that faced potential investors in South Africa. Additionally, growth opportunities were wasted by the political and economic policies of successive apartheid governments. These were incredibly damaging, to be sure, but an equally serious consequence was that they conspired to prevent South Africa's economy from adapting to changing global conditions. Take staple exports, for example: gold and other metals and minerals encountered deteriorating market conditions, but few efforts were made to develop competitive alternatives. So while South Africa's people have inherited a relatively open economy, there is little wherewithal to pay for imports over the longer term unless the economy begins to grow rapidly.

Despite immediate problems, the country's economy has great potential. South Africa has a competitive manufacturing sector in metal engineering and in pulp and paper. Moreover, the service sectors — of which banking, insurance, and tourism are the most important — also offer prospects for growth. There are vast untapped resources among our people that have to be identified.

A range of policy options can help fulfill South Africa's economic potential. These include developing effective education and training programs; attracting foreign investment in order to strengthen the country's technology and market access; instituting measured reform of trade policy to encourage domestic competition and lower the import bill; adopting a tough competition and antitrust policy to lower prices and raise business efficiency and, simultaneously, to generate opportunities in business among those previously excluded; and developing a range of initiatives to stimulate private-sector investment and restructuring.

In this regard, we might pause to consider an aspect of global change to which I have alluded and which will have a vital bearing on how, if at all, countries like South Africa are to fulfill their potential. Science and technology carry human progress and, as noted, provide footholds for national prosperity. Recent developments in these fields are baffling: like biotechnology, in which gene manipulation alone has huge implications in a range of fields that impact directly on health, food, and resources.

This decade will see the launch of an ambitious earth satellite observation system. It will provide new insights into areas that have a direct bearing on the prosperity of our people: climate change, environment, desertification, deforestation, and drought. Data management is the most critical component of changes that are still to come. When they do, new fields like communications technology will enable us to understand and manage many aspects of the changing world: migration, disease, urbanization, and water resources are only four of countless others. Planning will be enhanced by this knowledge. Significantly, too, this real-time information will create the capacity of countries and regions to communicate and, perhaps, avoid conflict.

The lesson is clear: not only South Africa but all the countries of the South need to be part of the breaking wave of technology. Our educational institutions need to carry forward the capacity of our people to enjoy the fruits that will flow from these developments. South Africans will have to harness and adapt the power of science; our universities need to be encouraged to remain competitive. The government is committed to establishing better communications with our scientists and to creating a new science advisory apparatus. But — and this is a warning — none of this can be achieved without real partnerships between the North and the South.

Innovative policies, like the development of science and technology, will not provide a quick cure to the country's economic afflictions; additionally, their implementation will take time. Given the political price attached to securing democracy, a number of short-term strategies will be needed to address areas of immediate concern.

But the essential components of international economic relations must nourish a broad development strategy. South Africa will need to strengthen its trade performance and its capacity to attract foreign investment. It will also have to examine the possibilities of obtaining technical and financial assistance from the developed industrial countries. South Africa's challenge is to offset skewed patterns of economic development; this, too, will not be easy.

A range of new forces influencing global change can alter the geometry of trade and acutely — and very frequently — turn the terms of trade. For South Africa and other developing countries, these have been increasingly adverse. As the century draws to an end, the producers of primary products are suffering severe economic hardship. Differentials between rich and poor countries are increasing. Devastated African economies — as one example — are pushed to the very edges of the international economic system. The increasing global purchase of the rich enables them to recast the institutions that regulate global economics in their own image, rather than for the benefit of all countries. Conversely, the majority of countries suffer a diminishing ability to influence a political process — which crucially affects the lives of their people — for no other reason than that they are poor. These are not peripheral considerations; they stand at the very center of international relations.

The rich countries are living in a glorious pool of permanent economic light. Beyond this rim of light, a secondary group of countries are found; they live in a kind of economic dusk. Further away, beyond the pool of light and the shadow, the greater number of countries and peoples of the world live in an economic darkness. Typically, images like this fail to capture the misery that these categorizations mean for billions of the planet's poor.

The international community cannot view this situation with any equanimity — a world in which large numbers of the population are condemned to be excluded, cast into the darkness because they are poor, can never be secure. For the world to be at peace, we will need the rim of the light to be extended.

The philosophy of my government on these issues is clear. We will seek to maximize the benefits that can flow from the present structure of international economic relations. We will also actively seek to reform — with the help of our neighbors, fellow Africans and the South — the existing rules of the road.

South Africa will approach the powerful international actors — like the World Trade Organization — in a vigorous fashion, not seeking confrontation and not acting defensively or as a supplicant. The country will place on the emerging agendas the concerns and the interests of Africa and the South. We will encourage the formation of alliances between countries of the South, particularly the role of organizations like the Nonalignment Movement and the Group of 77, which despite the ending of the Cold War remain important. It is not difficult to predict that new multilateral organizations, concerned with making the South more viable, will be brought to life. The countries in the shadows, like my own, have a responsibility to ensure that they help widen the arc of the world's economic lamp.

Full participation in the global trading system is central to securing South Africa's international economic relations. For the sake of our democracy we need to be in the pool of light. While striving to accommodate the concerns of the General Agreement on Tariffs and Trade (GATT) in regard to the high levels of protection in industry and to open our markets to external trade, South Africa will insist that this is a two-way process. We will take action against the products of countries that will not open their markets to South African products. The principle is clear: for the international trading regime to be effective, reciprocity is paramount.

The developed world, though, must also recognize the need of the less advantaged countries to build an infrastructure and to consolidate areas of the economy that are in their infancy. This is not to be confused with narrow protectionism.

A program of trade policy reform must, however, address the levels of protection and the development of effective export incentives that are internationally acceptable. As the Uruguay Round demonstrated, the growth of North-based trading blocs — such as the European Union and NAFTA — has weakened the position of developing countries, particularly those like South Africa, which are not members of any trading bloc.

South Africa is enthusiastically seeking new avenues for its exported manufactured goods, minerals, and agricultural produce. At the same time, the government is actively seeking to consolidate our long-standing relationship with the European Union, South Africa's largest trade and investment partner.

In addition, the country is examining the expansion and strengthening of its relationship with the United States, NAFTA, Japan, and economies of the Pacific Rim. Throughout these negotiations South Africa seeks the assurances from members of the major trading blocs on the issue of market access. Our location on a particular economic concourse, however, will impel us to simultaneously strengthen South-South ties in an effort to prevent further economic nationalization.

In this there are time considerations: any effort to force the reintegration of the country's trade regime into the global system will be resisted. Although it supports free trade, South Africa's government will not place the demands of others' sectoral interests ahead of the needs of the country's people.

Because of its importance to South Africa and the deep-seated dilemmas these economic issues raise for the South, I have dwelt on South Africa's international economic relations at length. For reasons that have run through these pages, economic growth, national development, and social reconstruction in South Africa and across the world require an engagement that is both effective and creative in international economic relations. A way must be found in which all countries can find their way into the light. Equally so, there is no pretending that robust economics are not conducive to development or — as some would have us do — wishing these into oblivion by the use of some fanciful ideological curse.

Facing the Twenty-first Century

The process we call global change is far from complete and its future is wholly uncertain. The international arena is a far more uncertain and even more dangerous place. The familiarity that once held the world together has come apart, and all about us new ways of engaging politics are under way. There are obviously no clear-cut answers to the range of new questions that are uppermost in the affairs of nations: as a result, all leaders need to be attentive to the continuous unfolding of events.

The world is truly global — what occurs in one country or continent seems programmed for elsewhere. The only salvation lies, therefore, through imaginative engagement with the forces that are transforming our world. All humankind — nations and individuals — are called to a moment of great creativity in the closing years of the twentieth century.

The common properties that South Africa brings to a world in deep transition reflect its past and its present. Our geographical location dictates a diplomatic role in Africa and a development role in our region. The imaginative deployment of "islands of skilling" can help the sea of illiteracy that faces the country's majority. Our capacity to influence events, however, will primarily depend on how we understand the lessons of struggle.

Our country — perhaps like no other — knows the challenges of diversity, democracy, disquiet, and development, the familiar litany of new world issues. We know them because our struggle has been for the world's future, not its past.

This is why I will end where I started: with the unforgivable sin of the personal. It is unlikely that I shall see much of the next century. I know, however, that the choices we now make and the crusades we now generate will shape — and reshape — the course of this nation's history, Africa's future, and human destiny. This is why facing up to the twenty-first century is the continuing challenge of my life's work.

His Excellency

Fernando Henrique Cardoso

President of Brazil

The Post–Cold War Era

A View from the South

Introduction: The End of the Cold War

The Cold War is over. This is a positive development by any measure. Never was international peace and security more at risk than during the grim decades of the Cold War. Any local or regional outbreak of violence ran the risk of escalating into all-out war between two competing blocs, either of which had the capacity to destroy the other. The stability of the international system was precariously maintained on the basis of mutual fear of destruction. Deterrence, rather than cooperation, was the prevailing concept.

This ideological confrontation permeated the domestic political context in many countries. This was particularly true in Latin America. Dissenting political opinion was mistaken for insurrection and then usually silenced with either coercion or violence by the military regimes in place. The doctrine of "national security" and the human rights abuses committed in its name were a painful side effect of the Cold War in Latin America. I myself was a victim of political persecution in my own country and was forced to live in exile for many years. I was then a professor of social science at the University of São Paulo.

Only within the conceptual framework of the global ideological conflict could I be considered any threat.

Countries in the South had little, if anything, to gain from the state of international relations during the Cold War. Issues of key interest to them such as development, disarmament, and the struggle for independence of former colonies not only were placed low on the international agenda but also were subordinated to the dispute between the two superpowers. The official flow of resources into developing countries most often took the form of military aid or arms-related financing. These fueled or ignited civil wars and regional tensions provoked by the quest for wider spheres of influence between the two superpowers. Though regional crises have always existed, during the Cold War they were exacerbated by an ideological dispute whose motives were entirely alien to the root causes of regional problems. The conflicts in Korea, Vietnam, Kampuchea, Afghanistan, Angola, Mozambique, El Salvador, and Nicaragua are only a few of the bloodier examples of such East-West tensions transposed to the South.

The collapse of the Soviet Union was precipitated by the disintegration of the political and economic systems prevailing therein. It was an empire held together by political oppression, persecution of minorities, fear, and a cumbersome bureaucracy. After years of military overspending, its economy was in shambles. A mix of economic mismanagement and the absence of a significant private sector prevented the Soviet economy from creating the conditions necessary for growth in the long run.

Freedom and the market economy emerged from the Cold War as widely accepted values. Latin America in general, and Brazil in particular, cannot but rejoice at this fact. These values reflect choices made by this region during the 1980s. To see these core values strengthened at the international level can only reinforce our inclination to be more in tune with the world, so that our growing participation on the global stage will be more harmonious than ever before. Just as the 1990 Conference on Security and Cooperation in Europe (CSCE) summit in Paris had supported democracy as the sole form of government acceptable to its member countries, so the 1991 Organization of American States (OAS) General Assembly in Santiago, Chile, endorsed a hemispheric commitment to democracy and approved a resolution by which the OAS Permanent Council should be convened in cases of unconstitutional interruption of the democratic political process in any of its member countries.

By freeing the international agenda of tensions that ultimately prevented truly concerted international action to the benefit of mankind, the end of the Cold War in the late 1980s was a long-awaited development. Countries in the South, including Brazil, had used many of their most prominent international statements during the preceding decades to call for an end to the global confrontation. From 1989 onward, they would no longer have to reiterate this call. Their attention would instead be drawn to new opportunities and new challenges.

The Post–Cold War Period:
Complacency and Frustration

Political events in the early post–Cold War years proceeded at a very fast pace. They initially tended to confirm the highest expectations that one could have nourished about the dawning of a new era in international relations. The year 1990 witnessed the dismantling of the Soviet empire and the reunification of Germany. Shortly after that, peace was achieved in parts of the world other than Europe.

Regional tensions abated or ended in Central America and in Africa. Free elections were held in Nicaragua in 1990 that removed the previous government from power and replaced it with a firm opponent. The conflict in El Salvador was settled through U.N. mediation on the last day of 1991 and sealed with the signing of the peace agreements in Mexico City in 1992. In Africa developments were also positive. By May 1991, the United Nations had helped the People's Movement for the Liberation of Angola (MPLA) and UNITA reach a peace agreement, allowing both for the two fighting armies to merge and for general elections to take place under international scrutiny. The implementation of this agreement, we now know, fizzled out later on. It nevertheless set a precedent for the Lusaka agreements of 1994, which are currently in the process of being enforced, with good prospects for the future. The end of the Cold War played a significant role in getting the white minority in South Africa ready to start talks with the black majority, with a view to rolling back one by one the pillars of apartheid. Only a few years ago, no one could have predicted that Nelson Mandela would be elected, and then sworn in, as the president of all South Africans.

Important changes were under way in the Middle East as well. Ancient hatreds had previously combined with stockpiles of deadly weapons to make the region the most likely stage for a direct confrontation between the two superpowers. In 1956 and 1973 that bleak scenario was not far from becoming a reality. Yet the miscalculation of Saddam Hussein, upon invading Kuwait in August 1990, found a different atmosphere in world affairs, which allowed for a sequence of events unthinkable during the East-West tensions. At the urging of the United States, a series of U.N. Security Council resolutions were passed that not only conferred international legitimacy on a coalition of countries for them to wage war against invading Iraq, but also inflicted upon it severe cease-fire conditions under resolutions 687 and 688. In addition, these resolutions created "safe havens" for Kurds in the north and for the Shias in the south of Iraq.

The international response to the Gulf conflict was viewed as proof that the U.N. Security Council, now unchecked by the veto of one of the superpowers, could be the core of a system of worldwide collective defense in cases of flagrant threats to international peace and security. The relatively successful U.N. engagement in other regional conflicts at that time contributed to reinforcing that view. On the other hand, the Gulf War cleared the way for the Middle East peace process. Syria was forced by the Soviet disengagement to seek improved relations with the United States during the Gulf War. The Soviet retreat from the region also caused the United States to look at Israel from a new perspective, no longer primarily as the single regional ally of the West and therefore deserving special treatment. The Madrid Conference ensued in October 1991, in which Syrians, Palestinians, and Israelis sat at the negotiating table. The peace process in the Middle East has continued to move forward in the years since then.

Events in the immediate post–Cold War period were certainly impressive enough. Yet there was a wave of triumph that seemed to be in excess of what would have been a justifiable optimism. Complacency about its own actions was to prove an enemy of the West, for it prevented the necessary international action to deal with other kinds of conflicts that were unfolding.

Ethnic rivalries. Religious intolerance. These driving forces of conflict, in principle, have nothing to do with ideology. Conflicts rooted in those uncontrollable forces were to prove a truly difficult test for the international community. The former Yugoslavia is a case in point. Like the Soviet Union, Yugoslavia was kept together only under authoritarian rule. It was no nation-state. When the long-repressed ethnic and religious rivalries were finally unleashed, the disintegration of Yugoslavia was inevitable. Whether or not the country should remain a single political entity is not, however, the point. What was at stake in the former Yugoslavia, particularly in Bosnia, was first the willingness, and then the capacity, of the international community to negotiate a political solution, to provide humanitarian relief, and ultimately to avert the likely bloodshed. The international community failed in all three respects, just as it failed subsequently in Somalia and Rwanda. Complacency had to be tempered with frustration over the images of Sarajevo's ruins, Somalia's hopeless violence, and a Hutu mother fleeing Rwanda in despair with her children.

The sort of wars we saw in the former Yugoslavia, Somalia, and Rwanda are the ones we are likely to be faced with in the post–Cold War period. We must recognize that this is a challenge we are ill prepared to cope with. To tame the forces leading to them is probably beyond the capacity of the international community. But the escalation of those wars should meet stronger resistance. If outsiders turn a blind eye to conquest or bloodshed, why should the warring parties refrain from escalating their violence? If they do not perceive any serious external interest in stemming atrocities, why then should humanitarian relief reach those in need of it? In fact, why then should they refrain from attacking the Blue Helmets? The present Bosnian quagmire has provided ample evidence of the need to rethink and strengthen U.N. peacekeeping and humanitarian aid operations. It has also shown multilateral organizations to be at a loss in seeking a satisfactory political settlement. The United Nations, the European Union, NATO, and the CSCE were all involved at one stage or another in trying to bring peace to the former Yugoslavia. None has been successful. There was no repetition of the effectiveness displayed by the Security Council during the Gulf War. A crucial reason for this lies in the present institutional architecture of world affairs, which is largely inherited from the Cold War years. It is now time to redesign it to meet the challenges ahead and to give it more legitimacy by opening its decision-making processes to more democratic participation by the international community.

After the Cold War:
New Issues, New Risks

The international agenda has gradually changed in the post–Cold War years. This is only natural. To the extent that the threat of an East-West war no longer exists, other issues are now getting more attention — human rights, drug trafficking, the environment, population growth, South-North migration, and displaced persons and refugees. These issues are each important and have an inherent merit: the focus on human beings and on the quality of human life on Earth.

World conferences have been held on such issues as the environment (Rio de Janeiro, 1992), human rights (Vienna, 1993), and population (Cairo, 1994). These conferences no doubt served a useful purpose and fostered understanding and cooperation in their respective fields. Despite the importance of those issues, approaches for dealing with them seem to vary widely between developing and developed countries. Where the former see opportunities for international cooperation from a developmental perspective, the latter — especially their public opinion — quite often perceive threats to their well-being and to their own security. Apart from that, the North tends to consider each issue in isolation. By contrast, the South usually focuses more on the interplay of the various issues, viewing them from an integrated developmental perspective.

Take, for example, the case of South-North or intraregional migration. Since extreme poverty, hopelessness, unemployment, demographic growth, environmental damage, and massive violations of human rights rank amongst the chief reasons for massive displacements of persons, which may have an adverse impact upon the destination country, should not these problems be attacked at their origins through a multifaceted, development-oriented strategy? Such an approach would place matters in the appropriate perspective of the commonality of interests between North and South.

The risk to be avoided is that of oversimplification of reality. The new issues on the agenda must not be regarded solely as threats to well-established patterns of well-being in parts of the world or as a motive for mutual accusations and recriminations among nations. Similarly, they must not simply replace the old fear of a nuclear holocaust as the new supposed threats to world peace and security. Cooperation is what is called for.

Cooperation must take new forms. Established patterns for managing international relations have become inadequate due to the very nature of the new issues on the agenda, which demand greater participation of actors other than representatives of national governments. I can hardly conceive of any meaningful work undertaken in the humanitarian or the environmental fields without the contribution of grassroots organizations.

They are a productive channel between government and society. They voice significant concerns that would otherwise remain unheard. They have allowed for greater transparency in the decisions taken by governments in international forums. And the links they create among themselves are also a new form of international cooperation. What a difference from the usual conduct of international relations in the Cold War, in which the overwhelming role played by government representatives, working against the background of ideological controversy, generally failed to build the confidence necessary for the more ambitious actions now made possible by a partnership between society and governments.

Beyond the Political Agenda:
Economic Competition and Integration —
New Challenges

The changes brought about by events in Eastern Europe and, later, by the collapse of the Soviet Union and the shift to a "unipolar" strategic system are much more political than economic in nature. They constitute a step in the evolution of international relations toward a permanently updated form of power politics among states and groups of states. They can also be seen as a reenforcement of historical tendencies alongside the other forces that have been driving history since the end of World War II: the growing economic interdependence among nations and the attainment of increasingly higher levels of economic competitiveness. Competition for a greater share of the world market has become an overriding concern, and any acquired share is regarded as a source of power among nations, replacing in a way the pursuit of territorial gains or strategic and military power. This is what explains, in a nutshell, the demise of the Soviet Union and its allies, the power of which was based essentially on military might.

The creation of the European Economic Community in 1956 and the relatively quick reconstruction of Japan showed that the years of absolute U.S. dominance of the world economy were coming to an end. Strategic bipolarism was being fundamentally transformed by a revival of a complex economic competition among the leading countries. Soon these were to be joined by newly industrialized and fast-growing developing countries in Asia and Latin America.

Viewed against this background, the post–Cold War period has revealed one crude reality that developing countries must bear in mind when reassessing their policies and goals: a world of tough economic competition that certainly would not end poverty automatically, nor would it lead to the closing of the gap between richer and poorer nations.

The international environment is a key element determining growth prospects for all developing countries. Obviously, countries in the South find themselves at different stages of development, and strategies pursued by them must take those differences into account. It is true that world economic output slowed down in the first few post–Cold War years, following the Gulf conflict and the disruption of centrally planned economies. But the latest indicators show that the world economy is now regaining speed. In 1995 not only developed and developing countries will grow; the so-called economies in transition are expected to post positive growth for the first time since 1989.

To the extent that its growth will continue to outpace that of the world economy, world trade will remain a dynamic force for creating jobs and wealth worldwide. It is thus in the best interests of all nations to preserve an open international trading system and to resist the dangers of protectionism, managed trade, or unilateral action in trade matters. A rules-based system, applied universally, is the best guarantee to ensure that trade will continue to foster economic growth in the future, as in the past.

The post–Cold War period has seen the conclusion of the GATT Uruguay Round of trade negotiations and the birth of the World Trade Organization (WTO). These are welcome developments. The main goal of previous trade rounds was to reduce tariffs, which were then the main barriers to the expansion of world trade. Tariffs having been greatly lowered, the focus of attention has shifted to subtler forms of protectionism and impediments to trade. The Uruguay Round dealt with some of those topics, such as intellectual property rights and market access rules (subsidies, dumping, safeguards). Others will have to be dealt with in the WTO. In our era of fierce global competition and of widespread adherence to free market economic principles, it is imperative that the WTO be expanded to include as wide a membership as possible. Global markets go hand in hand with global players.

Another feature of the post–Cold War era is the consolidation of regional integration agreements under looser (NAFTA) or tighter (European

Union, Mercosur) schemes. There is no denying that the movement toward a deeper economic integration preceded the end of the Cold War. To mention only one example, efforts to build what is now the European Union started in the 1950s. Still, the fact remains that regional integration has been a distinctive feature of the post–Cold War period. The early 1990s have seen the signing of Maastricht, NAFTA, and Mercosur as well as the announcement, in the recently concluded summits at Bangor and Miami, of negotiations to establish free trade areas in the Pacific region and in the Americas. A hemispheric free trade agreement in the Americas, as now envisaged, would have been virtually impossible during the Cold War, when countries in the region were a theater for guerrilla operations, at times aimed at each other.

Open regional integration creates additional trade flows without imposing barriers to outside trading partners. The creation of Mercosur was based on that principle. Even though Mercosur accounts for a growing share of Brazil's total foreign trade, the trade flows with other trading partners have been on the rise as well. No less important is the fact that integration creates a sense of mutual interests, cooperation, and solidarity. Recent events in the Mexican economy bear witness to that feeling of shared responsibility among countries belonging to an integration scheme. We must hope that this spirit can be applied to the global management of economic affairs. Therein lies a challenge — and also a new opportunity for strengthening the operational capacity of international financial institutions such as the International Monetary Fund and the World Bank at a time when financial transactions, like trade flows, have also become global in nature.

The Mexican situation highlighted one side of globalization that had received little attention: the disruptive impact of swings in public confidence abroad on an open economy as well as the vulnerability of these economies to such volatility. The lifting of capital controls facilitates the inflow of foreign resources just as it facilitates their rapid outflow whenever the perception — correct or not — becomes widespread that a country may face difficulties. Thus, misperceptions may occur and exact a heavy toll from any country whose economic situation would otherwise be intrinsically sound and which could stay on the right track with adjustments over a certain period of time. This side of globalization is one that must be examined more thoroughly so that adequate responses can be found.

The "Four Fundamentals" of the Post–Cold War Period and Responses to Them

Only a few years have elapsed since events in Eastern Europe changed the international setting. This period has shown that post–Cold War politics and economics are much more complex than previously anticipated by those who had indulged in hastily celebrating the triumph of a "new world order." Reassessing international relations and the role of diplomacy in the 1990s is of the utmost importance for developing countries. In my view, this task should take into account what I will refer to as the "four fundamentals" of post–Cold War international relations:

1. the economic globalization of production and capital flows on an unprecedented scale, requiring a search for new "comparative advantages" and putting competitiveness at the center stage of international affairs;

2. the leading role of international trade in goods and services in the creation of wealth;

3. the growing consensus — although far from absolute — in the international community around the values of democracy, human rights, sustainable development, and economic freedom, as well as an increasingly shared view of the economic policy instruments necessary to bring about sustained growth;

4. the increasing tendency toward regional integration under arrangements of various scopes.

It is against the backdrop of these fundamentals that one should examine the role played by the sovereign state as the main actor of international relations. Interdependence and globalization have not meant the negation of the nation-state. All four of the fundamentals actually project national capabilities of individual states. National power and assets still put states in a more comfortable position relative to other international actors. Nothing is new in this centuries-old relationship among sovereign states except for the fact that military strength, territorial dimensions, and population size are no longer the key attributes of power.

History, although dominated by a continuous power struggle among the strongest, has always allowed for states to seek sources of power other than the military. These are today called "soft power" by some scholars and embody such attributes of power as, among others, a skilled work force, a strong cultural background, a shared sentiment of national unity, and full command of modern technology and an ability to develop it. They may be "soft" only when compared with the "hard" power of maintaining large numbers of men in uniform and weapons of mass destruction. Yet in today's world, in which competition has all but moved from the military realm to the economic and technological fields, it can justifiably be argued that soft power takes increasing precedence over hard power.

Asian countries have provided a renewed example of how states can respond in positive ways to the external environment. The strategies pursued by them were not at all a direct response to the international political structure under a bipolar system. They were, rather, ways to take full advantage of new "windows of opportunity" created by widening international markets and the inflow of western capital after the first few post–World War II years. They found themselves better positioned than most countries when changes in the whole international structure accelerated in the late 1980s and early 1990s.

From whatever angle one looks at ongoing developments, there is no escaping the fact that the challenges represented by the four fundamentals above will require states to adopt a set of responses that combine the following elements: political stability through democracy and respect for human rights; macroeconomic stability; government efficiency and a strong and competitive private sector; sustained growth with better income distribution and sustainable use of natural resources; improved education and professional training; and a clear sense of inclusion among the poorer classes of society.

The accomplishment of these goals is no easy task, particularly for developing countries. Some of them, in the poorer regions of the world, must indeed pool their resources if they are to stand a chance of becoming viable states. In any event, the bulk of these efforts will have to be undertaken by the developing countries themselves. There is a good deal of homework for them to complete. A failure to redress social imbalances and income inequality will eventually result in loss of competitiveness and markets for their products, thereby limiting their growth potential and widening the development gap between such countries and their competitors in the marketplace. Lack of an adequately educated population is a major impediment to technological research and development. It thus puts a curb on the potential of any society to produce products with higher value added and condemns it instead to continue relying on either commodities or labor-intensive products. A society with sharp social and economic inequities is politically fragile. A sense of national cohesion is rarely to be found in those countries where the chasm between the haves and the have-nots is so wide as to generate violence rather than a sense of common purpose.

A View from the South: Brazil

Brazil has learnt the lessons of the past few years. During this century, with the exception of the "lost decade" of the 1980s in which per capita income remained stagnant, Brazil has had one of the fastest-growing economies in the world. After two years of around 5 percent growth in annual output and with similar prospects for the current year, Brazil is now in the process of resuming its past performance in a new context of economic stabilization coupled with an openness to international trade, capital, and investment flows.

Equally important is the fact that, unlike the so-called economic miracle of the 1970s, the current economic plan is being carried out in a Brazil that has reconciled itself fully with democracy. The economic plan itself was thoroughly discussed with various sectors of Brazilian society before it was undertaken. It is now being complemented with a firm emphasis on social questions. This is a top priority of my government. To provide Brazilians with equal access to education and health care is my long-term goal. Without it, our present economic growth will be no more than a temporary episode of academic interest to a handful of economists.

Brazilian foreign policy, for its part, is expected to play a major role in widening the country's options and opportunities. Brazil's restored role as a stabilized and growing economy, as well as a consolidated democracy, will have a positive impact on the country's bid for improved international and regional partnerships. Mercosur, now at the stage of a customs union, has made Brazil more attractive as a partner.

Several confidence-building measures in the areas of nonproliferation and nuclear cooperation with Argentina and the International Atomic Energy Agency, full participation in the Tlatelolco Treaty, and a firm constitutional commitment to the peaceful uses of nuclear energy have enhanced the country's credibility worldwide and broadened the opportunities for a freer access to technology.

At the same time and with a very pragmatic point of view, we aim to broaden our participation in the most important international decision-making bodies. Major economic decisions can no longer be confined to a small group of countries at a time of globalization of capital and trade markets. The same applies to the political decisions necessary to maintain world peace and security. Brazil certainly has a contribution to make in most international matters.

Conclusion:
A Time for Cooperation and Inclusion

The first few years of the post–Cold War era have simultaneously revealed new possibilities and risks. Facts are not readily discernible. They no longer fit any predictable mold. We were used to interpreting any event from an East-West perspective, and at times our way of thinking still has a long way to go before we can look at the new realities without any preconceptions. A freshness of spirit and an open-minded approach to international relations is what the post–Cold War period is really in need of.

Prospects for the remaining years of this century will be bright if world leaders are able to tackle the challenges posed by this period virtually free of ideological tension, a period offering unmatched opportunities for global cooperation on a broad array of issues that place the concerns of people and society at the forefront of the international debate. We know from experience the consequences of our unwillingness to act: brutal violence and misery continue to occur not only in remote corners of the world, but also at the very heart of developed societies.

It is time for an affirmative partnership. For this affirmative partnership to be truly successful, countries must enhance their own capabilities. Brazil is ready. In our case, enhancing our capabilities means social and economic reforms and a clear commitment to strengthening our citizenship. No country will be competitive and strong in the new set of international circumstances without a sense of belonging among all its citizens.

It may look like a paradox to see that hope has been brought back into international relations at a time when the grand utopias of the recent past have faded. The "new man" those utopias were supposed to create did not materialize. But the time is now ripe for the daily changes that really matter in order to improve the quality of life of mankind. The good news of the post–Cold War era is precisely that human beings have been repositioned at the center of our attention in international affairs.

Part 2

The International System in the Post–Cold War Order

His Excellency

Boutros Boutros-Ghali

Secretary-General of the United Nations

The United Nations in a Post–Cold War Order

In September of 1992, nine months into my tenure as secretary-general of the United Nations, I submitted to the General Assembly my first annual report on the work of the organization, emphasizing the new opportunities before the United Nations in the post–Cold War world. In my second annual report in September 1993, I stressed the host of new peacekeeping demands made upon the organization as a new dimension of conflict erupted in states around the world. During the period covered by my third annual report, I sought to correct the common misperception of the United Nations as an organization primarily dedicated to peacekeeping, and this is what I would like to further expound upon in this essay.

Economic and social questions have long occupied the major part of U.N. efforts. Such work has become all the more important today precisely as conflicts are increasingly recognized to have economic and social origins. Thus, in the midst of its efforts to contain and resolve immediate conflicts, the United Nations is deepening its attention to the foundations of peace, which lie in the realm of development.

In my 1992 report, "An Agenda for Peace," I outlined suggestions for enabling the United Nations to respond quickly and effectively to threats to international peace and security in the post–Cold War world. In our peace operations and in our efforts to face the new dimension of conflict, the United Nations continues to test "An Agenda for Peace" in action every day. Lessons from this experience continue to emerge, and a positive process of evolution can be discerned, moving toward ever more effective ways of maintaining international peace and security in the post–Cold War era.

Journeying into uncharted territory, the United Nations has encountered vast challenges. Genocide, ethnic cleansing, and crimes against humanity of a hideous nature have returned in new forms to haunt the world community. Effective means for putting a permanent end to these atrocities remain to be found. Yet the world organization continues to learn how to resolve crises and alleviate suffering in new and desperate situations. Each peace operation has taught us more about handling the range of novel problems — and opportunities — that the post–Cold War era presents.

Increasing our responsive capacity to immediate crises is clearly not enough. As ethnic violence plagues many states, corrosive economic and social problems erode the authority and sovereign power of others and spread across political borders. The United Nations must renew and strengthen its commitment to work in the economic and social fields as an end in itself and as the means of attending to the sources of conflicts. In the altered context of today's world, the definition of security is no longer limited to questions of land and weapons. It now includes economic well-being, environmental sustainability, and human rights protection; the relationship between international peace and security and development has become undeniable. Yet, while we have seen some progress toward peace and conflict management, we have seen little concerted action toward development. In the midst of urgent efforts to deal with outbreaks of violence and sudden disasters, it is the task of the world community to redefine and bring to fulfillment the idea of development as the long-term solution to the root causes of conflict.

As part of this effort, I recently presented the General Assembly with a report and recommendations entitled "An Agenda for Development." These recommendations explore the multiple dimensions of development and the multiplicity of actors engaged in the development task. Rather than proposing specific solutions, we must seek to provide a comprehensive framework for thinking about the pursuit of development as a means of building foundations for enduring human progress.

Peace, the economy, the environment, society, and democracy are interlinked dimensions of development. Peace provides the most secure context for lasting development. A growing economy generates the resources for progress. A protected environment makes development sustainable. Healthy social conditions strengthen the social fabric, reinforcing peace and development. Democracy fosters creativity, good governance, and the stability that can maintain progress toward development over time. All five development dimensions function together in an interlocking and mutually reinforcing way. This suggests that development will require vigorous action in line with a comprehensive vision — a vision that incorporates, integrates, and facilitates progress all along the entire range of development issues.

Looking to the sources of conflict, we see that the agenda presented to the United Nations by today's world is greater in complexity and scale than at any other time in the history of the organization. The task is daunting and may seem overwhelming as we step into the future without history's guide and in the presence of so much stress, misery, and violence. This is not cause for despair, however, but for the utmost dedication, determination, and lively commitment. The dimensions of development are in reality concepts that express the highest aspirations of human life. In attending to the sources of conflict through the pursuit of a comprehensive vision of development, we have the opportunity to realize greater potential for all humanity than ever before.

For the United Nations, this translates into an opportunity to bring together, in a strongly coherent and unified fashion, the original aims of the world organization. Peace, justice, human rights, and development — the original aims expressed in the U.N. charter — can all be pursued most effectively within a comprehensive vision. The new international context and the multidimensional nature of the challenge call for multilateral action and an integrated approach. In both mission and mandate, the United Nations is uniquely suited to this task, encompassing all dimensions of the development challenge.

As a forum for discussion and awareness-raising, as a tool for cooperation and decision making, and as a vehicle for promoting multilateral action, the United Nations can help forge the necessary global consensus.

The world organization also has the capacity to set internationally agreed-upon standards and to undertake operations through its global network of field offices. In these respects, there is no alternative to the United Nations as an active force for development.

To this end, the 1995 World Summit for Social Development in Copenhagen and the fiftieth anniversary year of the founding of the United Nations present historic opportunities that must be grasped.

As globalization transforms today's world in many positive ways, social ills such as crime, disease, drugs, unchecked migration, poverty, unemployment, and social disintegration have emerged on a regional and international scale. The magnitude of these challenges, coupled with the blurring of national boundaries through advanced communications and global commerce, render states and their governments decreasingly able to face or solve these problems alone. The United Nations, its member states, and other actors in the world community must seize the opportunity to construct an international consensus on social development and then commit themselves to a practical plan for international action.

The fiftieth anniversary of the founding of the organization invites the United Nations, its member states, and the peoples of the world to appreciate and strengthen the accomplishments of the past, to recognize and meet the challenges of the present, and to design and implement a plan for the United Nations of the future. Drawing from the lessons of the past and the challenges of the present, we have the potential to create new ways to use the original mechanisms provided by the charter within the emerging global context. Above all, we now possess an exhilarating challenge and an invaluable opportunity to forge a global consensus behind development, in all of its dimensions, as the most lasting foundation for international peace and security and as the greatest hope for all humanity. We must attend to the immediate problems of conflict, under all circumstances keeping in mind the aspects of development that must be strengthened. The peoples of the world look to the United Nations as the institution indispensable to the success of these efforts.

In the new international context, we initially set out together with determination to achieve peace and security, economic advancement and social equity, democracy and human rights. The enormity of tasks undertaken, however, soon forced us to acquire a new realism — an awareness that we have embarked upon a long path toward progress that will be marked by both successes and failures.

Today we have a deeper understanding of the sources of trouble in our world. We now know that security involves far more than questions of land and weapons. We further realize that the lack of economic, social, and political development is the underlying cause of conflict.

As in all cases, recognizing the problem is the first crucial step. Next comes action based upon that recognition — dedicated, determined, and sustained action toward development in all of its dimensions. In redefining and bringing to fulfillment a renewed vision of development, we can begin to get at the roots of conflict. In the process, we can create a new system of international cooperation. We can build enduring foundations for a secure, just, and creative era for all humanity. This is the primary mission of the United Nations in its second half-century.

This great project cannot be fulfilled without a continuing commitment to it on the part of all nations. Such a commitment must rest on a conviction on the part of all peoples of the United Nations that the world organization is capable of comprehensively addressing global issues of peace, sustainable development, and social justice.

Such a commitment can be achieved through the process of democratization within states, among states, and throughout the international system. Democratization means a guarantee of free participation, and the extent of this process can be measured by the commitment of member states to participate in the work of the United Nations. Today that commitment is far from satisfactory, as evidenced by the fact that in 1994 only 17 of 184 member states made good on their assessed financial commitment to the organization in a timely fashion. This is a matter of gravely needed resources, but it is more profoundly a matter of setting priorities. The record reveals that full and responsible participation in the United Nations is not a top priority on the agendas of most member states.

Only the expressed will of the people can impress upon their governments the importance of committed participation. By deepening U.N. involvement with, and responsiveness to, the concerns of grassroots movements and nongovernmental organizations, support for the United Nations can be strengthened from the ground up as governments feel the urging of their people for a truly effective and universal United Nations.

The acts of the United Nations must carry the authority of the peoples of the world, acting in concert through the member states of the organization. Its purposes derive not from a minimum of political consensus but from the principles of common humanity, the values enshrined in the charter. The extraordinary challenges and possibilities of this moment in time require the most dedicated and far-reaching response. To this end, member states must recognize in the United Nations the projection of the will, the interest, and the most profound dreams of their citizens.

The realization is dawning that for human beings around the world, in every land and of every background, the United Nations is even more than an instrument of peace, justice, and cooperative development among nations: it is the repository of hope for humanity and the future. That hope deserves our deepest continuing commitment.

His Excellency

Shri P. V. Narasimha Rao

Prime Minister of India

Challenge and Opportunity in the Post–Cold War Era

Building an International Environment Supportive of Democracy

Nature of Global Changes

During the past few years, the processes of history have suddenly accelerated, transforming the international landscape beyond recognition. What is especially remarkable is, first, the global scope of the change and, second, the pace of the change.

Another notable feature of the change is that several contradictory trends are in simultaneous motion. On the one hand, there are integrative trends fired by developments in technology and the emergence of a global marketplace. On the other hand, there are disintegrative forces at work, fracturing national entities along ethnic, religious, and even tribal lines. There is a welcome surge of democracy and concern for human rights all over the globe. At the same time, the pervasive lack of development and the growing poverty in many parts of the world are already creating conditions for the return of totalitarianism. And while the end of the Cold War has erased the likelihood of an East-West confrontation, the North-South gulf threatens to make the world a grotesque and extremely ugly place to live in, if living is at all conceivable.

It is against this background that I have chosen the theme for this essay. The post–Cold War era has thrown up several new and difficult challenges. At the same time, however, we have before us a rare historic opportunity to reshape interstate relations in a manner that underscores the positive trends and avoids the threatening and negative features.

Features of an
Effective New Structure

What should be the main features of the new structure of interstate relations? Here, by interstate, I mean total and multilateral. Quite clearly, it must be a structure capable of dealing with challenges that are global in scope. These include issues that affect the interests of the vast majority of countries, such as environmental degradation, weapons of mass destruction, cross-border terrorism, and drug trafficking, to name a few. There are also other issues that are specific in location but may nevertheless have a global impact. Thus, the famine and civil war in Somalia, even if it is in a distant part of the world, impinges upon the consciousness of people all over the world.

Secondly, not only must our structure be geared to global challenges, it must also be capable of responding promptly and effectively to the rapidity of change. Problems must be contained before they degenerate into chaos. Crises must be arrested and reversed before they turn into tragedy.

Does our national experience provide us with any pointers in this regard? I think our experience as democracies certainly does. Democracy is effective precisely because it offers a mechanism through which a national consensus can be evolved behind preferred policies. Democracy allows for orderly change. These same principles must now be extended to interstate relations mutatis mutandis. International cooperation to deal with global challenges will be effective only if it is backed by international consensus. Such a consensus can be evolved only through a truly democratic and multilateral process, with the participation of equal and sovereign states.

Need for a
Representative Security Council

You may ask whether the United Nations does not offer precisely such a mechanism for international cooperation. Yes, the United Nations is capable of becoming an instrument for global action, provided it pays greater heed to the principles of democracy. We recognize the need for a Security Council that is capable of swift action to uphold international peace and security. However, the element of accountability that is integral to the concept of democracy is missing from the current functioning of the Security Council. If the Security Council is to be accepted by the international community at large, as legitimate and important, as an impartial instrument for safeguarding international peace and security, then its actions must be seen to represent the collective will of the General Assembly. Its actions in enforcing compliance will have greater acceptability if they are seen as representing a larger collectivity rather than the inclinations of a few powerful nations. It is for this reason that India, for one, has argued for an expansion of the Security Council to make it more representative of the much larger membership of the United Nations today. We have also advocated greater accountability to, and participation by, the U.N. General Assembly in the maintenance of international peace and collective security.

I mentioned several sets of contradictory trends in the world today. Let me deal with some of them.

For several years now, we have been witnessing increasingly stronger trends toward regional integration. The world has become a global market but is increasingly organized in interlinked regional clusters. The emergence of a single Europe is the most successful manifestation of this trend, but similar groupings are emerging in North America and the Asia-Pacific region as well. Even South Asia is finally beginning to put substance into its own regional organization — the South Asian Association for Regional Cooperation (SAARC).

Dangers of Ethnic Fragmentation

As against this trend, however, we are witnessing the breakup of nation-states along ethnic and religious lines. There has been a tremendous upsurge in ethnic particularity and religious extremism that threaten to rip apart the national fabric of several states.

In actual fact, however, less than 10 percent of the 170 states in the world today are ethnically homogeneous. Only about 50 percent have one ethnic group that accounts for more than 70 percent of the population. Once the present nation-state is called into question on the basis of ethnic or religious particularity, it is difficult to see where the process will stop.

Fragmentation has already set in motion forces that will cause even more fragmentation. This is already happening in several parts of the world and resulting in chaos, violence, and bloodshed. Ethnic or any other form of centrifugalism is therefore a counterproductive process in a vast majority of cases. It will not solve the problems that are alleged to have triggered it. On the other hand, there will be more problems—and more intractable ones at that. The quest for homogeneity would, in most cases, prove a mirage. The world has to live, and learn to live happily, with plurality. In other words, the trend of ethnic fragmentation should stop—in the interest of mankind. But why does fragmentation become such a powerful urge? Most often, it is a strong sense of grievance regarding exploitation of one group by another through force for a long time. When the element of force weakens and disappears, the urge to separate asserts itself. The exploitation is often economic or political, perhaps both. But it is often forgotten that the same exploitation can and does continue in a uni-ethnic society as well. In other words, ethnic or other distinctiveness is only a pretext for exploitation and not its real cause. If one pretext is removed, another will take its place. The solution thus lies in moving toward a nonexploitative society wherein the availability of opportunity is reasonably well distributed. But since exploitation is often done through violence, a nonexploitative society is possible only under conditions of nonviolence. Mahatma Gandhi conceived of and propounded a society of this nature.

I have tried to explain this aspect at some length because the same principle would apply to a world order consisting of many societies and groups. The relations among states should thus be reorganized on nonexploitative and nonviolent lines. Of course, this will take time, a long time perhaps. Even the acceptance of this pattern is not going to be easy, treading as it will upon the toes of many age-old exploitative forces and interests. Nevertheless, I am not aware of any alternative pattern that would be viable.

Development Strategy

As a democracy, India has welcomed the popular upsurge that swept across the globe, bringing freedom and opportunity to peoples of countries long suppressed by unrepresentative governments. Here it would be wrong to assume that this resurgence of democracy in several parts of the world is a permanent and irreversible condition. There is nothing automatic about democracy. It is a political form that has evolved over many centuries.

There is a certain temper, a certain way of thinking, that lies behind the institution of democracy. Democracy needs to be nurtured. It is not a ready-made garment that fits everyone. It needs to be consciously evolved and practiced.

Similar considerations are relevant in devising an appropriate development strategy. The experience of many countries indicates that a market-oriented economy is best suited to bringing about an efficient allocation of resources — and consequently more rapid economic development. We ourselves have therefore given a strong market orientation to our economic policy, reducing the degree of government control over productive activity and providing an environment that encourages the spirit of enterprise in our people. However, the role of the state in economic life will continue to be crucial. There is no mechanistic equation between a free market and economic development, just as a free market is not necessarily equal to democracy. This is particularly true in developing countries, where neither the affluence of the few nor their philanthropy can be assumed to extend all the way down to the base of the pyramid. Large numbers of our population are outside the operation of market forces, and state intervention is necessary if we are to alleviate poverty and distress for these sections of society and to raise their living standards, at least in the foreseeable future. Besides, in developing countries the state often has to play an active role to create the conditions in which markets can work — for example, by providing the necessary infrastructure and often even institutional support, not to mention conditions of law and order, conditions of equal opportunity, and conditions of fairness in society as a whole. These are the things that need to be ensured even for a free market economy to function in a state.

Nurturing Democracy

If this is the case, then the international structure we seek must be very different from the direction in which we are presently headed. First, we must recognize our responsibility for supporting and nurturing democracy everywhere. The fragile institutions of democracy in the developing world as well as in countries that have just emerged from the collapse of the socialist system are threatened most by economic deprivation and lack of development. All these countries are reorienting their economic policies to utilize the many advantages of market orientation. But we must not assume that this reorientation alone will solve all problems, independent of the international environment. We must also not assume that this reorientation is going to be automatic or easy or that it can be accomplished within a short time. It will take its time, it will take its effort, it will have its ups and downs, and it will pass through many bumps before it really arrives. Such economic reorientation takes time to have its full effect, and in this process all these economies can be greatly helped by appropriate international support. They need a greater injection of financial resources to support their reform efforts. They also need assured access to markets in industrialized countries. Their opening up to the world will be most effective only if the world also opens up to them. All this calls for renewed commitment to multilateral international cooperation. Unless this is done, we run the risk of discrediting economic reform as well as democracy in many countries. I am sure you are aware of the trends that are threatening to develop in some of these countries where the advent of democracy, the advent of liberalization, the advent of opening up has not produced results in the short run and people are getting restive. So some result is necessary to give them hope that there is a possibility of much more to come. I am not recommending anything to anyone. I am only trying to analyze the way people's minds are working in these countries because we have all these inputs coming in from these countries. If such skepticism really takes hold, namely that nothing is going to happen, the road to totalitarianism will not be very distant. This is the danger I would like to point out, for the fragility of democracy itself is a hurdle. If there had been democracy in these countries for the last two hundred or three hundred years, they would take all the ups and downs in stride. But today when there is a sudden change in the system and the change has not been properly assimilated and internalized, what is needed is the result in the short run, however slight, however symbolic, however halting. But if the result is not there and people are worse off than they were three or four years back, then there will be the danger of a backlash.

North-South Cooperation

Building an international environment supportive of democracy and helping countries overcome problems of economic transition must therefore be the aim of the international community. So it is a great responsibility —

the responsibility for the whole world. For the system of democracy to take root in the whole world, this is the real measure of the responsibility implied in this. In the final analysis, democracy within nations can be sustained only if there is democracy among nations. If certain countries with relatively greater political, military, and economic power seek to exploit the current fluid situation, to perpetuate their dominant status, then others will feel obliged to resist at some point through whatever means are available. Totalitarianism finds its best argument in national insecurity and a perception of threat.

Similarly, economic development must again be put at the very center of the international agenda. The international economic environment must be conducive to growth, and the trend toward a truly global marketplace must be promoted and not retarded by protectionism, unilateralism, and discriminatory trade practices. Over the past several years, the principle of multilateralism in trade has been seriously eroded. Development, which was recognized as a central concern in the multilateral trading system, has now been pushed to the sidelines. If we are to sustain democracy and development throughout the globe, then there is no alternative to a genuinely multilateral, nondiscriminatory, and development-oriented trading system.

It is in this context that India, along with other developing countries, has been advocating the urgent resumption of the North-South dialogue. Cooperation between the North and South is crucial if we are to successfully meet the compelling challenges that confront us. Confrontation will not bring any advantage to either side. During the U.N. Conference on Environment and Development, we did manage to avoid confrontation and were able to evolve workable compromises to our mutual benefit. The successful conclusion of the Chemical Weapons Convention is yet another example of North-South cooperation. These efforts were successful because they were multilateral efforts, with balanced obligations and benefits, universal in scope and nondiscriminatory in character. These are the models we must follow in the future.

Seen against this perspective, there is little prospect of success in efforts being made by some countries to create a two-track world in which a handful of affluent countries will monopolize access to technology and sophisticated weaponry while the rest of the world is hemmed in by all manner of restrictive regimes and conditionalities. The danger of nuclear proliferation, for example, can hardly be countered by a regime that perpetuates nuclear arsenals among a handful of countries. The route to be followed here is the same as in the case of the Chemical Weapons Convention. Our approach must be universal in scope and nondiscriminatory in character.

India's Future Relations
with Its Major Neighbors

Taking China first, I am quite satisfied with our relations as they exist today and as they promise to develop in the future. We do have one problem. We have had it for a long time. This is the border question. We decided to put into motion a mechanism that would take care of that question, and that is now being done. There is a Joint Working Group that examines the question of the border in all its ramifications while not holding up our relations in other fields. We have had very fruitful exchanges and visits as well as co-operation in some areas with China.

What one should remember in facing the realities is that the conditions and problems in India and China are more or less similar. The direction in which solutions could lie are more or less the same. So whether one likes it or not, when it comes down to discussing matters, you find that you agree. Sometimes you are surprised how much you agree. This is the reality.

As for the former Soviet Union, there is no such thing as a former Soviet Union, unfortunately. The former Soviet Union had very good relations. But we don't want those relations to become former relations; we want those relations to endure with the successor states of the former Soviet Union. That is one decision we have taken.

A number of heads of state of the southern republics have visited India. Whereas in the past we were dealing with one country, the Soviet Union, now we have to deal with several other countries. On their side, goods have to be delivered by three, four, five countries today where they were delivered by only one several years back. So there is a necessary transition going on the other side, with all the uncertainties that accompany a transition. But the end result, I think, after a year or two is going to be that we will stabilize our relations with all these successor states and we will have by and large no problem. We will have to change the pattern of our cooperation according to the changed circumstances. This exercise will have to be undertaken — I have no doubt about that — and the process has in fact started. A few setbacks are occurring here and there, but on the whole I do not find any insurmountable difficulty in reestablishing our good relations with the successor states of the Soviet Union.

There is another point that needs to be remembered — that India has age-old relationships with some of the southern republics of the former Soviet Union. In fact, they date back to a time before the Soviet Union itself came into existence. So we do not have any problem with some of the republics, and we are going ahead with reconstructing our relations along new lines. It will take time, but I have no apprehensions about any insurmountable difficulty appearing along the way.

I do not share the conclusion that there is significant instability in Central Asia, although we are conscious of the troubled situation in Tajikistan and on the Tajik-Afghan frontier. The other countries of the region are stable and are coping with their developmental problems as best they can. For this, we are providing whatever assistance we can, given our own limitations. The possibility of fragmentation, not just in Central Asia but elsewhere too, is a serious issue and needs to be addressed collectively. I believe that any fragmentation along ethnic lines or any forced revision of existing frontiers will have serious consequences and should be resisted by all the countries in the region so as to preserve peace and stability in our neighborhood.

Pakistan, of course, is a special matter. Pakistan and India have a special relationship as they belong to the same subcontinent. They became two countries despite a common people. Even today blood relations by the millions are spread over both countries. The languages are common. The culture is common. The history is common. The commonality between the countries is so great that it is very difficult, once you leave India and Pakistan and go to a third country, to distinguish between an Indian and a Pakistani.

But then there are two countries. If they are two countries, each country has to have some distinctive identification of its own. I mean, that is the aspiration of every country, what every country asks itself: how am I different from the other? what is my identity? These are questions that history will have to solve. We are too small, too transient, and forty years is too short a period for the identity of a new country to emerge.

Meanwhile, we have problems. We are neighbors with China, Pakistan, and Bangladesh, and we are having all the problems that neighbors can have — such as disputes over borders and water rights. As for Kashmir, it is part of India and always has been, right from the start — on August 15, 1947.

Before that, Kashmir came to India, and it is a part of India. Pakistan thinks that Kashmir should go to Pakistan because of its Muslim majority. My response — and India's response — is this: what do we do with states where there is a Christian majority? where do we send them? This is an absurd situation. We are a secular state. We have Hindus, Muslims, Christians, Parsis — all the religions of the world are available in India. I can't send people to different countries based on religion and maintain only one community or one religion in India. That is not my philosophy at all. The basis of the Indian state is secular. If the basis of the Pakistan state is different, then I cannot help it. Pakistanis have every right to have whatever philosophy they like. But my philosophy is that I absorb everyone. Indian history is witness; for thousands of years we have been absorbing cultures from abroad and also sending our own culture outside. There has been so much give and take, so much interchange of cultures, it is just not possible for any Indian mind to accept that only people belonging to one religious denomination should inhabit a country and no one else should come. That's not the philosophy of India.

Scholars who have an idea of how the Indian mind, the Indian vision, has developed over the millennia should easily perceive that whatever we wanted, we wanted for the whole world. There is no ancient text in India that says that something good should happen only to India. Every text says that it should happen to mankind, to the whole world, looking upon the whole world as one family. These ideas are inherent in Indian thinking. We cannot help it. We think only along those lines.

Yes, we are a nation-state. We have our interests. We fight for our interests. We make friendships. Sometimes there may be a tiff here and there. All that is true because we are in a modern world. But what is essentially India is something that needs to be understood. We have not annexed any territory or other countries at any time in modern history. India is a totally nonaggressive state. But if India is attacked, India is always ready to answer. So these are the traits of the Indian mind, Indian thinking, and Indian history, and these are the answers we have to give to any of the questions raised in regard to our relations with our neighbors.

His Excellency

Tariq Aziz

Deputy Prime Minister of the
Republic of Iraq

The Post–Cold War Era

"Facts and Prospects"

When Ronald Reagan became president of the United States in 1981, he started a great campaign against the Soviet Union, calling it "the Evil Empire."

During that period and before, the Soviet Union and the other communist regimes were, in most cases, blamed by the United States and the West for the insecurity, upheavals, civil wars, and other disturbing situations in the world. Communist and socialist theories and policies were blamed for the economic problems in the communist states and those of the Third World nations that were inspired by such theories and policies.

Less than a decade later, that "Evil Empire" collapsed. All the Eastern European communist regimes collapsed, some before and some after the collapse of the Soviet Union.

The Bush administration, along with other western leaders, analysts, and writers, regarded those historical events as the greatest victory to have happened, since the end of the Second World War, for democracy and free market economy over totalitarianism, communism, and socialism.

Bush and his administration started to talk widely and enthusiastically about a "New World Order." Great expectations were raised and promises made by U.S. and other western leaders about the spread of democracy in the world, economic development on the basis of a free market economy, and peace and order in the world under the active role of the United Nations, with the political and military leadership and resources to be provided by the United States and other western powers.

The Bush administration, feeling that this new situation provided it with great opportunities, mainly in the Middle East and the Arab Gulf region, exploited the events following August 2, 1990, to create the conditions and pretexts for waging a devastating war against Iraq and subsequently taking over the whole region (Saudi Arabia and the Gulf states) and its resources, mainly oil.

A few years have gone by now, and one cannot help wondering whether the world in general, and the United States and Western Europe in particular, are "better off" than they were during the period before the collapse of the "Evil Empire" and the end of the Cold War.

In November 1992, eleven months after the collapse of the Soviet Union and twenty-three months after the Gulf War — which Bush regarded as his and America's greatest victory in decades — the American voters were not impressed by all those "great" achievements of the Bush administration. They abandoned him for a new leader who has never admitted any role in those American "victories" but focused mainly on the economy.

Although the American ruling establishment enjoys under the new circumstances a world status in political and military terms that it has never enjoyed before, this status has not been reflected in the life of the ordinary American citizen and the welfare of the nation as a whole. The major problems of the past, economic and otherwise, have continued, and the main debate currently prevailing in the United States is not about how to benefit from the gains of the end of the Cold War but about various domestic problems that have nothing to do with any of the aspects of the Cold War. In Western Europe none of the ruling parties or leaders who were in power during the collapse of the Soviet Union — and who, like George Bush, rejoiced in those developments — could enhance their political status as a result of victory over communism. People elected their ruling parties and presidents for domestic reasons.

The economic situation in the whole of Western Europe did not improve as a result of the collapse of the Soviet Union and its political, military, and economic bloc. The same economic problems remained and in some cases worsened.

In the former communist states of Eastern Europe no country can now claim a significant economic improvement during the last five years. In fact, those countries are now facing more economic difficulties than they were facing under the communist regimes. Their economies have been further aggravated by such chronic and typically capitalist diseases as inflation, unemployment, and organized crime. With the exception of more political freedom, nobody in those countries can claim that a great positive change has been achieved since the collapse of the old regimes.

In Poland, Hungary, and Bulgaria, the old communist parties changed into social democratic parties and regained power through free elections, which shows that the rulers under the old regimes were not as unpopular among their people as the American and western propaganda claimed before the end of the Cold War, picturing those nations as slaves living under the yoke of communist rulers.

The political relations between the heir of the Soviet Union, the Russian Federation, and the United States did not develop into the alliance envisioned in the euphoria of 1991 and 1992. The geopolitical facts as well as national interests that largely governed Soviet foreign policy are reemerging as the dominant factors in shaping the foreign policy of the Russian Federation. Only the communist ideology of that policy has disappeared.

After almost five decades of peace and tranquility in the whole of Europe during the so-called Cold War era, Europe is witnessing a real and vicious war in the former Yugoslavia. The United States, Western European nations, NATO, and the United Nations have so far failed to stop the war and bring about a peaceful solution to the conflict. Prospects for the spread of violence in the Balkans cannot be ruled out.

In the other parts of the world the scene is no better. It is, in most cases, even worse. In Afghanistan the civil war that was an outcome of and a proxy for the Cold War conflict has developed into a devastating and chaotic situation. During the Soviet presence in Afghanistan there still was a "state" of Afghanistan; now, several years after the pullout of Soviet troops, Afghanistan is a heap of rubble.

The only relatively positive development in Asia is the limited success in containing civil war in Cambodia. In other Asian countries no positive achievement could be credibly related to the end of the Cold War. The same situation and the same problems persist as before. The prospects of new conflicts and crises are by no means less now than they were during the period of the Cold War. The same thing could be said about Latin America.

In Africa, the situation is different. Africa, with various young states, suffered more than any other continent from the atrocities of both the Cold War era and the post–Cold War era. That continent was a battlefield and laboratory for the disastrous practices of communist and pro-western politicians who were supported and patronized by their mentors in both Moscow and Washington and other western capitals. The whole continent, with very few exceptions, is facing a disastrous future in all areas: political, security, economic, and health.

In the Middle East, or the Arab world, no Arab patriot can in any way be reasonably convinced that the situation now is better than it was in the seventies and the eighties. Some pro-American and pro-western politicians and writers might say the opposite; but those politicians and writers are much more unpopular and isolated in their own societies than the pro-American and pro-western politicians and writers who were in command before the Second World War and the short period thereafter and who were later toppled by nationalist revolutionaries.

From the coast of the Arab Gulf to the coast of the Atlantic Ocean, all the Arab states, without exception, are now poorer and less secure than they were before the end of the Cold War and before the war against Iraq. None of the Arab states can realistically believe that the coming years will bring a better situation.

The "peace process" that was officially launched at the Madrid Conference in October 1991 is regarded by the parties concerned as the main positive achievement in the Middle East in the post–Cold War era. But an impartial and objective assessment of this process since its start will show that it is by no means a smooth process, and very few leaders in the area are showing confidence that it will realize a permanent and truly durable settlement acceptable to all parties. Most of the optimistic statements made about the prospects of this process are wishful thinking at best.

During the past period a tremendous number of problems and crises have emerged in this process, most of them of a crucial nature. Nobody can say with any degree of confidence that a satisfactory solution has been reached to any of them. Most of the solutions have merely been temporary arrangements or hasty agreements resulting from the pressure of events or attempts to avoid escalation. The basic and most critical issues — such as the right of the Palestinians to an independent state, the status of Al Quds, the Israeli withdrawal from the Golan Heights — are not yet seriously addressed, and the gaps between the parties concerned remain huge. When the peace process started, especially after the Gaza-Jericho agreement, high hopes were raised about the prospects of economic development in the countries engaged in the process, especially for the Palestinians, as the big prize for peace. These hopes have not yet materialized and few people still believe that they will materialize in the future. The United States did not offer to the hopeful parties significant economic assistance to bolster the status of the leaders engaged in the process and generate for the peace process the popular support it badly needs. Aid from the European Union states is not enough to create significant change. The wealthy Arab countries are no longer as wealthy as they were, and their economic and financial support is very small. The international private investors are still hesitant to invest large amounts of money because of the spread of violence here and there and the uncertainties about the whole situation. The ordinary citizen on both sides has not felt the benefits of the process.

Both the United States and the Soviet Union were mentors of the Madrid Conference and subsequently of the peace process. The Soviet Union collapsed three months after that conference. The Russian Federation inherited the role of the Soviet Union in this issue, as it did in many others, but up to now the role of Russia in the peace process is minimal and sporadic. It is clear to all parties concerned that the United States is the only mentor in this process.

The European Union and major European states like France have been deliberately excluded from playing a direct and tangible role in the process. George Bush chose the weak Soviet Union as a partner so that it would be easier for the United States to play the most dominant role. But for decades the Arabs have been complaining that the United States could not be an impartial broker in any peace settlement between Arab states and Israel because Israel is a U.S. ally while U.S. relations with the Arab states are of a second-rate nature, even when it comes to America's best Arab friends. Moreover, Israel has great influence inside the United States in shaping U.S. policy toward the region and can exert tremendous pressures on the U.S. administration, Congress, and the media, while the influence of the Arab lobby in the United States is negligible, if it exists at all.

The Clinton administration, especially after the November 1994 congressional elections, when the president's party lost its majority to the Republicans, has become more vulnerable to the Jewish lobby in Washington. Now both the president and the Republican presidential candidates are competing to win Jewish American support. In some cases, they have even gone far beyond Israeli demands and tactics, becoming more royalist than the king!

This has aggravated the already existing imbalance in the peace process and left the pro-American Arab leaders in an embarrassing situation.

The most tangible and politically significant result of the process is that the whole situation, after more than three and a half years since the convening of the Madrid Conference, is getting more and more unpopular both in Israel and in the concerned Arab countries, and the leaders championing this process on both sides are losing political ground. Their positions are vulnerable and their future is very much in question.

The extremists on both sides who reject the whole idea of a peaceful settlement between Israel and the Arabs are increasingly active and are resorting to violence, which makes the process more difficult and more vulnerable and increases the burdens and pressures on the leaders of both sides.

It is not my wish to sound pessimistic here about the world situation and the prospects of the post–Cold War era. But as a citizen in a nation that is severely suffering from this situation, as an Arab, and as a citizen of the Third World, I can hardly express satisfaction or optimism about the current international situation.

Several years after the collapse of the Soviet Union, very few people still agree with the Reaganites that it was an "Evil Empire." This is not a tribute to the Soviet Union or to communism, nor is it an attempt to come to their defense. I have never been a communist. I have always been critical of communism. Our government in Iraq had good relations with the Soviet Union in many respects, but we were not in agreement with the Soviets in many ideological and political areas. We strongly criticized the Soviet Union when it invaded Afghanistan. The Soviet Union and some communist regimes in Eastern Europe encouraged and supported the communist party in Iraq against our government. We have had difficult times with these countries on various occasions. I met with many Soviet leaders—

Brezhnev, Kosygin, Podgorny, Gromyko, Ponomariov, and others — during the seventies and the eighties. The degree of agreement between us was not very large.

But it is a fact that when the Soviet Union existed and was internationally active, my country and many other countries, especially in Asia and Africa, enjoyed a greater degree of independence, had better prospects for economic development, and were more secure. The reason was not that the Soviet empire was a good empire, but that it provided a global political, military, and economic equilibrium sufficient to maintain balance in the international situation.

The two dominant blocs at the time, western and eastern, were facing each other in all realms of rivalry and competition. In those circumstances each of the two blocs and their two leaders — the United States and the Soviet Union — had to be careful about their policies toward, and relations with, the majority of nations, particularly those that had not aligned themselves with either camp. In order to avoid a shift in the balance of power, if any of those nations showed signs of moving from a position of nonalignment to an alliance with either of the two blocs, both the United States and the Soviet Union would make great political efforts to avoid antagonizing that nation and would begin to show it greater attention and respect.

The balance of power that prevailed between the two blocs throughout the long period from the end of the Second World War to the collapse of the Soviet Union produced what was, relatively speaking, the most secure period witnessed by the world in modern times. Although several wars occurred during that period — such as the Korean war, the Vietnam war, the Arab-Israeli wars, the two wars between India and Pakistan and others — most of those wars, with the exception of the first two, were short wars, and most of those situations were under control through the mutual desire and joint efforts of the two superpowers. When the Korean war ended without gains to either side, the cease-fire remained effective for decades to come. When the Vietnamese war ended, there were no further military activities or threats. The cease-fires between the Arabs and the Israelis were mostly respected by both sides with the help of the two superpowers. In most cases the two superpowers found it in their mutual interest not to allow a conflict between their allies or proxies to spread; they had the means and capabilities to contain them and, in some cases, to put an end to them.

However, to criticize the current post–Cold War international situation will not by itself provide solutions to the present problems. It is necessary to have a clear analysis of the situation, an analysis that might contribute to finding the ways and means to improve the situation.

What is important to the majority of nations in the world is not to idealize the post–Cold War era but rather to institutionalize the practices that have ensued during these past few years. The other important matter is to define the role of the United States in the current international situation.

As for the role of the United States in this situation, it should be stated from the very beginning that there is a great difference between the situation which resulted from the Second World War and that which resulted from the collapse of the Soviet Union. During the Second World War the United States and its allies, including the Soviet Union, fought a long and bloody war to defeat Germany, Italy, and Japan militarily, economically, and ideologically. The efforts and sacrifices in that battle were tangible and enormous. Therefore, the victors who emerged from that war deserved the status and the privileges of the victors. The United States played the most significant role in that conflict and later played the sole significant role in providing economic assistance to Europe to recover the tremendous losses it had suffered during the conflict. Nobody questioned the "leading role" of the United States during that war and after; it was a justified role achieved by great sacrifices, efficiency, and tremendous help to others. The so-called American or western victory in the collapse of the Soviet bloc is a superficial one. The Soviet Union did not collapse as a result of efforts by the United States and Western Europe. That collapse actually came as a surprise to them, more similar to an earthquake than to a planned and anticipated result.

Therefore, the emergence of the United States in the leading role after the collapse of the Soviet Union — a role that the Bush administration hastily claimed — was rather an unexpected opportunity than a deserved status or privilege. The United States itself was not prepared for it, and there is no certainty that it can hold on to it.

In a few years' time there was enough proof that the United States had failed to play the role of the sole leader of the world for its own good and for the good of the world at large. Even the best friends of the United States cannot convince themselves that the role it has played as the sole leader or the sole superpower has brought positive results to them and to the world. The United States is now in conflict with many countries, most of them supposed allies, for economic and other reasons. The apparent characteristic role of the United States as a world leader is that of a primitive giant, always threatening the use of military and economic punishments. Most U.S. positions toward international issues are regarded by friends and foes as lacking wisdom, rationality, and realism.

It is very much desirable now in the whole world that the United States should consider seriously and honestly abandoning the idea of becoming the sole world leader and trying honestly and realistically to come to terms with its real capabilities. The current international situation that emerged from the sudden and unexpected collapse of the Soviet Union should not mislead the United States into overestimating those capabilities or further inflating its arrogance. The United States simply was not and is not prepared to play the role of the sole world leader. It does not have the moral, political, economic, and cultural potential and capabilities it needs to lead the world for the better. It does not have the military capabilities for that either, although U.S. military power is the mightiest in the world. It certainly does not have the will to make the same human and economic sacrifices it did in the Second World War. It can still play a significant role in international affairs, but it cannot play that of the sole leader. The world in general should not encourage this role or give it moral and political support.

There is a serious moral and political necessity for other participants to play their natural and desired roles in shaping the international situation. Russia's growing ambition to be more independent of the United States and to have its own view of world affairs is a positive phenomenon. Those who criticize Boris Yeltsin and his foreign minister, Andrei Kozyrev, for this independence are biased and wrong. The world needs a powerful, independent, and internationally active Russia. This is not a call for a return to the Cold War. It is neither realistic nor desirable to hope for a return to the previous international situation. What has gone is gone. The Soviet Union, along with its vast and powerful bloc, is history. Russia itself is not interested in returning to its Soviet past, and such a return is not welcome to those nations that have abandoned their fantasies about communism and similar ideologies. A strong, independent, and active Russia is needed for the world to regain the sort of balance it has lost since the collapse of the Soviet Union — to no one's benefit.

The status of China as a big power should be assessed as a positive factor. The world in general and the Third World in particular need a strong and internationally active China. The isolation of China within its own borders and within its own economic concerns can only be a negative phenomenon.

The world needs Europe as a balancing power against the inflated role and wrong policies of the United States on various international problems and issues. Nobody should realistically imagine Europe facing up to the United States as an enemy; but the world needs Europe, with its rich heritage of civilization and long experience and knowledge in international affairs, to moderate and rationalize U.S. policies on various international political, economic, and security issues and to tell the United States, when necessary, where to stop.

As for the Third World nations, the new international situation should not drive them to hastily abandon the political systems, economic practices, and regional and semi-international organizations they adopted and created in the past decades after independence. Those political systems and economic practices should not be regarded as the product of the Cold War era, to be abandoned after the end of that era. Although reform and new thinking are always needed, these systems and practices were in most cases the outcome of a national need to protect their independence and to provide requirements for development compatible with the realities in their societies, which basically differ from those in the American and Western European societies.

The Movement of Nonaligned Countries, the Organization of African Unity, the League of Arab States, and other groupings created in the past are not a product of the Cold War era and should not be regarded as such. There were genuine reasons for their existence in that era, and those reasons still exist now.

If the current inflated role of the United States is contained by both American and international efforts, if the roles of Russia, Europe, and China develop positively, and if Third World nations maintain their independence and national characteristics, the end of the Cold War could be a prelude to a better international situation, free from the menace of nuclear war between the two superpowers and free from the ideological war between the two major ideologies of the past — communism and capitalism. But if the current situation persists for a long time, it will be difficult to anticipate an international situation that is characterized by peace, tranquility, and real development.

Part 3

The United States and the
Commonwealth of
Independent States in the
Post–Cold War Order

The Honorable

James A. Baker III*

Former Secretary of State,
United States

Selective Engagement

Principles for American Foreign Policy in a New Era

Today's state of world affairs resembles the periods of revolutionary science described by historian Thomas Kuhn, periods marked by the consignment of one scientific paradigm to oblivion and the emergence of another to replace it. Kuhn's concept of paradigm can shed light on the uncertainties we face in world affairs today. He stresses the twofold nature of any paradigm: as an explanation of reality and as a tool for problem solving within that reality.

With the eclipse of communism and the collapse of the Soviet Union, the United States has, in a real sense, lost its paradigm for international affairs. As we look to the future, we must learn to do without the explanation of international affairs that the Cold War provided and the tool for problem solving, known as "containment," that saw us through ultimate victory in it.

From Disengagement to Selective Engagement

This essay was drawn from remarks made at the James A. Baker III Institute for Public Policy at Rice University.

Today we are moving into the century's third great period in U.S. foreign policy. The first lasted until 1941, with a brief interregnum during World War I. During this period, U.S. foreign policy was guided by the principle of disengagement. The term is more accurate than the usual one, "isolationism," because it better captures the historic folly of the period. This is because the United States, as World War I demonstrated, was never truly isolated. Its size, large domestic market, and relative geographic remove, however, allowed the United States to indulge in the fantasy of isolation. By the 1930s, that fantasy had grown frayed. Worldwide depression, the emergence of fascism, and the development of new weaponry had begun to erode even further the already shaky foundations of isolationism. Still, it took the shock of Pearl Harbor and the rigors of world war to rid the United States of its illusion. By disengagement we had sought to isolate ourselves — and failed.

The second period began with America's entry into World War II. In it, U.S. foreign policy was driven by what could be termed compulsory engagement. First fascist, then communist aggression thrust the United States onto the world scene. The advent of nuclear weapons raised the international stakes to unprecedented heights — not only our way of life but our lives themselves were at risk. We had no choice but to accept this reality. It was hard to argue the case for disengagement with tens of thousands of nuclear warheads targeted on the United States by a hostile Soviet Union. In addition to the magnitude of the Soviet threat, there was its pervasiveness. Communist aggression made the entire world a field of contention. West and East competed, not just politically and militarily, but economically, technologically, and socially.

Today, with the end of the Cold War, we are entering yet a third distinct era in U.S. foreign policy. That policy should be guided by the principle of selective engagement — a principle that embraces the freedom of action that we enjoy with the end of the Cold War but recognizes the continued imperative of U.S. leadership in the global arena. Selective engagement, or, indeed, any effective principle for foreign policy, must be based on rigorous analysis of the world and our role in it. The first step is a clear comprehension of the complex global trends shaping our world today. The second is a sober assessment of U.S. interests. The third is a pragmatic recognition of competing U.S. objectives. And the fourth is a firm understanding of the tangibles and intangibles of American power.

Global Trends:
Living with Ambiguity

Let me begin with the powerful global trends that are sweeping our world today. In the geostrategic realm, the demise of the Soviet Union has decreased the risk of global thermonuclear war while increasing the possibility of lesser, but still dangerous, regional conflict. International power has been diffused and international discipline loosened. Under these circumstances, the proliferation of weapons of mass destruction raises the possibility of a "New World Disorder" with a vengeance.

In ideology, there has been a similarly ironic effect. The collapse of communism as a world force has spawned the rise of ultranationalist movements and leaders that threaten their citizens' freedom and their neighbors' security. Serbia's Milosevic and Russia's Zhirinovsky are just two prominent, if particularly sinister, examples of the reemergence of fascism as an international force. More generally, nationalism has created a potential zone of conflict that stretches from the Balkans through the Caucasus and into Central Asia.

In the diplomatic arena, the end of the Cold War has created the possibility of new international partnerships, most notably between the United States and Russia. But it has also strained the Western Alliance that fought and won the Cold War. With the end of the Soviet menace, North America, Western Europe, and Japan are looking at each other less as political partners and more as economic competitors.

In economics, the rise of interdependence has both increased prosperity and, perversely, raised the domestic political stakes for trade and investment issues. The passage of the North American Free Trade Agreement (NAFTA) and the conclusion of the Uruguay Round mark welcome victories for the forces of economic liberalism. But the proponents of protectionism remain strong throughout the industrial democracies, particularly as the United States, Western Europe, and Japan face the ever-growing competition provided by the dynamic economies of East Asia.

Finally, the scientific and technological revolution has changed everything from the way we look at man, to the way we work, to the way we make war. The emergence of information as a commodity has altered forever the nature of our domestic economies as well as the terms and intensity of international competition.

These trends are ambiguous and, indeed, often contradictory. They suggest the extent to which ours is a complex, indeterminate world. At present, no single trend is dominant, and the nature of the new order far from set. In the late 1940s or early 1950s, in striking contrast, U.S.-Soviet rivalry would have led and, indeed, overwhelmed any list of international trends. This makes it critical that we pursue a strategy that is flexible enough to cope with today's turbulence.

American Interests:
The Need for Proportionality

Such a strategy, in turn, depends on a careful assessment of U.S. interests. On one level, of course, America's interests are simple and largely uncontested. Based upon the well-being of our citizens, they include security, prosperity, and promotion of American values. Move from generalization to specificity, however, and we enter at once a far more complex area.

Preventing, containing, and, where possible, resolving regional conflict is, for instance, clearly a general American interest. Just as plainly, however, America's specific interest in avoiding conflict on the Korean peninsula differs in type and magnitude from our interest, for example, in promoting a peaceful settlement in Angola. War in Korea would immediately involve thousands of U.S. troops and, given North Korea's dangerous game of nuclear hide-and-seek, the potential use of atomic weapons. In short, all interests are not equal. Specific policies must reflect this fact. Above all, they must be proportionate to the U.S. interests involved.

The Clinton administration's difficulties in Haiti and Somalia can be traced, at least in part, to the lack of such proportion. In Somalia, especially, we saw what could be called "mission creep." What began as a limited humanitarian mission grew to an ill-considered exercise in nation-building with deadly consequences. This does not mean that we have no interests in either country. Clearly, the United States does have an interest in encouraging democracy in Haiti, just as we do in averting human suffering in Somalia. But those interests are not of sufficient importance to squander American lives or fritter away American prestige.

Only a sense of proportion permits us to craft appropriate policies. We cannot solve every one of the world's problems. What we can and must do is focus our attention and resources on the key challenges to our real vital interests. These include consolidating democracy and free markets in Eastern Europe and the former Soviet Union, containing regional conflicts and stemming the proliferation of weapons of mass destruction, strengthening an open global economic system, redefining the Western Alliance, and renewing American leadership. All these challenges share one common characteristic: our success or failure in meeting them will directly affect the lives of Americans for years and decades to come. There is no better definition of a vital American interest.

Objectives:
The Importance of Balance

As we pursue American interests, however, we must recall that our approach to a specific country, region, or issue can possess competing and sometimes contradictory objectives. Often our interests themselves will conflict — sometimes our long- and short-term goals. It is important that we recognize these competing objectives. By doing so, we can make an informed choice among them, or, preferably, craft a policy that balances them.

American policy toward China is a case in point. Any list of U.S. interests in China would include protection of human rights, market access for U.S. firms, and Chinese cooperation on a range of international security issues, especially nonproliferation. Yet, given the regime in Beijing, an absolutist policy on human rights would undercut both our commercial interest and our interest in denying North Korea nuclear weapons. Moreover, U.S. efforts to promote human rights in China by diplomatic isolation and economic sanctions risk a backlash by the Chinese regime that would actually damage our long-term goal of Chinese democratization.

Faced with such a circumstance, the Bush administration developed a China policy that pursued, through a mix of incentives and disincentives, all our major interests in China. That policy seemed unsatisfactory to many, especially in the human rights community, but we had no real alternative without surrendering other important U.S. interests. Balance in our policy toward China was critical and remains so.

The United States has faced yet another test of our ability to balance objectives: expanding the membership of the North Atlantic Treaty Organization (NATO). Clearly, the United States has an interest in the independence of the newly democratic states of Eastern Europe. This independence can be best guaranteed through full NATO membership. Just as plainly, however, precipitous Eastern European membership in the alliance could play into the hands of ultranationalists in Russia and damage the cause of reform, another important U.S. interest. Faced with these competing objectives, NATO has essentially temporized on the issue of Eastern European membership. By so choosing, NATO has deferred, by default, to reactionary elements in Russia.

I am convinced that a more innovative approach to NATO membership can better serve our interests both in Eastern Europe and Russia. Promoting Eastern European security and Russian democracy are not mutually exclusive. Specifically, I believe that NATO should offer immediate full membership to select central and Eastern European countries (for example, Poland, Hungary, and the Czech Republic) and leave membership open for the remainder of the new emerging democracies in Eastern Europe and the former Soviet Union, including a democratic Russia, once it institutionalizes democracy, free markets, responsible security policies, and a commitment to Helsinki principles. Such an approach would help consolidate democracy where it has already taken firm root — in Warsaw, Budapest, and Prague — while giving the other emerging democracies a concrete incentive to accelerate reform through the "carrot" of full NATO membership. Instead, the alliance has accepted a false choice between reform in Russia and security in Eastern Europe, missing an opportunity to promote both.

Power:
The Imperative of Credibility

Assessing interests and balancing objectives, however, are not enough. There must also be a firm understanding of the nature and exercise of U.S. power. Today, the United States enjoys a preeminence in world affairs unique in history. That preeminence is perhaps most decisive in the military sphere. With the collapse of the Soviet Union and the demise of the Warsaw Pact, the United States no longer faces a global enemy. Our victory in the Gulf War demonstrated a capacity to project overwhelming military force half a world away. In short, U.S. military supremacy today goes unchallenged. Any aggressors contemplating action against the United States must include the certainty of defeat in their calculations.

America's international stature is also rooted in its economic strength. Our workers remain the world's most productive. Our export sector is the world's largest. And, with congressional approval of NAFTA, the United States enjoys a market of over 350 million consumers.

But the wellsprings of U.S. influence transcend military might and economic vitality. They include a third, intangible source: credibility. Our allies look to us with trust for a reason. Three times during this century, in two world wars and one cold one, the United States stood forthrightly with its friends against aggression and for freedom. More recently, President Bush declared that Saddam Hussein's invasion of Kuwait would not stand and made good on America's pledge.

Economic strength and military might are necessary but not sufficient causes of U.S. power. There must also be a willingness to use that power consistently, decisively, and effectively. That willingness, that credibility, has been a crucial element of American leadership since World War II. However, if this leadership is to be sustained, U.S. military might, economic power, and credibility must be maintained.

In defense policy, the United States must reassess any further cuts in force levels and preparedness. Twice before, after World Wars I and II, the United States neglected its armed forces. We and the world paid a price. As recently as the late 1970s, ours was a hollow army of doubtful readiness and dubious morale, a state of affairs that took years to reverse.

America's economic might, too, must be husbanded. Global interdependence has raised international competition to a new and feverish pitch. How the United States addresses key domestic issues, such as the budget deficit, restructured health care, and educational reform, will directly affect not only the prosperity of our citizens but our international influence.

But it is America's credibility that today is most at risk. Over the last two years, empty threats to use force in Bosnia, missteps in Haiti, and the tragedy in Somalia have all raised doubts about our resolve. These doubts go beyond U.S. policy in the Caribbean, the Balkans, or the Horn of Africa. When the United States acts or fails to act, no matter where, the whole world watches and draws lessons. Every time the United States issues an empty threat or fails to insist upon solemn international obligations, American power diminishes.

This lack of resolve in our foreign policy derives from not only confusion over our interests in this new era but also a fundamental uneasiness with the concept of U.S. power. Comfort with U.S. power is a precondition to its competent exercise. During the Cold War, virtually every use of

American power could be understood and explained to the American people as a response to the danger of Soviet totalitarianism. Today, of course, that argument is obsolete — and no similarly compelling calculus of force has emerged to replace it.

Whether America uses its power alone or with others must be based on pragmatic considerations. Alliances, whether formal or informal, and multi-lateral organizations, such as the United Nations, all represent means, not ends, in the pursuit of U.S. interests. Properly understood, multilateralism, coalition-building, and unilateral action constitute instruments by which a strategy of selective engagement can be pursued.

We need a choice, not just of policies but of instruments to implement them. Sometimes, as in support for a settlement in Cambodia, the United Nations will be the most appropriate vehicle. Other times, as in support for reform in the former Soviet Union, we will have to form ad hoc coalitions with like-minded states. And, as it did in Panama, the United States must always be prepared to act unilaterally when necessary, the oldest and still surest test of a great power.

Our action against Iraqi aggression in the Gulf provides a model for the effective use of American power. It included unilateral action in our deci-sion to dispatch troops to Saudi Arabia in the immediate aftermath of the invasion of Kuwait. It embraced the creation of an ad hoc coalition, first to enforce economic sanctions, then to finance and fight the war against Sad-dam Hussein. And it included the resort to multilateral institutions like the United Nations to rally world opinion and ensure universal compliance with Iraq's political and economic isolation.

Freedom of Action
and American Leadership

When we speak of "selective engagement," the term itself explains much. First, it recognizes the idea of a United States actively engaged in inter-national affairs. It embraces the concept of a United States not just in the world but of it. Soviet expansion may have compelled U.S. engagement after World War II, but postwar America's achievements were not limited to fighting and winning the Cold War. A global liberal economic regime, partnership with former adversaries like Germany and Japan, and the cre-ation of a truly international community of democratic values spanning three continents and two great oceans were all, in a sense, part of the Cold

War. But in another sense they transcended it. All were the products of U.S. engagement. And U.S. engagement remains no less imperative in today's world of fierce economic competition, burgeoning instability, and renascent fascism. In sum, the "engagement" aspect of selective engagement recognizes that disengagement today is simply not an option.

Second, selective engagement stresses that U.S. engagement means making choices — that is, selecting how, when, and where we will engage. With the emergence of the United States as the world's sole superpower, we enjoy unprecedented freedom of action. In stark contrast with the Cold War, we confront today no single overwhelming threat to our interests. Ironically, the United States can do so much today that we are tempted to attempt everything — or do nothing at all.

This freedom makes it all the more imperative that our nation's leaders set clear, coherent, and comprehensive criteria for making these vital decisions. Above all, we need to act in proportion to our interests, seek balance in our objectives, and remain credible in the exercise of our policies.

Making History by Solving Problems

I make no grand claims for selective engagement. Other, more ambitious approaches may bring better theoretical order to today's uncertainties. Candidates range from that old standby, balance-of-power realism, to neomercantilism, to the latest multilateral iteration of Wilsonianism, to that newest entry, Samuel Huntington's "clash of civilizations." But it might be wise for all of us to focus less on grand theory and more on conceptual tools for the nitty-gritty work of solving problems. There are enough of them — from Bosnia, to North Korea, to the historic events that seem to unfold daily in Russia — to keep us occupied for years.

For, at heart, foreign policy is not so much about creating a new world from a blank slate. Rather, it is about making a better world — a freer, more democratic, more secure, and more stable world — from the rough, uncomfortable, and unpredictable reality of human action and human choice. It is about making history — because what is history, fundamentally, but the record of human decision?

I have always approached the conduct of foreign policy in this way — a reflection, perhaps, of my own bias as a practitioner rather than theoretician. But a problem-solving approach to foreign policy is also justified by the revolutionary circumstances in which we find ourselves. The contours of the current era are only slowly emerging. A little intellectual modesty is in order — and a little reading of history.

In retrospect, new eras seem to emerge fully formed from the periods that precede them. At the time, however, the reality is different. Five years passed between the end of World War II and the promulgation of containment as official U.S. policy in the NSC-68 document — five years that appeared chaotic to those who lived through them. Like us, they were finding their way, and, like us, finding themselves as they did so.

We would do well to remember something once noted by Dean Acheson, who served at the highest levels of the State Department from 1941 to 1953, a period that in some respects provides a compelling parallel to our own. In his incomparable memoir, *Present at the Creation*, Acheson wrote that the task before the United States after World War II appeared only a "bit less formidable than that described in the first chapter of Genesis." The same can be said of the task confronting U.S. foreign-policy makers today. As we look to the daunting tasks ahead, it might be useful for us to reread Genesis and remember that even God, wise beyond all human comprehension, took creation a single day at a time.

The Honorable

Andrei Kozyrev

Former Foreign Minister of the
Russian Federation

Russia in the Multipolar World

The main distinctive feature of the world free from the bloc confrontation of the Cold War era is the extraordinary variety of cultural, political, and economic forms of state development. This trend is clearly visible in the former USSR and Eastern European countries after the demise of communism. Totalitarian regimes that denied the very right of peoples to have national interests exceeding the bounds of communist ideology have vanished to cede their place to over twenty new states seeking to enhance the specific spiritual and economic potential of their nations. The same trend is gaining momentum on the global scene. The end of the superpowers' confrontation has brought out of the shade the formation of several centers of dynamic economic development, including those in the so-called Third World. Many developing countries that were seen before as "pawns" in the Cold War have become independent participants in international politics.

Now it is already obvious that the world of the twenty-first century will be neither unipolar nor bipolar. It will be multipolar. First of all, because the rejection of the superpowers' rivalry brings to the forefront the factor of economic, not military, power. The importance of several "engines" of world development is being drastically enhanced, namely of such integration associations as the European Union, the North American Free Trade Association (NAFTA), and the Association of Southeast Asian Nations (ASEAN). Integration links that reemerge within the Commonwealth of Independent States (CIS) are called upon to play an important role as well.

Second, the very nature of contemporary international problems makes it vital to seek their solutions on a multilateral basis. Acting alone, no one — not even the most powerful state or the most effective military and political union — is able to cope with the threat of the proliferation of weapons of mass destruction, to solve transboundary environmental problems, to eradicate international terrorism and narcobusiness.

The international system has lost its illusory equilibrium, which was based on the "balance of terror" between the two hostile blocs. However, it has an opportunity to gain internal stability based on common universal values of democracy and human rights, which are shared by the increasingly wide range of states in their commitment to the universal principles of international law, economic integration, and interdependence. It is the enhanced role of these factors that can bring to life the basic principle of multipolar world structure — unity in diversity.

That is why I do not believe either in the fatalism of the "conflict of civilizations" notion proclaimed by some politicians or in the inevitability of the North-South confrontation predicted by others. The civilization disparities may not by themselves be the cause of international conflicts. The source of the overwhelming majority of modern crises in the world lies within states themselves and not in interstate relations. The international community has to cope with a situation in which states are on one side of the barricade and the problems they are facing are on the other side. Here we have a strong incentive for interaction and cooperation.

Nevertheless, the formation of a multipolar world is not by itself a guarantee of international stability and security or of sustainable economic growth. The danger of escalating rivalry between ethnic and regional interests is quite real. It threatens to throw the world back to a new "mutual deterrence" and even to a system of hostile alliances, replicating the pattern of the year 1914. New threats, stemming mainly from aggressive nationalism, are pushing in the same direction. The events in former Yugoslavia and in a number of "hot spots" in the former Soviet Union have demonstrated what kind of barbaric chasm we are being drawn into by ethnic intolerance elevated to the rank of state policy.

The growing social and economic crisis in vast regions of Asia and Africa remains a critical factor of instability. It is not accidental that the bloodiest and most prolonged clashes take place in the poorest countries, such as Afghanistan, Somalia, Ethiopia, Sudan, and Rwanda, where they sometimes lead to the disintegration of the state as such. The maintenance and, in a number of regions, the escalation of conflict potential is accompanied by the growing danger of the proliferation of weapons of mass destruction and devastating conventional weapons.

The existing mechanisms of international cooperation still fail to give timely and efficient responses to these challenges. After World War II, the democratic world, united in the face of the danger of totalitarianism, quickly formulated a common strategy. The Marshall Plan played a core role in the economic restoration of Western Europe, and the doctrine of containment made it possible to pool forces for repelling the Stalinist expansionism.

Today democratic nations are again in need of a common strategy. This need is dictated by the very scope of the task they are facing, namely the transformation of an unstable post-confrontational world to a stable and democratic one.

New Russia has oriented its foreign policy toward contributing to achieve this task, for in it we see a natural external continuation of our internal reforms. The transformation of an overarmed and self-isolated empire to a normal democratic state open to the world community is our main contribution to international security and stability.

It is needless to say in what an arduous and painful way this transformation proceeds. No doubt it will take us a lot of time to fully heal our economy of structural distortions inherited from the hypercentralized totalitarian system and to remedy our society of spiritual vacuum and imperial syndromes. But it is important that democratic and market mechanisms are starting to operate and to actually change people's way of life. A new generation of Russians already perceives the freedom of speech and press and free elections as a matter of fact, while only recently it was just an impossible dream. As for social life, while a decade ago the Soviet reality was symbolized by long queues of people lining up for essentials, today they are queuing rather for shares of private companies and privatized state enterprises.

Now the transformation process in Russia has actually progressed to the point where no return to communist totalitarianism is possible. However, the fundamental issues of Russia's future and of its role in the world remain unsolved. The reforms continue to be endangered, and this time the dangers emanate from political forces acting not under communist but rather under nationalist and at times neofascist slogans. They thrive on a national humiliation complex of a certain part of Russian society that developed as a result of the collapse of communism and disintegration of the USSR.

Until recently, the struggle between the democratic and imperial options in Russian politics, advocated respectively by the executive authority and the Legislature — i.e., the president, elected directly by the people, and the Parliament, being Soviet in origin — took the form of an open confrontation. This confrontation led to a tragic denouement in October 1993 when the leaders of the former Supreme Soviet provoked bloody incidents in Moscow.

The situation has radically changed since December 1993. A constitution was adopted in Russia, which served as the basis for elections of a new Parliament. Thus, the foundation of a new democratic Russian statehood was laid down, without which no reform is conceivable. The signing of the Civil Accord among major political and social forces on the initiative of President Yeltsin in May 1994 has created prerequisites for the country's development in the environment of civil peace.

This also creates new conditions for the formulation of foreign policy. The Russian democrats would lose the right to call themselves democrats had they ignored public opinion. It is precisely for the hearts and minds of the public at large, which play a decisive role under democracy, that the struggle between advocates of the democratic and imperial options is being mounted. This constitutes the main feature of the current stage as opposed to everything the West got accustomed to in the previous decades. For the first time, the policy of Russian reformers themselves and their friends abroad is to be shaped with due regard for how it is perceived inside Russia.

The task of the Russian democrats is to convince public opinion that the national interests can be realized only within the framework of a democratic and open foreign policy and that a great Russia is the Russia of Sakharov and not of Zhirinovsky. If the West is willing to assist us in solving this problem, it should shape its policy toward Russia in such a way as to demonstrate to the Russian public that the world needs Russia as a strong partner, occupying its merited place in the family of free and democratic states based on the rule of law rather than as a "sick man" of Europe and Asia. The policy accommodating these aspirations will be the best contribution of the West to the stability of Russia and the world and will most effectively block the revival of "Russian imperialism." In contrast, the estrangement of the West and attempts to screen it off from Russia with new "iron curtains" and "sanitary cordons" will only create a fertile soil for nationalist and imperial extremism. This is why a partnership with Russia can only be characterized by equality rather than paternalism.

Russia's contribution to the creation of a safe democratic world is realized, first, through its role as the major warrant of stability in the former USSR.

The breakup of the Soviet Union has left us and the whole world with problems of an unprecedented geopolitical scale. The success of our efforts to avert the worst—i.e., recurrence of the Yugoslav tragedy in the territory of a nuclear superpower—can be attributed to the fact that we abandoned the imperial course and did not attempt to restore the union state by force or to revise the boundaries. Similarly, we rejected the opposite calls "to withdraw" from the former union altogether and to retreat into ourselves in self-isolationism. We chose an arduous path but, in the final analysis, the only correct path: reforming the space of the former USSR on a new, voluntary basis—i.e., through the CIS.

The very name incorporates two principal and interrelated elements of our policy. On the one hand, it is the recognition of sovereignty and independence of the former Soviet republics. On the other hand, and no less important, it recognizes the need for close cooperation among the CIS countries, given their economic, political, cultural, and humanitarian interdependence.

Despite all the complexities of the commonwealth's development, it has already begun to live up to its name. Strengthening of trends toward reintegration in the economic sphere has become a reality. Restoration of economic ties among the CIS members constitutes their considerable joint contribution to global economic stabilization, which significantly reduces the need of this region for external financial and economic assistance. The necessary conditions to enable the commonwealth to become an attractive partner in large-scale investment cooperation are gradually being created.

Transition to partnership relations with leading democratic powers of the world has become the second major direction in our diplomatic efforts. Addressing a meeting of thousands in Moscow just after the abortive August putsch, I proclaimed as an official foreign policy line the theses that I had put forward earlier in the mass media only as a supposition: for democratic Russia, western democracies are natural friends and, in perspective, allies, just as they were enemies for the totalitarian USSR. This line, met with understanding by our western partners, has been reflected in many Russian treaties and agreements with the United States and the Western European states; it has also materialized in their support of Russian reforms and in the development of cooperation on key international problems.

The positive consequences of our turn toward partnership with the West have already influenced the world situation to the full extent. After signing the SALT-2 treaty and the agreement between Russia and the United States on mutual nontargeting of missiles, it was possible to achieve a real breakthrough toward strategic stability in relations between the two major nuclear powers. Partnership relations have been established between Russia and NATO, the two most powerful military entities in Europe. Russia is joining the "Club of Seven," transforming it into the political "Eight."

Nowadays we find ourselves at the next stage, in which the most important thing is the specific contents of the partnership rather than its symbols. And here, indeed, we sometimes have to use tough language and to defend our legitimate interests as other states do, which no one can suspect of pursuing an "imperialist" line. However, nowadays, as before, the strategic policy of Russia is aimed at the establishment of partnership relations with other "poles" of world politics, at the formation of a system of cooperative democratic management of international relations.

We focus our efforts on the following principal directions.

Promotion of respect for human rights throughout the world. The notion of the existence of an inseparable link between the preservation of peace and a society's degree of openness and respect for human rights, which was regarded by the communist regime of the USSR as an inadmissible challenge to itself and its ideology, has become one of the fundamentals in Russian foreign policy. The rights of a human being to life and to basic civil freedoms have a universal character. No national peculiarities can justify the refusal to abide by generally accepted norms in the field of human rights. Therefore, we should not disregard attempts to erode these norms by creating separate concepts of human rights for the "North" and for the "South" or by opposing some categories of rights to others.

Russia advocates human rights in all countries, without any exception, where they are flagrantly violated. We cannot accept any reference to the principle of noninterference when rights and freedoms of individuals are violated. Universalization of the norms of humanitarian law is all the more necessary as mass violations of human rights have not ceased but have acquired a new dimension and an alarming scope. Now they mostly relate to discrimination and expulsion of, if not direct violence against, ethnic minorities.

The world community is already turning its face toward this threat. An important step in this direction occurred in 1993, when, at Russia's initiative, fifty-three European, American, and Asian states—members of the Conference on Security and Cooperation in Europe (CSCE)—adopted a declaration firmly condemning all forms of aggressive nationalism, racism, chauvinism, xenophobia, and anti-Semitism. However, this is only the beginning of work that is so badly needed by hundreds of millions of people belonging to ethnic or linguistic minorities in dozens of countries throughout the world. A serious problem today is the violation of generally recognized ethnic minorities' rights in Latvia and Estonia, where nearly one-third of the "nonindigenous" population—Russians, Ukrainians, Belorussians, and Jews—either find themselves in the position of being immigrants deprived of civil rights or simply being "squeezed out" from these countries through a kind of legislative "ethnic cleansing."

The Russian leadership does not consider the Russian-speaking population as a means of restoration, by force, of the USSR or as a kind of the "fifth column" in the new independent states. We demand respect for generally recognized international standards in the field of human rights with regard to all peoples and ethnic minorities in the CIS and Baltic states without any exception. Thus the issue relating to the Russian-speaking population is not the subject of a particular dispute between the former republics of the USSR but is rather a problem to be solved with the participation, on a legitimate basis, of the international community.

During the period of confrontation, human rights were the focus of the struggle between the forces of democracy and totalitarianism. In a new multipolar world they should constitute a basis for bringing together peoples and civilizations of the West and the East, the North and the South. Only then will the world make progress in attaining the goal proclaimed by the founders of the United Nations: "to reaffirm faith in fundamental human rights, in the dignity and worth of the human person."

Preventing proliferation of weapons of mass destruction. The threat of a global conflict has faded away, but a new threat is emerging: there is a risk that weapons of mass destruction will proliferate throughout the world and reach the zones of destabilization and regional conflict. Parties to these conflicts do not hesitate to use the most sophisticated types of weapons, not only against each other but also against the civil population. There are abundant tragic examples: the "war of cities" waged by Iraq and Iran against each other, missile bombardments of Israel and Saudi Arabia by Iraq.

Proliferation of weapons of mass destruction and the missiles for their delivery poses a direct serious threat to the security of Russia. Along the borders of the CIS, in the Middle East and South Asia, powerful interests in certain countries seek to acquire missiles and their production technologies, while some of them do not even try to disguise their nuclear ambitions. Some states have chemical ammunitions in their arsenals; others can easily set up their production.

To remove the threat of proliferation of weapons of mass destruction, Russian diplomacy is acting in three directions. First and foremost, we are trying to settle political conflicts that are nourishing the regional arms race. Russia is willing to promote normalization of relations between India and Pakistan, as well as between the Korean People's Democratic Republic and the Republic of Korea. To find a comprehensive solution to security issues on the Korean peninsula, we have suggested that an international conference be held with the participation of both Korean states, Russia, the United States, the People's Republic of China, and Japan. Our efforts to settle the Middle East conflict involving near-nuclear states are producing the first encouraging results.

The second direction relates to steps aimed at enhancing the regime of international trade in arms and military technologies. And here the problem of restricting trade in ballistic missiles and their production technologies has come to the forefront.

As a first step on the international scene, Russia has declared its intention to join the Missile Technology Control Regime (MTCR). This was mentioned in a statement by Boris Yeltsin, dated January 29, 1992, on Russia's policy in the field of arms limitation and arms reduction. In early 1993 the Russian government adopted a special regulation dealing with control over the export of missiles and missile technologies. It was based on the MTCR rules and norms.

For Russia, compliance with the MTCR rules entails considerable financial and economic costs. We had to revise a number of large-scale contracts concluded by the former USSR—in particular, the contract for the supply of missiles and missile technology to India. When taking this painful step, we were guided by broad international security interests. Therefore, we are entitled to count on other exporters of missile technologies to adopt a similarly responsible approach to their obligations and to provide Russian producers equal access to the world market of space services.

Finally, the third direction of our efforts to prevent the spread of weapons of mass destruction is to impose an international legal ban on the development and production of chemical and nuclear weapons. A real breakthrough here was the opening for signature in January 1993 of the Convention on the Prohibition of Chemical Weapons. Russia was among the first nations to adhere to this instrument.

At present, a priority task for the international community is to strengthen regimes that support nonproliferation of nuclear weapons. Transition from bloc confrontation to multipolarity in the world entails complicated problems. The previous limitations (bloc "discipline") are no longer effective. They should be replaced by new ones that increase the effectiveness of the Treaty on Nonproliferation of Nuclear Weapons (NPT).

The comprehensive nuclear test ban should become one of these important limitations. Russia was among the states that initiated negotiations on that problem, which started in January 1994. Early elaboration of a respective treaty will help to solve the issue of giving the NPT permanent status as advocated by Russia.

Peacemaking. The "new generation" of conflicts in the former USSR turned out to be an unprecedented challenge to the world community. Here the deterioration of the situation to a Yugoslavian scenario could lead to major ecological disasters and to uncontrolled migration of huge quantities of weapons throughout the continent, including the most fatal ones. Chaos and instability in the Eurasian sphere threaten to make it a free-transit passage for the narco-mafia and terrorism to Europe.

The international community cannot protect itself from these threats using old means such as the expansion of military alliances, the establishment of isolated "security zones," the provision of nuclear guarantees, or the buildup of military might. It is in the common interests of Russia and the international community to extend all-European standards of civilized and responsible behavior to the new independent states of the former USSR and to integrate them into the CSCE framework. One should not forget that the southern border of the CIS is at the same time the border of the CSCE zone.

The local conflicts in nearby regions are increasingly affecting the everyday life of Russia. In many cases, it is the Russian-speaking population in the states of the former USSR that becomes the victim of ethnic conflicts. In 1993 alone, the country gave refuge to more than two million people. Their settlement in new places of residence cost the Russian Federation government and local authorities 51.5 billion rubles in 1992 and 1993. This is a heavy economic burden for any country, all the more so for Russia, which is experiencing a difficult transition period. The mass inflow of refugees has reanimated the long-forgotten threat of epidemics of dangerous diseases. Tides of organized crime from "hot spots" are reaching Russia. Therefore, it is quite natural that Russian society is preoccupied with the situation in those zones of conflict.

Russia is "doomed" to play a special role in maintaining peace and stability in the former USSR. Imperial ambitions are not the point here; the point is that no foreign state — far or near — and no international organization is able to take the place of Russia, simply because peacekeeping efforts in the region require large resources. At present, over 18,000 Russian servicemen participate in four peacemaking operations in the CIS territory.

Our actions in the CIS zones of conflict are based on the principles of international law: respect for sovereignty and independence of the states involved in conflicts, noninterference in their internal affairs, recognition of their territorial integrity while respecting the rights of ethnic minorities. In all these situations Russia does not impose its peacemaking services but acts only at the request of the legitimate governments of the states concerned. All peacekeeping operations (PKO) conducted by Russia are transparent for the world community and keep a constant liaison with the U.N. and CSCE observer missions.

However, the approach of these organizations as well as that of many of our foreign partners still lacks consistency and is characterized by duality.

They seem to be torn between an understanding of the real significance of the Russian peacemaking mission and concern that it could serve as a pretext for the revival of Russia's "imperialist" ambitions. As a result, instead of support for our peacekeeping efforts, we sometimes witness attempts to draft various speculative schemes and "criteria for assessment of Russians' actions," which only lead us away from practical work.

Meanwhile, what we really need is a common long-term international strategy for peacemaking. Our principal goal should be prevention of conflicts. Universal principles of participation in peacemaking efforts should also be elaborated. They should include, in particular, the principle of a just distribution of the burden of peacekeeping costs, inter alia in the territory of the former USSR. We could discuss the establishment of a voluntary fund and the issue of taking into account the peacemaking expenditures, borne by the former USSR, when assessing contributions to the "traditional" U.N. PKO. Similar cooperation could be arranged within the framework of the NAC.

Global economic reunification. The confrontation policy of the Cold War era resulted in economic division of the world. The orientation of the former USSR and its allies to the autarchic development seriously affected both the living standards of our peoples and the growth rate of the world economy in general.

Now unique conditions have been created to incorporate into the economic interdependence system a region with a population of 500 million people. The key problem here is the integration of Russia into the world economy. Its solution will not only help to move forward Russian reforms — which, in itself, would be an important stabilization factor for the international system of states — but will also provide a strong impetus for cooperation in the most promising fields, from peaceful uses of outer space to solutions of the energy problem.

The long-term strategy of economic partnership that we proposed to the "Big Seven" meets these goals. Our list of priorities includes forms of Russian participation in the international economic relations that neither require additional external financing (including the lifting of discriminatory restrictions on Russia's international trade) nor lead to the external debt growth (promotion of direct investments, debt restructuring), but result in a broader cooperation between Russia, the International Monetary Fund, and the World Bank.

Special attention should be paid to strengthening the social orientation of international cooperation projects. It is important to increase, as soon as possible, support for privatization and structural adjustment of the economy in Russia and to assist small and medium-scale enterprises. Thus, it is necessary to recognize that Russia should be granted a nondiscriminatory position in the international markets, with abrogation or revision of legislative acts restricting its access to these markets. This would serve not only our interests but those of our creditors; an increase of Russia's export earnings would help service its own debts and those of the former USSR.

For centuries, the term "multipolarity" was associated with rivalry of "power centers" that balanced between war and peace. Now the end of confrontation and ideological antagonism gives mankind a unique chance to use the creation of a multipolar world for the promotion of constructive cooperation in the economic, scientific, and cultural fields. A global breakthrough to diversity of means and forms of peoples' development will make the world truly united and secure for all.

His Excellency

Nursultan A. Nazarbayev

President of the
Republic of Kazakhstan

Kazakhstan and the Commonwealth of Independent States

Inevitable Integration in the Post–Cold War Order

Mankind eagerly awaits the twenty-first century. The Cold War has come to an end. The global ideological confrontation between the two superpowers and their satellites, which previously threatened the planet with nuclear holocaust, has now become part of history. Yet does this mean that today's world has become safer and more stable?

Regrettably, the hope that the collapse of totalitarianism and the subsequent demilitarization would automatically bring to the nations of the world prosperity and confidence in their future has proven altogether illusory. In the new political reality there is no end to military conflict. Furthermore, there has been a disintegration of the former system of collective security and a consequent upset in the balance of geostrategic interests of states constituting the now deceased Soviet bloc as well as that of their former adversaries.

In the situation that has developed one cannot help feeling seriously concerned about the efforts made by certain political theoreticians to fix, in the international social conscience, a stereotype according to which mankind is gradually getting involved in a new global confrontation — never mind whether it is a "war of cultures" or a "war of economies." Allegations that countries and nations have no alternative but to experience a new breakdown of world civilization are, in fact, none other than a recurrence of the confrontational mentality. The crux of such an approach is to justify the right of the most powerful to settle their problems at the expense of the vital interests of their partners. The new world order, if based on this principle, is certain to be neither long-lasting nor durable, for it inherently generates conditions for potential conflicts both between them and those countries which are forced to be part of any sphere of influence.

Misunderstanding or ignoring this obvious truth invariably brings about a clash between the states, as it might trigger a whole sequence of local conflicts which, given the unstable balance of forces and interests, is capable of exploding into warfare in today's world.

Small wonder that a formidable responsibility rests on the heads of state and governments of those countries that are participants in the negotiating process. They are bound to overcome racial, ethnic, and religious barriers, mistrust, and economic egotism. They should soberly and courageously face the reality and shape the world order based on principles of humanism, equality, and good will. The world order appears to be, for the first time in human history, in a position that allows harmonious development of nations without suffering from a waste of intellectual and material resources for the benefit of military competition. Beyond any doubt, this would generate favorable circumstances for the convergence of world economies and cultures.

The fundamental basis for such a world order should, no doubt, become an ever greater expansion of the number of those who participate in the global system of responsibility, which should include both developed and developing countries. Great powers, for their part, could have acted as guarantors of the efficiency of the negotiating process, as those of all the states honoring general principles and standards of the new international system. We are bound to build this new world order, resorting to all opportunities without exception, and we should set up regional security zones, take all preventive measures to adequately anticipate potential conflicts, and win over broad circles of world public opinion in settling this crucial problem.

In our day remains the no less serious problem of ideological confrontation between certain states. As a rule, it is of a purely ideological nature and essentially predetermines antagonistic relations between the states at issue. It is the solely pragmatic approach in the dialogue between the subjects of the conflict, substantiated by mutually beneficial cooperation, that is capable of removing enmity and bringing the states out of political deadlock.

This is essentially the goal that Kazakhstan pursues in its convening of a Conference for Interaction and Confidence Measures in Asia (CICMA), a regional forum whose noble mission is to prevent conflict-fraught situations through constructive cooperation of its member states. If a conflict does erupt, the organization should strive to localize and neutralize the nascent threat. An Asian analogue of the Conference for Security and Cooperation in Europe (CSCE), the CICMA possesses a number of specific features determined by certain peculiarities of the Asian region, including inherent contradictions and territorial problems. Yet as a member of the CSCE and a supporter of the inviolability of its cardinal principles, Kazakhstan advocates within the framework of this international entity more effective mechanisms to influence the complex political processes unfolding in Europe.

As is well known, so far the CSCE has neither a mandate of its own nor sources of funding to successfully engage in conciliating current conflicts, particularly armed ones. The CSCE in its present-day form experiences substantial difficulties in ensuring implementation of its ten basic principles, for until now no adequate mechanisms existed for carrying them out. So it becomes evident in this context that in the matter of conciliating conflicts on the vast European continent, it is not enough to rely on the United Nations alone.

An urgent necessity has arisen for a comprehensive security system specially designed to summon the efforts of all the available international and regional agencies. The CSCE should help overcome the difficulties the United Nations had to face after the collapse of the socialist camp when its activities were essentially reduced to that localization of numerous armed conflicts.

One has to admit nowadays that the political context of processes unfolding in the post-Soviet sphere acquires tremendous significance. After disintegration of the system of international security based on the nuclear parity of the Soviet Union and the United States, the new independent states have to single-handedly settle a formidable problem — defining forms and ways of transforming the self-contained, isolated communist system into an open democratic society. And although each of these states has preferred a way of its own and its own reference points along with its own share of responsibility for regional security, none may claim the right to contest this choice, imposing its will through economic, political, or military pressure. Indeed, the situation that has shaped up in each of the post-Soviet republics is so specific and delicate that it would not suffer any rude interference. These countries are in the process of transition; they are just on the way to forming their statehood. There is an inevitable disease of growth for which no immediate remedy exists. What they need is peace, economic cooperation, and domestic stability.

The political evolution of the former Soviet republics, which has been so closely followed by the West, has brought about substantial alterations in the geopolitical landscape of the post-Soviet space. Russia, as a nucleus of the CIS, has been virtually thrown back to the East and is currently at the crossroads. What way should its geoeconomic development take? As for Kazakhstan, its geopolitical situation is that of a young independent state, the nature of which is determined by a number of factors, including its tenuous geographic position in the central Asian region; the enormous length of common land borders with Russia and China (two world nuclear powers whose populations total 1.3 billion people); exceedingly rich deposits of natural wealth; the availability of nuclear testing grounds and a cosmodrome; and the enormous sparsely populated territory.

Small wonder that it is of vital importance for the republic to provide itself with a dependable belt of confidence and good-neighborliness all along the length of its border. Kazakhstan, a land with no territorial claims to any of its neighbors, is firmly committed to a peaceful policy, and it is only natural that it is permanently engaged in expanding the infrastructure of its relations. The young state has acceded to the Nuclear Nonproliferation Treaty (NPT), voluntarily abandoning its arsenal and obtaining international safeguards for its security.

It is no secret that the problem of modernization of the new independent states of the CIS, their territorial integrity, and stability has surpassed regional borders, turning into a major problem for the world community. The fact that the countries of the CIS have joined the European negotiating process and their consequent emergence on the world stage as equals make the problem of their integration within the CIS framework ever more topical.

The CIS is not a state; it is not some supranational formation but a mechanism of regional interaction adequate to actual circumstances and comparable with the European Union. Yet, if European integration is based on the gradual advance from economic integration to a comprehensive political interstate partnership, the Soviet pattern functioned in a reverse sequence — from political unitarianism to a self-contained, closed economic system. This is why one should accept, as inevitable, that the process of the overall acquisition of sovereignty in the former USSR republics has not only brought about a collapse of the once-single political space but also triggered grave and unprecedented economic crises that befell all the new independent states without exception. It is far from fortuitous that integration processes within the framework of the CIS have acquired a pronounced political coloring owing to their close economic cooperation.

Yet for no apparent reason these positive developments — which are, in fact, extraordinarily vital for CIS participants — are sometimes interpreted by certain outside observers as a wish to revitalize the old empire. Only one argument can refute these misgivings: consolidation of economic, political, and cultural relations among the new independent states is essentially one of the most powerful factors stabilizing domestic policy and the social situation in these republics. The tried and tested path followed throughout the world is that of integration. Yet we are supposed to proceed in the reverse direction. The idea utterly disregards the fact that our nations have much in common. It is actually a purely political situation. Kazakhstan consistently advocates the idea of economic integration of the CIS member states without infringing on the interests or sovereignty of the other states. Kazakhstan fully honors the principle of noninterference in the internal affairs of each nation as well as the rights of each nation to manage its own destiny. None may argue this choice, for it incarnates Kazakhstani people's striving for freedom and prosperity. And, besides, the will of the nation is a sacred thing.

However paradoxical, Asia, being one of the potentially "explosive" continents, is developing its economic potential at a dynamic tempo and is expected in the foreseeable future to catch up with the West. Accordingly, the orientation of Kazakhstani foreign policy is that of developing well-balanced relations both with European and Asian states. While consolidating its position within the framework of the European Union, Kazakhstan, however, would strive to comprehensively expand its cooperation with the countries of the Asian-Pacific region. Therefore, if political relations linking the republic with the European Union are in fact a priority, then economic interaction with countries of Southeast Asia may well be regarded as long-term and promising.

One of the most serious concerns threatening mankind today is militant nationalism and fundamentalism. The genuinely unique experience gained by the peoples of Kazakhstan in interethnic and interreligious cooperation enables it to avoid interethnic conflict. This notwithstanding, general world developments testify to an ever-growing presence of these pernicious processes. Even civilized Europe is shaken with convulsions of fratricidal butchery in Bosnia. Regrettably, eventual efforts made by the world community to stop the bloodshed ended in failure. It is worth noting that collective CIS peacekeeping forces have succeeded in localizing civil war in Tajikistan through securing the Afghan-Tajik border. Similarly, all is being done to bring the opposing parties back to the bargaining table. Much is also being done to conciliate the conflict in Nagorno-Karabakh. The most crucial goal is to prevent escalation of any conflict and to anticipate its eventual development, given the bloody Yugoslav scenario.

I would like to emphasize in this context that, in its peacekeeping activities, the United Nations might have substantially broadened its support by drawing from regional international agencies, including those operating in the Commonwealth of Independent States. We cannot afford to let any state assume the role of international policeman (as was the case in the past on more than one occasion). Peacekeeping forces should be impartial to any of the adversarial parties. By joining the efforts of all the countries of the world, we are bound to elevate the role of U.N. preventive diplomacy, to establish sort of a system of pre-crisis notification meant for timely removal of the deepest causes of nascent conflicts.

No small impact on the eventual political reality may be wielded by the relations between the great powers. For Kazakhstan, just as for any other central Asian republic, it is of paramount importance that members of the Nuclear Club — the United States, Russia, and China — be capable of setting up a stable balance of political, economic, and military interests in the region. Otherwise, foreign policy pursued by the new independent states would lose its orientation with respect to the aforementioned powers. The states in question would lose the actual perspective of the world leaders' involvement in settling cardinal issues of the independent states. The time when the vital interests of the superpowers in some particular region served as a pretext for interference in the internal affairs of sovereign countries should be long gone and done with. Otherwise, nothing will come of our intention to build a new equitable world — a reliable groundwork for the well-being and happiness of future generations on Mother Earth.

His Excellency

Leonid Kuchma

President of Ukraine

Ukraine

*Identity in the
Post–Cold War Era*

Politics, as a rule, gives no unambiguous answers to the fundamental question of the post–Cold War order regarding whether or not the world has become a more dangerous place since the collapse of the Soviet Union. Of course, the global security system changed drastically after the bipolar world disappeared and confrontation between the two political systems ceased to exist after the demise of the USSR.

The global Cold War division lines have disappeared, along with the threat of planetary nuclear catastrophe. Gone is the excruciating fear of a possible demise of mankind in a thermonuclear duel that plagued the world for half a century. Most important, though, is a radical change in the psychology of vast numbers of people, including politicians and the military. They no longer regard the East or the West as a symbol and a source of evil, and no longer clench their fists and weapons at the thought of the opposing social and political system.

Thus, the level of security grew significantly in the global sense, or, to be more exact, the level of global tension and confrontation noticeably subsided in the world. However, I would not consider myself a pragmatic politician if I could not make calculations in politics. Even the most elementary calculations produce dramatic conclusions. Today, the number of local military conflicts has grown exponentially compared with those in the era of global confrontation. A thousand times more people die in those conflicts.

It appears that everything, both in life and politics, has to be paid for. We had to pay in local and regional fears of many hundreds of thousands of people, if not millions, for the end of global confrontation and planetary fears. Decades from now, historians will probably give an unbiased analysis of the entire process of the rise and evolution of the Balkan, Caucasian, and central Asian conflicts. It is only then, based on an impartial analysis, that we will be able to say whether there was an opportunity to avoid those conflicts during the collapse of such a huge social and political entity as the former USSR.

The historians will probably say that the blame was on politicians and their inapt decisions. They may presume that the blame could have been on the objective reasons. An enormous amount of social, national, religious, and ethnic energy is released at the collapse of the huge state formation, which feeds ruthless conflicts, military clashes, and social dramas and tragedies. Today it is clear that many threats of a regional and local nature replaced one paramount threat to the entire world. It is very hard for me to judge whether this price is acceptable and such change of threat levels optimal, or whether a shift in the cause of threat from political to nationalistic, ethnic, or religious ones can be regarded as progress.

As a politician, I certainly understand that the removal of a threat to the existence of humankind is a fundamental breakthrough in the development of human history. But as a person who is aware of the deaths of many thousands of people and who daily sees those tragedies on the television screen, I would consider it cynical to say that the world has become more secure and comfortable for man to live in. I believe that many politicians tend to forget that the man in the street is equally scared of dying, either in a global war or a local military clash.

In summary, we can assume that after the Soviet Union disintegrated, the world not so much witnessed the change of the volume of threat to humankind but rather the structure of that threat. This conclusion leads us to assess how to improve international security. International security can be significantly upgraded in case a new structure of world threats is brought in line with the traditional all-European and global collective security systems. I think that the existing collective security systems — such as NATO,

OSCE (Organization for Security and Cooperation in Europe), and others — do not yet fully employ the mechanisms and forms of action that are required of a new world order. Born at the time of global confrontations, these institutions are not yet ready to prevent, forecast, preempt, and eliminate on-site, local hotbeds of tension. I believe that the urgent common goal of all democracies today is to find and work out adequate ways of preventing and extinguishing local conflicts. I am deeply convinced that none of the local conflicts should be disregarded or ignored. A small infection can spread into a total poisoning of the whole body. Similarly, world wars grew out of the so-called "small" conflicts.

Dangers Confronting Ukraine

When estimating the level of security of one or another country, experts usually single out the following fundamental threats: territorial claims to that country from its neighbors, separatism, the degree of tensions between ethnic communities, and, finally, terrorism. Fortunately, none of those extreme threats is typical for Ukraine today. Neither of Ukraine's neighbors presented official territorial claims to Ukraine during the time of its independent existence. More than that, good-neighbor relations with surrounding states and their mutual understanding of the significance of the principle of inviolability of borders continue to gain strength.

Separatism, as an intention of some region to fully secede from Ukraine, also does not exist in its pure form in our country. There does exist certain instability in several regions — in part, in Crimea. Our actions in relation to Symferopil are directed primarily toward preempting further development of such instability. The sparks lit by the autonomy's authorities should not ignite the fire of a broad conflict. It will be an easier and more humane task to prevent such a conflict than to localize burgeoning political emotions.

In Ukraine there are regional political movements that demand a certain distancing of the region from the center. There are also separate extremist factions that favor a reshaping of Ukraine's map. However, I would repeat that there is no all-powerful, well-organized separatist movement in Ukraine. In recent years, Europeans, in part observers of the post-Soviet states, have learned only too well what dangers and consequences separatist movements can harbor.

No doubt, we have regional instabilities, but those instabilities stem not from the political aspirations of some regions to split Ukraine but rather from criticism of the nature and rate of economic reform pursued by the central authorities. We still continue to search for an optimal structure of the central authorities and harmonious relations between the central power and local government. There are certainly many problems in this area, but they have no fatal or destructive nature for Ukraine.

The relations between ethnic communities in Ukraine — such as between the Ukrainians and the millions of ethnic Russians — also have never given birth to extreme problems that could threaten the existence of Ukraine. Today, numerous studies — in particular, international studies — indicate a high level of integrity for Ukraine's multinational society. The formation of a single Ukrainian nation sharing common values and a common destiny as a state will certainly be a lengthy process, but it has started and is continuing successfully.

Finally, terrorism, which is becoming a plague in many countries, luckily has no tradition and, I hope, no perspective in Ukraine. Nevertheless, we believe that we must always be on the alert against such a threat at a time when terrorism can use even nuclear weapons and their components as its instrument. We are ready to cooperate and do cooperate with all countries that seek effective ways to eradicate terrorism as a social and political phenomenon.

I would again reiterate that today there are no extreme challenges that would directly endanger the existence and calm in Ukraine. Yet this does not mean that life is free from clouds in Ukraine. The archaic political system inherited from the past, which combines obsolete legislative bodies — the Radas — with the reformist executive branch, undoubtedly presents a serious threat to the very existence of Ukraine. The economy provides another example of a similar nature. The transition from the socialist economy to a market economy requires immense organizational effort, financial support, and huge social costs. That is why we welcome and appreciate any assistance from abroad that decreases the level of tension in the social sphere.

Direction of Ukrainian Foreign and Military Policy

The formation of an independent Ukrainian state is taking place at a difficult time, characterized by a transition from the Cold War and interbloc confrontation to the creation of a new world order that must be based on cooperation, interaction, and stability. The multifaceted nature of the transition period dictates the singularity of Ukraine's foreign policy.

Our most important task is to overcome Ukraine's dissociation from the European states. This policy is aimed at creating reliable guarantees of Ukraine's external security, using Europe's best experience in building a truly democratic state, and engaging international assistance to fight the economic crisis for the sake of market reforms. We regard Europe as an integral entity, a common home for all nations and countries that live on the continent. History gave all Europeans a chance to unite. It is important that we do not lose that chance but make the unity come true.

Ukraine regards its participation in the future all-European security system as a major foreign policy guarantee for its national security, and rates its cooperation with such European structures as OSCE, NATO, the European Union, and the Western European Union as a major priority on its foreign policy agenda. This approach has been recorded in the "Basic Guidelines of Ukraine's Foreign Policy" and "The Military Doctrine of Ukraine."

At the subregional level, Ukraine is persistently expanding ties and cooperation within the framework of the central and Eastern European region, with member states of the Black Sea Economic Cooperation and its Parliamentary Assembly and with Northern and Baltic Councils, where Ukraine speaks out for deepening ties between all member states.

On a bilateral level, Ukraine is primarily interested in maintaining close and varied relations with countries of central and Eastern Europe, with new independent states, and with former republics of the Soviet Union. We are close to those countries and peoples not only geographically but also due to our common historic past and economic, cultural, humanitarian, and other links. As those links are renewed on new principles of equality and mutual benefit, Ukraine insists upon only one condition: we are against the renewal of domination by any state, against imposing someone's will upon other nations.

We are convinced that the ongoing reform process in Ukraine directly relates to the problem of stability and security in Europe. Along with Russia and the United States, Ukraine therefore actively cooperates with other European countries, in part with member states of the European Union. In addition to other reasons, such cooperation is important for Ukraine from the psychological point of view. It is important for the people of Ukraine not to feel excluded from the club of European nations, to be able to count on their support and friendly attention so that they can see a perspective for the future. It would be easier for them to resolve the difficult social problems that arise in the course of the reform. That would also make less acute the issues of ethnic minorities, conflict, and the geopolitical orientation of the population.

Success in bringing about reforms and better living is far from being a domestic problem of Ukraine. It is hard to foresee all the negative consequences that would directly affect the stability of Europe unless there are changes for the better in Ukraine's domestic life and its cooperation with the world at large. Of extreme importance for Ukraine are economic relations with European countries both on a bilateral and multilateral level. Ukraine will continue to develop and deepen its overall cooperation with the European Union along the lines of a step-by-step integration of Ukraine into the all-European economic space. However, we understand that time, effort, and desire of all interested sides is needed for Ukraine's full-fledged inclusion into the contemporary European process in all its integrity.

The strengthening of trust and confidence is yet another area where such an approach can serve as a key to the solution of many international problems and a path to accord. The establishment of a zone of security and cooperation in the center of Europe as well as better understanding in the military and naval fields in the Black Sea are the concrete foreign political initiatives that Ukraine sponsored in order to create a climate of trust, stability, security, and cooperation in the regions that border Ukraine and that are sensitive to contemporary changes on the European continent.

Ukraine believes that western, northern, central, and Eastern Europe must act as one entity. Bilateral and regional efforts should unite European states. These efforts must be coordinated in timing and expression of political decisiveness for all Europeans to reach one goal — to create a Europe integrated on the basis of three dimensions: democracy, well-being, and security.

Part 4

Regional Divisions in the Post–Cold War Order

His Excellency

Dr. Kamal Kharrazi

Ambassador Extraordinary
and Plenipotentiary of the
Islamic Republic of Iran;
Permanent Representative
to the United Nations

Iran's View of the Post–Cold War Era

*Continuity and Change
in the Region*

It is becoming increasingly difficult to resist subscribing to the idea that the end of the Cold War did not bring about a new world order. The image presented of such a new world order was one of an evolving international consensus that was to embrace all that countervails against the political-military confrontations of the old bipolar system. Euphemisms of democracy, freedom, market economy, pluralism, and freedom of choice were used to persuade the international community that we are on the threshold of an order whose hallmark could not but include, inter alia, a global partnership for peace, along with security and prosperity founded on general principles of consensus, all-inclusiveness, interdependence of historically dissimilar units, and, above all, abandonment of power politics in the conduct of international relations.

However, the unfolding events of the last few years, and particularly the manner in which major international players conducted themselves in respect to these events, has left little doubt that at this juncture of history such an idealistic new world order is far-fetched, if not a mere chimera. This view is not grounded in an inherent pessimism in human potential to manage its affairs in the context of such an ideal global order; rather, it is a realistic assessment of the current state of world politics, still characterized by power politics and hegemony of the powerful.

The events since 1990, particularly those in the Persian Gulf, the former Yugoslavia, Somalia, and Rwanda, combined with the responses and conduct of major international policymakers toward them, make it abundantly clear that the much-celebrated phrase "new international order" has been coined by those who perceive themselves the victors of the Cold War and as such justified in appointing themselves the "global Leviathan." However, this mentality goes against the tide of contemporary history. The modern trend now is for populations to restrict their own national governments in every possible way, thereby taming the real Leviathan — let alone a global Leviathan, which is an oxymoron in and of itself.

Attempts at assuming total control of world affairs by certain countries that are powerful in terms of their military capacity clearly indicate the continuity of the Cold War mentality. As such, they are bound to fail because they totally disregard the inherent diversity of human society and its inalienable right to freedom of choice. Furthermore, economic giants like Germany and Japan, a United Europe, and a dynamic, post–Cold War developing group of states — including its Islamic component which, in response to the Islamic resurgence, has adopted a more active and vocal stand — are formidable factors that preclude supremacy and total control of world affairs by a global Leviathan. Furthermore, such hegemonic attempts rob the international community of opportunities for positive development and growth of the human condition, which the end of the Cold War initially presented.

The end of political and military confrontation between the two superpowers, therefore, did not put an end to power politics, but rather gave rise to a renewed thirst for world power and control founded on the fallacious notion that might makes right. As a result, it would be fair to conclude that the current state of world politics has no semblance of any order, particularly at the global level, notwithstanding the ostensible expressions to the contrary circulated primarily out of Washington.

Immediately following the end of the Cold War, the United Nations gained some renewed spirit when it was viewed as an effective international authority to resolve regional conflicts and reshape the conduct of international relations in the new era. An effective United Nations was thought to be able to operate on the basis of international wisdom, withstanding aggression in the context of collective security, peacemaking, and peace-building. A prime example of such a renewed United Nations was the reversal of Iraq's second aggression against one of its neighbors in the Persian Gulf. Despite the excesses in the use of force against the Iraqi forces and civilians, which gave rise to some concern about the conduct of such operations, the determination of the allied forces led by the United States to stop Iraq's aggression was viewed as indicative of a rejuvenated United Nations.

However, the subsequent events in the Balkans, particularly the continued Serbian aggression against Bosnia and Herzegovina, dashed all hopes for an effective United Nations. The practical acquiescence of the United States and the halfhearted measures of its allies in NATO under the U.N. banner, which allowed the Serbs to continue their aggression and onslaught with impunity, pointed to the fact that an international order remains secondary to and, in fact, a function of the differing national interests of those who formulate international policies in the post–Cold War era. An international order vis-à-vis important international issues is in limbo. France's support for loosening the sanctions against Iraq, despite the determination of the United States to keep them in place; policy differences between the United States, on the one hand, and the United Kingdom and France, on the other, about the debilitating issue of Bosnia; the retreat from Somalia; and the tacit indifference to the slaughter of hundreds of thousands of people in Rwanda all point to a marked absence of an international order.

The double standard applied by the U.N. Security Council in attending to regional conflicts, such as reversing Iraq's aggression against Kuwait in a surprisingly short time as opposed to allowing Serbian aggression against Bosnia Herzegovina to drag on after three years with no prospect in sight for a just and equitable solution, casts a shadow over the United Nations. Therefore, the paralyzed U.N. system of the Cold War period has become an effective vehicle only when certain permanent members of the Security Council select it to be so in order to advance their foreign policy objectives, and it remains in the abyss when their policy objectives do not coincide. The incapacitated United Nations of the past is in danger of becoming the unpredictable United Nations of the next millennium.

If the United Nations is to maintain its authority as a truly international organization, it needs to enhance its role and authority to meet the global expectation of it as a truly international organization where all member states, comprising all world cultures, have meaningful input into its modus operandi and future. Thus, democratization of the U.N. system in order to bring it into accord with contemporary realities is fundamental if this international body is to remain viable fifty years after its birth. If the flag of the United Nations is not to become a flag of convenience, then the misuse and selective use of its system by the major powers should desist forthwith. In this respect, the secretary-general's agendas for peace and for development are important first steps that should be viewed as an integrated approach to challenges facing the world community.

Underdevelopment and the less than favorable North-South relations bear directly on international crises and the peacemaking efforts of the United Nations. In response, the United Nations must devise a framework for more cooperative North-South relations, on the one hand, and foster a culture of multilateralism as well as regional economic, political, and security arrangements on the other. Under such circumstances, the United Nations will move toward creating an international climate where infliction of undue influence and pressure on its process by the major powers will become less likely.

As indicated earlier, development of a new international order is a reasonable goal, where the decision-making process for our increasingly smaller and more interdependent world would not only be transparent and all-inclusive but also democratic. However, in light of the temptations seized upon by the powerful states to seek total control of world politics, the development of a decent international order will clearly require a long, interactive process counterbalancing assertion of rights and demands of equality by the developing states with resistance to such demands by the industrial states. This process will inevitably entail give and take and require learning and relearning by western countries and developing countries alike about the virtues and endurance of an order premised on multilateralism, good-faith negotiations, consensus-building, and recognition of the legitimate interests of all in a healthy, international climate free from pressure and power politics.

A significant outcome of the end of the Cold War has been the emergence of a trend in the developing world, kept in check during the Cold War, of self-confidence and assertion of its values and priorities in order to achieve a reasonable parity with the industrialized states in shaping the future landscape of world politics. Despite the insistence of the western states on maintaining the status quo, the pattern of history, as manifested in the abolition of slavery and the demise of colonialism, is working in favor of the developing world to rise above the second-class world citizenship that it is now accorded.

A preliminary indication of this new trend is the vigor with which the developing states have asserted their concerns and priorities and contributed to the final decisions at major international conferences in the last few years. Examples include the 1992 Rio International Conference on the Environment, where the developing states incorporated the interrelated concept of sustainable development in the final documents of the conference; the second World Conference on Human Rights, held in Vienna in 1993, where the developing states underscored the need for recognition of cultural diversity in the world while acknowledging the universality of all human rights; and the 1995 World Summit on Social Development, where the developing states asserted their definition of absolute poverty and highlighted the imperative of international efforts for its elimination as a prerequisite for social development.

These three international conferences indicate the contemporary trend of the developing countries' self-assertion, their energetic and constructive contribution to the international policymaking process, and, at the same time, their recognition of the need for a final compromise on issues and perceived interests. Notwithstanding the fact that the processes of these conferences were not free from power politics and behind-the-scenes influence peddling, all things considered, the new trend is an indication of a burgeoning international climate in which a new mode of conduct of international relations may evolve; that is, international policymaking and standard-setting will no longer be the exclusive domain of the West, but a common responsibility of the world community as a whole.

The Islamic Republic of Iran, for its part, has practiced what it preaches. Its constructive role and good-faith negotiations and contributions in many international conferences, including those mentioned above, are clear examples of Iran's recognition of global pluralism, balance of interest, and meaningful compromise. Furthermore, Iran's active and serious participation in the deliberations of the 1993 Convention on Prohibition of the Use, Production, and Stockpiling of Chemical Weapons, the 1994 International Conference on Population and Development, and the 1995 Conference on Review and Extension of the Nuclear Nonproliferation Treaty, provide further indications of this new trend. Iran's constructive role in bringing together the differing views of the western and developing states and its help in achieving consensus on many international policy decisions are generally recognized facts.

Iran's foreign policy objectives and practices in the region are other indications of how Iran intends to deal with challenges and opportunities of the post–Cold War era. In this context, the Islamic Republic of Iran has played a constructive role in promoting the culture of regionalism in the Persian Gulf, central Asia, and the Caucasus in terms of economic development and cooperation as well as conflict resolution.

Notwithstanding the general support of Saddam Hussein in his war of aggression against Iran, which for some Arab states of the Persian Gulf included logistic and financial support in billions of U.S. dollars, the Islamic Republic of Iran recognizes the fundamental need in the region for a new beginning. Iraq's second aggression in a decade against another neighbor added to the complexities of the region and made a new beginning all the more necessary. Hence, ever since the establishment of a cease-fire in the Iraq-Iran wars, the Islamic Republic of Iran has tried to promote bonds of cooperation and friendship with Arab states of the southern Persian Gulf. The critical importance of promoting stability in the Persian Gulf area, as well as maintaining the freedom of navigation in that strategic waterway for the economic vitality of littoral states and stability of world economy, is universally recognized.

In order to expand regional cooperation, the Islamic Republic of Iran has been encouraging closer cultural, economic, and social ties among the littoral states of the Persian Gulf to build the foundation for establishing a regional mechanism to deal with security issues, threat perception, and other concerns. The climate in the region following the allied war against Iraq and the ensuing massive presence of U.S. forces in the region years after the war, combined with the chronic U.S. hostility toward Iran, have all led to a situation where Iran's initiatives for regional decision making have not yielded the desired progress.

U.S. portrayal of Iran as a threat against Arab states of the Persian Gulf, in which Tehran is seen to have embarked on military buildup, sought nuclear weapons, and supported international terrorism, is deceitfully designed as a divisive, post–Cold War policy to deny the legitimate and inherent interests of Iran. Of course, such U.S. policy also helps sustain lucrative weapons and defense contracts in the Arab states of the Persian Gulf at a time when, because of cuts in U.S. defense spending, many American weapons production complexes are going bankrupt. The policies and practices of the United States in the Persian Gulf more closely resemble those of a bully on unfamiliar turf than those of a superpower attempting to develop a new world order on the basis of a balance of legitimate interests.

Iran's defense expenditure, despite eight years of war, loss of equipment, and normal attrition, is quite modest and has been disproportionately low compared with that of its neighbors, whether expressed as per capita or as a percentage of its gross domestic product. For instance, according to the 1994 issue of the *Congressional Research Service Report for Congress: Conventional Arms Transfers to the Third World*, while Iran made $5.7 billion in arms transfer agreements in 1990–1993, Saudi Arabia made $35.1 billion in arms transfer agreements for the same period. Saudi Arabia's arms transfer agreements were equally high for the period 1986–1989 — $32.6 billion — before the allied war to evict Iraq from Kuwait. Contrary to official U.S. assertions of Iran's allegedly massive military buildup, authoritative publications of both European and U.S. research institutes confirm our contention. (For a review of military expenditures in the Middle East, see Brassy's *The Military Balance 1993–1994* and the Congressional Research Service's report on conventional arms transfers to the Third World for the period 1986–1993.)

The campaign of disinformation by the United States about the alleged existence of a secret nuclear weapons program in Iran should also be seen in the context of power politics. In point of fact, Iran's peaceful nuclear program is consistent with the Nuclear Nonproliferation Treaty (NPT). Routine as well as nonroutine inspections of Iran's nuclear facilities by the International Atomic Energy Agency (IAEA) have confirmed that Iran is in full compliance with both the NPT and IAEA's Safeguard Agreement. Indeed, those countries with the technical know-how have undertaken under the terms of the treaty to assist other signatories to develop peaceful nuclear technology. Cognizant of the dynamics of nuclear proliferation, Iran has been a staunch proponent of enhancing the monitoring regime and capabilities of the IAEA.

As a major country with the longest shoreline in the Persian Gulf and established interests in the millennia of its civilization in the region, Iran views U.S. policy in the Persian Gulf and its confrontation of Iran as slipshod and marked by short-sighted capriciousness. It is in this context that the Islamic Republic of Iran has made the following concrete suggestions to allay security concerns in the region, real or induced: establishment of the Persian Gulf as a zone free from all weapons of mass destruction; transparency in arms transfer and exchange of reports on military holdings within the regions; consideration of a ceiling for defense spending and arms imports; and development of security arrangements for the Persian Gulf through regional cooperation on the basis of assuring defensive capabilities with a minimum number of armaments and in accordance with the mandate of Security Council Resolution 598.

Iran has additional investments in regional cooperation and stability to its north, where it has been an active partner in the international efforts to find peaceful solutions to conflicts and violence in Afghanistan, Karabakh, and Tajikistan. Iran also spearheaded an effort to expand the membership of the Economic Cooperation Organization (ECO), founded by Iran, Pakistan, and Turkey, to include the newly independent republics of the former Soviet Union; the ECO now consists of eleven countries in the region and is recognized as a growing and important regional organization. In this way, it has managed to successfully negotiate and pursue the implementation of several important projects for regional cooperation and development: preferential tariffs protocol among ECO members, the ECO Shipping Company, ECO Air, a gas pipeline from Turkmenistan to Europe via Iran, and, above all, preparation for the trans-Asian road and railway network.

On March 17 of this year, the southern leg of Iran's railway network linking Europe, the Caucasus, central Asia, and the Persian Gulf was inaugurated by President Rafsanjani in a ceremony attended by presidents and senior officials of many states from the greater region. The 700-kilometer railway, connecting the port city of Bandar Abbas in the Persian Gulf to the main Iranian rail network, was completed at a cost of about one billion dollars and turns Iran into a regional transportation hub. In his speech at the inaugural ceremony, President Rafsanjani, underlining the importance of efficient transportation networks in developing a free market economy and regional cooperation, offered the use of the Iranian railway network to regional states: "Our brothers on the southern shore of the Persian Gulf who are also interested in being linked to areas north of Iran could easily access this railway."

Iran views promotion of free trade and economic cooperation among members of the ECO as a guarantee of greater stability in the region. As the natural bridge between the Persian Gulf area and central Asia and the Caucasus, Iran is committed to strengthening peace and stability in the larger region through expansion of the scope of economic cooperation between the ECO and its neighbors. As an Islamic country, Iran aims to bring economic prosperity and political stability to the region through expansion of regional economic cooperation, friendship, and recognition of a balance of legitimate interests for all concerned.

This process is gaining momentum and strength as Iran continues to consolidate its internal coherence, institutionalize its governing system, and further its economic growth. Iran is determined to fulfill the role that geography and history have placed upon it in this strategic region in an orderly and friendly environment. Consistent with its rich Persian-Islamic civilization, the ultimate objective of Iran's domestic and foreign policies is to develop an independent, democratic, and prosperous Islamic country devoted to peace, security, and prosperity in the region and beyond. If the achievements of the seven years since the cease-fire in the Iraq-Iran war are any indication of the future, then Iran is on the right path.

His Excellency

Fidel V. Ramos

President of the Philippines

The Age of People Power in the Pacific

The story that made the rounds a few years back, about world leaders meeting with the Creator, has now been overtaken by events. The deity apparently granted President Gorbachev of the Soviet Union, President Bush of the United States, and Prime Minister Shamir of Israel one question each about the future.

"God," asked Gorbachev, "do you think the USSR and the United States will ever end their rivalry?"

"Yes," replied God, "but not in your lifetime."

Then Bush asked, "Do you think we in America will ever see friendship between blacks and whites?"

And God answered, "Yes, but not in your lifetime."

Finally came Shamir's turn. "God," he asked, "do you think there will ever be peace between Jews and Arabs?"

"Yes," said God, "but not in my lifetime."

Since then, both the Soviet Union and communism have collapsed; black-white relations are taking an upturn under President Clinton, and — most surprising of all — the Israelis and the Arabs are actually talking peace, even while the four personages in the apocryphal heavenly summit continue to be alive and well.

Given these epiphanies, I find it hard to agree with the pessimists who say the end of the Cold War has merely complicated for the democratic countries the problems of security and peace they faced when the Soviet Union presented them with a monolithic enemy. Multipolar systems, which the world has once again become, are certainly more unstable than bipolar ones. But surely none of today's problems is more dangerous than the threatened nuclear confrontation between the United States and the Soviet Union, which might have brought Armageddon upon all mankind. In fact, for the richest and most settled portions of the globe — the democracies of Western Europe and the two Americas — the fear of war has been abolished; and their peoples can look forward to lives of peace, political freedom, and increasing wealth.

It is true that present-day disputes in those regions of the world still in turmoil are all the more volatile because they could work themselves out without the restraints the superpowers had imposed. But if increasing anarchy and violence in Bosnia and Rwanda are one premonition of the future of this turbulent zone, the Pacific Basin's increasing prosperity and expanding civil liberties in its post–Cold War stability are another, more optimistic intimation of the prospects for the Third World.

The end of the Cold War has also given us in Asia the chance to take command of our own fortunes. "For the first time in a century and a half," says the Australian scholar Paul Evans, "the future of Asia will primarily be determined by Asians."

Asia's New Role

The U.S. Navy's withdrawal from Subic Bay on November 24, 1992, ended an era during which, for 421 uninterrupted years, there had been no single day that foreign troops were not based on Philippine soil. Our country's emergence from under America's wings gives us Filipinos the opportunity after centuries of colonial passiveness to make our own history. Like any other coming of age, self-determination is complex and difficult; but it is also exhilarating.

The Dwindling Need to Resort to Force

We may all take some time to realize how much the world is changing because of our all-too-human tendency to deal even with the new in accustomed ways. But a basic change is developing in international relations. The change I see is that, in increasing portions of the globe, the resort to force is less and less necessary. Mutual security will more and more depend not on arms or military alliances but on interdependent economies.

If, in the age just ended, great powers typically progressed from economic strength to military power, today no democratic state need aspire to hegemony, for it can attain its goals through peaceful commerce and integration in the community of nations. Our world is no longer a world of "sea-lanes" and "choke points." Command of the sea is no longer necessary to acquire and preserve foreign markets and sources of raw materials as it was during the age of imperialism. A truly global market has arisen, founded not on force but on mutual benefit.

Democracy's Dawning in East Asia

East Asia's growth, unprecedented in economic history, is also reshaping the politics of the region. Everywhere in our part of the world we have been seeing the immense political power and moral authority that ordinary people can exert, just by standing up together for their rights. East Asia is in a new age of democratic participation — the age of "People Power."

Of course, there are those who say that Asia is not going to be civilized after the methods of the West, that Asians will prefer (at least for some time yet) to be ruled by authoritarians who make the economy grow rather than by democrats who can't say "no" to special interests. But this kind of cultural relativism is being refuted by middle-class activists from Beijing to Yangon. Everywhere in East Asia, people are giving up their tranquility and sometimes staking their liberty on the belief that there is something more to life than an unending spiral of individual gratification.

East Asia leads the worldwide movement of peoples in the developing countries, having awakened to their political entitlements, dismantling authoritarian and statist systems. The Philippines itself reclaimed its civil liberties in February 1986 through a nonviolent uprising after fourteen years of strongman rule. Our peaceful "People Power" revolution of 1986 became the model for other middle-class libertarian movements from Eastern Europe clear to Chile in Latin America.

Flashpoints and Danger Zones

Of course, not all countries are opening up to the global economy at the same time or the same pace. In almost every continent there are isolated states whose economies are typically outside the influence of the global market. To contain them we need a whole new framework for regional security to replace the Cold War structure that has been brought down.

Nuclear Stalemate
in the Korean Peninsula

The largest and most urgent security issue in our part of the world is the nuclear stalemate in northeast Asia. Only in the Korean peninsula do the deepest security interests of all the Pacific powers — the United States, Japan, China, and Russia — intersect.

The forty-four years that have passed since the Korean War broke out have not dissipated its ideological passions. (As a combat platoon leader in a Philippine Expeditionary Force sent to fight under the U.N. flag, I myself served in Korea in 1952.) An uneasy armistice still separates North and South at the 38th parallel.

Given the tensions in the Korean peninsula, do we have time to fall back on the "gradualist and phased reunification plan" first proposed by Kim Daejung some twenty years ago? Kim proposes unification in three stages — lasting altogether fifteen to twenty years — starting with a confederation of the two independent governments, progressing to a federation, and, finally, leading to a unitary state such as existed before partition, but one founded on democracy and an open market system.

Like other concerned bystanders, our own Association of Southeast Asian Nations (ASEAN) can only counsel patience and continued peaceful dialogue to the U.N. Security Council and to Washington in the high-stakes game with Pyongyang. Fortunately, the worst seems over: the protagonists seem to be settling down to serious talks. To start these off dramatically, summit meetings between the two Korean leaders, Kim Young Sam of the South and Kim Il Sung of the North, have been agreed on. If they begin to break down the logjam of enmity between the two states, economic and political relations in the peninsula can begin to flow more normally.

A relatively peaceful unification, the only lasting solution to instability in the peninsula, will give the new Korea the demographic weight to become a regional power—a combined population of close to 70 million and an army of 1.2 million, backed by an economy already experienced in heavy industry. But, as in Germany, regional power will come only at the end of a long period of reconciliation and consolidation, which the South must largely fund.

The Korean nuclear crisis also bolsters the emerging theory that the proliferation of nuclear weapons is by now unavoidable and that the world community's emphasis must shift to preventing their use. Right now, ten countries are believed to possess nuclear weapons. By the beginning of the next century, that number could reach twenty-one. Fortunately, through ASEAN and its new regional forum, we still have the chance to keep Southeast Asia free of nuclear weapons and to make it a zone of peace, freedom, and neutrality.

*Other Flashpoints
in Southeast Asia*

In Cambodia a coalition government chosen through elections supervised by the United Nations is still too weak to put down ideological and personalist factionalism. The country's peace will be fragile until the radical Khmer Rouge is brought into the political process; but reconciliation is complicated by the interests of outside powers. ASEAN and the United Nations must remain engaged for some time still in Cambodia.

In Myanmar, Yangon's military rulers are moving to end their country's isolationism. This gives the East Asian community the chance to broker a political settlement between the generals and their middle-class opposition, led by Aung San Suu Kyi. In Vietnam, it is in ASEAN's collective interest to encourage and support the effort to open up the economy and to incorporate Vietnam into its regional institutions.

*Competing Claims
to the Spratly Islands*

The Southeast Asian flashpoint most liable to flare up is Chinese-Vietnamese rivalry in the South China Sea. The two still have mutual grievances unresolved from the Indochina War. Another reason the issue may come to a boil is China's apparent need for new oil fields, which the waters around the Spratly Islands are believed to contain.

I see no substitute for consultations, along the lines proposed by the Indonesians, to produce a consensus among the six claimant states, which include Malaysia, Taiwan, Brunei, and the Philippines. The sea-lanes passing through the Spratlys are so widely used, increasingly also by China, that a conflict there would affect the entire Asia-Pacific community. I believe it is in this context that President Clinton expressed to me Washington's determination to oppose any resort to force in the Spratly Islands dispute.

I have proposed that all the claimant states and other Southeast Asian nations jointly study the demilitarization of the South China Sea. A freeze on all destabilizing activities should be accompanied by other confidence-building mechanisms — for example, by cooperative undertakings in marine research, fishing and environment protection, joint patrols against piracy, and other development ventures. The philosophy of sharing that we should follow is to consider the resources of the Spratly Islands the common heritage of all the nations and peoples on the peripheries of the South China Sea.

A Southeast Asian Arms Race?

Several governments in the region are building up and modernizing their arms inventories, raising anxieties about a Southeast Asian arms race. In fact, clearance-sale prices offered by western suppliers in the aftermath of the Cold War thaw, ironically led by the Cold War protagonists, seem to be a greater impetus than perceptions of specific outside threats. My own government understands why such an arms buildup is going on at this time among some of our neighbors. But we do need greater transparency in weapons acquisition and in overall defense policies to ensure that the modernization of arms inventories does not become provocative.

No to Narrow Nationalisms

Generally we must do all we can to ensure that the new world order does not result in a resurgence of narrow nationalisms, that many small conflicts do not replace the single big one.

In the past, we in the Philippines mistakenly equated nationalism with economic self-sufficiency. Now we are painfully and belatedly removing the barriers erected by successive governments against foreign investment and multinational industry. We have also redefined our concept of national security in nonmilitary terms. We now regard national security as founded ultimately on our country's economic strength, its political unity, and its social cohesion. And our concept of security is to seek security together with our neighbor countries and not against them, to build together not mutual deterrence but mutual support and confidence.

The Regional Role of the Great Powers

Outside influences — cultural, trade, and military — have impinged on Southeast Asia for at least a thousand years. In our time, the United States is the most important of these influences. Despite its withdrawal from its air and naval bases in the Philippines, a network of mutual-security pacts and access arrangements allows its planes and ships to use Southeast Asian bases in time of military need.

Japan has been our example and ideal since the Meiji era, not only for its amazing growth but for its success at modernizing under the shield of its traditional culture. China, still not a status quo power, remains inscrutable to most Southeast Asians, who were the historical objects of its southern expansion. As for Russia, its internal problems will prevent it from being a major player in East Asian politics for some time. President Boris Yeltsin's inability to initiate a settlement between Russia and Japan on the so-called Northern Territories issue shows the strength of right-wing nationalists in Moscow. But what is certain is that, as Richard M. Nixon wrote just before his death, "Russia will inevitably be strong again. The only question is whether a strong Russia will be a friend or an adversary."

A new balance among the great powers has yet to be established in the Asia-Pacific region. The quality of the relationships between the United States, Japan, China, and Russia will be crucial for the stability of the Asia-Pacific region in the twenty-first century.

What Regional Role for China?

Between 1974 and 1994, China's economic growth rate quadrupled, and it could double again by 2002. By 2010, China's economy might well be the world's biggest. China is already a major trading nation, of increasing importance to all the countries of the Asia-Pacific region. In keeping with its economic modernization program, China has also shown greater openness toward the regional economy. Under these circumstances, China's efforts to launch a blue-water navy and to acquire air-refueling capacity for its air force may merely be steps toward acquiring the military trappings appropriate to its new status.

But China's expanding economic and military power rests on grave internal instabilities. In stark contrast to industry, agricultural output is largely stagnant, because it may have reached its productive limits; the country is likely to be a big importer of food in the new century. Far too many people — 800 million peasants — depend on the land. China's population, now well over 1.1 billion, still has to shift from being a source of weakness to being a source of power. Rivalries are acute between coastal and interior provinces. The generational transition is almost upon us as Deng Xiaoping and his comrades disappear from the scene.

How soon will China's galloping growth bring about political liberalization? I think it likely, as the British diplomat Richard Evans predicts, that Deng's passing will give rise to a new "paramount leader" and that the enhancement of personal freedoms for the Chinese people will precede, by many years, the institutions of electoral democracy. We in Asia all have a vested interest in China's peaceful transition to economic and political pluralism. At the very least, China's restoration to the status of a great power will unavoidably renew its attraction for Southeast Asia's Chinese communities. Our *hua ch'iao*, because of their wealth, their entrepreneurial talent, and their regional networks, are vital elements in Southeast Asia's development efforts. They need to show that their basic loyalties are with their home countries and not their ancestral one.

Japan as a "Normal" State

Japan is becoming the predominant influence in Southeast Asia trade, foreign aid, and direct foreign investment. Our economies are increasingly tied to Japan's in various hierarchical roles. And our new middle classes are becoming an increasingly important market for its exports. Within Japan itself, the national leadership is debating the country's evolution into a "normal" state — a change which, among other things, calls for developing a ratio of military to economic power comparable to those of other large, rich countries.

Even now Japan has not entirely come to terms with its past; but we cannot set it apart in mutual suspicion and mistrust. The better way is to bind it, as we must bind every regional power, into our network of cooperative organizations. For this reason, my government supports Japan's bid for a permanent seat on the Security Council, which should enhance its political integration into the world community. And we Filipinos have no apprehensions about Japan's taking a more active role in Asian security cooperation.

Recession of the Pax Americana?

Anxiety was raised throughout Southeast Asia by the dismantling of the U.S. bases in the Philippines. The fear that potentially aggressive regional powers may be drawn into the power vacuum is undoubtedly real. But I think it will prove groundless. Demography, economics, and national security firmly anchor America to the Asia-Pacific region.

Preventing the Asian mainland from being dominated by any single power is a permanent and primary objective of U.S. foreign policy. America's two-way trade with East Asia is well over $300 billion, a third more than with Europe. Not just trade but a great wave of Asian migration has nudged the United States even closer to the western rim of the Pacific. By 1990, Filipinos had become its largest ethnic Asian population. By the year 2000 they should number over two million. For many Filipino families, Philippine relations with the United States will continue to be "special," whatever turn the official relationship may take.

America's own concept of its role in the post–Cold War world is still not fixed. There has always been a tug of war between moral concerns and national interest in U.S. foreign policy. Nixon echoes this idealist strain in his last book: "As the last remaining superpower, no crisis is irrelevant to our interests. . . . Enlightened people cannot be selective about condemning aggression and genocide."

By contrast, the realpolitiker Henry Kissinger insists that national interests and not moral sentiments must be Washington's framework for dealing with the new multipolar world. He argues that the United States can best serve the cause of democracy abroad by practicing its virtues at home, just as in the early days of the republic when Jefferson thought "a just and solid republican government" in America would be "a lasting monument and example" for all the peoples of the world.

A Concert of Powers

I myself believe the end of the Cold War gives the world community the opportunity not only to remove the threat of force from international relations but also to achieve unprecedented prosperity. But our world cannot exploit this chance without a unifying vision and the will to achieve it. Only the United States can supply that vision and that will, expressed as a global alliance for democracy. The United States can be the motive force of a concert of powers dedicated to keeping peace in the world through multilateral action. Ideally this central coalition should be housed in the U.N. Security Council, where it can assert the moral authority of the world community.

In East Asia, specifically, we need America's continuing engagement to complete the cycle of reassurance and mutual confidence we are setting up. We need the United States to help us build a regional framework that encourages enlightened self-interest but prevents any single power from dominating the region.

Economic Issues in East Asia

No region of the world has used its peace dividend from the thawing of the Cold War more wisely than East Asia. According to the latest figures from the Economic and Social Commission for Asia and the Pacific in Bangkok, the region has just had another good year. It grew six times faster than the global economy did in 1993. Some experts estimate that by 2020 East Asia's economic output is likely to exceed that of North America and the European Union. Even more significant is East Asia's unique partnership between the state and entrepreneurs, which has enabled a country like South Korea to defy the conventional economic wisdom that resource endowments determine future income and to dare create its own comparative advantage — by sheer political will, intelligence, and entrepreneurial drive.

Regional stability, which is the foundation of East Asia's amazing growth, is built on the emergence regionwide of a market system and on the recognition by all our countries of the need for regional peace if internal development is to continue. Growth poles — the newest of them grouping Mindanao, Brunei, eastern Indonesia, and East Malaysia in the East ASEAN Growth Area (EAGA) — are teaching our local peoples the virtues of working together. And interregional trade now binds our countries all the way from Russia's Far East and Japan down to Australia and New Zealand.

The Politics of World Trade

Apart from increasing trade among ourselves, securing continued access to markets and technology must now become the most vital and common concern of ourselves and our regional partners. For the danger is real that in world affairs, trade will replace war as the continuation of politics by other means.

For instance, the United States and France insist on a "social clause" on workers' rights and labor conditions in the global trade pact under the Uruguay Round of the General Agreement on Tariffs and Trade. This might well turn into a disguised form of protectionism, which ASEAN considers an inappropriate remedy to the widespread practice in poor countries of allowing the exploitation of their cheap labor to create jobs. Trade and economic issues should be separated from political issues such as human rights and should not be subjected to political conditionalities. Otherwise, rich and strong countries might impose all manner of political conditionalities on the smaller and weaker economies, conditionalities that in practice become used as new forms of protectionism or even neocolonialism.

We in ASEAN — Brunei, Indonesia, Malaysia, Singapore, the Philippines, and Thailand — have formed our own free trade area, AFTA, which is meant to give our six countries the economic weight and the attractiveness to investors that we need to become a major player in the future world. But we in ASEAN do not see the globe as divided into friends or foes. We do not see business competition as a barrier to economic cooperation. And we do not intend to shut ourselves away from the world. Today's Asia-Pacific has several circles of economic cooperation of which our six countries are also part; these circles include the East Asia Economic Caucus (EAEC), encompassing Northeast and Southeast Asia; and the Asia Pacific Economic Cooperation (APEC), which brings together countries on both shores of the Pacific Ocean.

Shared Regional Problems

The Philippines, much like Peru, the unwilling host to the world's last Maoist insurgencies, has been a source of worry to its neighbors these last twenty years. By way of a peace process being resolutely pursued, we have now put our political instability behind us. Peace talks with our military rebels and our Muslim secessionists are ongoing. Negotiations with our Maoist insurgents only await the settlement of their factional quarrels.

Economic growth on the scale and speed that some of our plural societies have been experiencing is by itself destabilizing. Disintegration of traditional communities releases disorder, delinquency, and frustration that typically expresses itself in racial, ethnic, and religious antagonisms, tribalism, and separatism among those social groups left behind by growth (at least temporarily), particularly if governments neglect to ensure that growth is, as much as possible, broad-based and equitable. "Tribal" groups in our plural societies are turning inward to protect distinct ethnic identities from the homogenizing influences of the international culture. And middle classes created by development are increasingly asserting their civil rights against authoritarian governments. All of these problems we see to some degree in East Asia.

The Rise of Fundamentalist Religion

Fundamentalism, in Christianity as well as in Islam, is rising, as believers seek religious certainty against what they see as the materialism and pornography of the modern world, a certainty that they do not see the institutional churches delivering. For many East Asians, personalist religion has also become a social anchor in the midst of tidal changes in personal relationships. In West Malaysia a fundamentalist state government threatens to impose traditional Islamic punishments for moral crimes. Even in Indonesia the state is hard put to maintain its secular character. In my own country, Pentecostal sects are undercutting the authority of the established church; and a so-called fundamentalist Islamic group, the Abu Sayaff, is being denounced by both our Muslim and Christian communities for its terroristic and criminal acts.

Potential Low-Level Problems

Potential low-level problems between Southeast Asian countries include the legal and illegal migrations of workers (of which the Philippines is a major source); environmental degradation; AIDS and other pandemics;

traffic in prohibited drugs; and piracy in parts of the South China Sea. On all of these problems, subregional and regional cooperation is urgently necessary. The exploitation of migrants could embitter relations between neighbor states unless humane legal arrangements for "guest workers," who have virtually no civil rights, are agreed on.

Then there are environmental problems, for which East Asia is already notorious: the world's highest rate of deforestation; the highest intensity of energy use per unit of gross domestic product; the highest emission rate of carbon dioxide into the atmosphere; and the worst rate of soil degradation. All of these problems call for cooperation across national and regional borders.

Security Cooperation in Southeast Asia

The promise of regional peace pursued by ASEAN'S founders since 1967 has turned into reality. As they foresaw, ASEAN has become a stabilizing influence, most notably in the former Indochinese states, as well as an effective counterpoise to big-power ambition in Southeast Asia. Its mediation in Cambodia helped bring about the withdrawal of Vietnamese forces and subsequent elections under U.N. supervision. In 1992 in Manila the Socialist Republic of Vietnam and the Lao People's Democratic Republic acceded to the Treaty of Amity and Cooperation that the ASEAN powers had signed in Bali in 1976. ASEAN has also become the focal point for security cooperation in East Asia, initially through its Post-Ministerial Conference (PMC) and, beginning in July 1994, through the ASEAN Regional Forum (ARF).

The ARF, a consultative body to deal with security questions in the region, has on its agenda a full range of security matters, from arms transfers and military exercises to the movement of refugees and illegal migrants across borders. Its membership of eighteen countries includes all the powers interested in the region. In addition to the six ASEAN members, Australia, Canada, China, the European Union, South Korea, Japan, Laos, New Zealand, Papua New Guinea, Russia, the United States, and Vietnam are all participants in the ARF. Through the PMC and ARF, we hope to build the regional architecture for the ASEAN ideal of a neutral and nuclear-free Southeast Asia.

A Web of Bilateral Security Ties

The ASEAN Regional Forum will supplement the web of bilateral security ties that already bind our countries. These ties range from military-access arrangements to joint military exercises and intelligence exchanges; from border-patrol agreements to cooperation in campaigns such as Indonesia, Malaysia, and Singapore have launched against pirates in the Straits of Malacca. China and Japan themselves now meet yearly on their bilateral security problems.

I recently proposed a military and defense complementary fly scheme for ASEAN. It calls for sharing expertise in defense technology, ordnance servicing, materiel procurement, and military database building. As the first step, I proposed greater transparency in defense policies and security concerns, including the exchange of defense white papers and the opening of a regional arms registry.

Because security issues are complex and often area-specific, a security forum for the entire Asia-Pacific region seems impractical, at least for the moment. Toward those countries that keep themselves apart, our best approach is not "containment" but "constructive engagement." We need to draw them into the web of regional collaboration that shapes our common interests, reinforces our common values, and regulates our common behavior.

Building a New Structure for Security

The advanced democracies in the rich western world may have outgrown balance-of-power politics, resolving their conflicts on the basis of shared economic and political interests. But our own strategy in the post–Cold War period must be to try and arrange among ourselves an internal balance of political and economic power sufficient to ensure our collective stability and regional peace.

We may expect the U.S. military presence to continue in Korea and Japan for some time still. Apart from these forward bases, however, U.S. strategy now emphasizes the rapid deployment of sea-air-land power, as in the Iraq-Kuwait war. But U.S. intervention is likely to be much more selective in the post–Cold War period, particularly in its commitment of ground troops, and any future exertion of U.S. power is likely to be part of a concert of powers acting through the United Nations.

As the Singapore diplomat Peter Ho points out, "We can no longer expect the United States to underpin by itself East Asian regional security. But there will be difficulties with either Japan or China taking up the slack — Japan because of the Pacific War, and China because of the historical tributary relationship and the Chinese populations in Southeast Asia. Thus our only recourse is to strengthen our own network of linkages."

In this effort to set up interlocking networks of cooperation in East Asia, ASEAN shows how shared values and interests can build the mutual confidence on which mutual security is best founded.

ASEAN as the Core of One Southeast Asia

Over the past quarter century, ASEAN has gathered our six countries together — like rice stalks in a sheaf at harvest time — in common action to accelerate the economic growth and cultural development of Southeast Asia and in a spirit of equality and friendship. In doing so, ASEAN has merely confirmed Southeast Asia's ancient sense of unity — in ethnicity, culture, and aspiration.

In our time, ASEAN's task is to build a stronger base for interdependence. If we do not convert into interdependence the chain of cooperation that has brought our economies together, then our separate countries — each one alone — may not stand up to the complexities and intense competition of the world economy. Unification alone will give our countries the cultural variety, the economic weight, the technological talent pool, and the internal market they need to become major players in the future world.

Preventing Our Countries from Becoming Pawns of Big Powers

If Southeast Asia's integration and unity is our shared dream, our countries are also being pushed to it by harsh realities. Regional unification has many political and economic compulsions. The strongest political compulsion is to prevent our countries from once again becoming pawns in the power politics of the great powers. The end of the Cold War, the recession of ideological rivalries, and the return to a multipolar world have freed every great power to pursue its own interests. And peace in the world will have to depend once again on reconciling or balancing these competing interests. Separately, few of our countries have the weight to stand by themselves in this kind of realpolitik. The majority will have to attach themselves as clients to bigger patrons.

In this sense, unification will strengthen the region as a whole against strategic uncertainties, particularly since the relationships among the big powers with interests in Southeast Asia—the United States, China, Japan, and Russia—are still evolving in ways difficult to predict. Even a unified Southeast Asia may not assure us complete control over our own fortunes. But, as the Indonesian thinker Jusuf Wanandi has said, "Only a united Southeast Asia has a fighting chance to face external pressures and to play a role in influencing the development of our region."

Only unification will enable us to move toward our dream of a nuclear-free Southeast Asia, a Southeast Asia that is a zone of peace, freedom, and neutrality.

The Building Block
of a Global Community

The strongest economic compulsion for unification is that our countries could otherwise be condemned to inferior roles in the hierarchical division of labor in the world economy. In the old days, economically weak nations became outright colonies. Today they may be formally independent; but they are, in reality, still mere hewers of wood and drawers of water for other peoples.

Trade becomes equitable only when both sides can enforce "reciprocity"—a roughly equal access to each other's markets and productive capacities. Separate, our countries cannot hope to be strong enough to do so. But together we have "a fighting chance" to stand up against the best in the world. Unification will give our individually small economies the larger market they need for competitive scale and for creativity to flourish. And a unified Southeast Asia can strive to be the building block of a global community.

Even without outside compulsions, unification still makes sense; it will relax some of our internal tensions. For one, the present-day division of Southeast Asia into "rich" and "poor" countries is the recipe for regional instability and local conflicts. Then, too, unification will enable us to convert our large populations from a source of weakness to a source of power. Finally, our tremendous store of metals and energy sources gives us a good shared base for growth. For example, Malaysia and Thailand between them produce a third of all the world's tin. Our region has great reserves of natural gas as well as geothermal and hydroelectric potential. And we can learn to harness the riptides and thermal power of our surrounding ocean which, in the Sunda Shelf alone, also produces a third of all the fish harvested in the developing countries.

Adopting the Region's Interests for Our Own

Unification may be inevitable, but moving toward it will still take all the political will, all the collective sense of purpose, all the idealism of our leaders. And the reason is that not every country will benefit equally from unification at the start. In their dealings, as we know, states usually recognize no motive beyond their national interest. The operating doctrine in power politics is that the state must seek its survival in an essentially anarchical international system, in which there is no freedom for the weak.

But, in this case, we must do more than look after the component interests of the member states. From the very beginning of this venture, all our countries must adopt as their own the interests of the region as a whole. If we do not agree there is a higher purpose than the immediate national interest that unification will serve, then we shall be bargaining ceaselessly over the fine print — over every little detail, every little concession. Then Southeast Asian unity will become a product of our least common denominator instead of rising buoyantly from the ties of blood, language, and culture we share.

Our leaders who founded ASEAN in 1967 were wise to proceed with the initial stages of regional integration without first resolving bilateral issues like the Sabah dispute between Malaysia and the Philippines. Our leaders today can build on this principle of transcending local disputes, of not allowing regional unification to wait on their solution. Building on shared regional values and on the needs, desires, and hopes of our peoples, our leaders can together achieve a synergy, an effect of which each country is individually incapable. Modernization and economic growth, which unification should speed up, can reduce so many of our problems to irrelevance, no matter how large they may loom in our calculations for the moment.

How Southeast Asia's Unification Can Begin

If it is to get anywhere, unification must begin, not in some grandiose political scheme, but in organic and practical ways, following the grain of history and custom. It should not compete with national sovereignties and identities. But it must equip itself with a framework for regional trade and mechanisms for regular consultations, for resolving internal disputes, and for resisting outside encroachments. And the groundwork must begin in our time. Unification, in my view, best begins with subgroupings — growth triangles and polygons of opportunity cutting across national borders, among areas with strong economic complementarity and historical associations. From these small beginnings, unification can develop through ever larger and ever widening circles of cooperation.

Our immediate task is to flesh out our vision of Southeast Asian unification with practical programs that will strengthen our separate countries' habits of cooperation. And cooperation can start with joint ventures on political, social, economic, and security infrastructure that will benefit the entire region. For instance, we could decide to accelerate the full implementation of AFTA and our agreements on a Common Effective Preferential Tariff from their present fifteen-year terms (from 1993) to seven years, or until the year 2000. We could extend accession to the Bali Treaty to Cambodia and Myanmar, in addition to Vietnam and Laos, as their first step to full membership in ASEAN.

We could intensify social and cultural exchange by setting up a Southeast Asian university system with centers of excellence in almost every country or by venturing collectively to preserve the cultural monuments of Borobodur, Angkor, Hue, Pagan, and the Ifugao rice terraces, which are, after all, the common heritage of all Southeast Asians. We could push collective projects like the development of the Mekong River and its tributaries and the breaching of the Kra Canal. And through a Southeast Asian Development Corps we could offer young Southeast Asians the chance to learn about the region's problems and their solutions at first hand.

Our Own Message to the World

According to the American security scholar Zbigniew Brzezinski, every great power that has appeared on the world scene has brought a message of worldwide relevance, derived from its own inner moral code, defining a "shared standard of conduct as an example to others," a message that transforms raw power into leadership that commands moral legitimacy. Perhaps Southeast Asia's own easy tolerance of religious and social diversity — sharing as we do cultures of pluralism — can be our message to the future world. And in a globe where ethnic, tribal, linguistic, and religious violence is breaking out, this is no mean message to mankind.

Reducing Poverty through Growth

Ultimately East Asia's security will depend on the continued growth of its economies. Through much of history, the world has been hostage to poverty, tyranny, and war. Force has commonly arbitrated relationships among nations. But over the past generation and a half, we have seen how economic growth, together with human development, can make countries safer as well as richer; we have seen how force in international relations can give way to the more benign regime of mutual benefit. In Western Europe, North America, Australia and New Zealand, and parts of Latin America, poverty, by being confined to ethnic or cultural underclasses, has become virtually invisible; and tyrannies have been replaced by democracies among which war has become outmoded as an instrument of competition.

Yet large portions of the world, particularly in Africa, continue to be "zones of turmoil." In these unhappy places, the condition of man is "a condition of war of everyone against everyone." East Asia lies in the intermediate zone: its peoples have not entirely escaped poverty, the fear of violence, or the reach of arbitrary governments. But continued economic growth, which over the long term brings about political liberalization within a sustainable framework, will enable the East Asian states eventually to enter the world's "zones of peace." At that point we can replace security arrangements based on the military balance with mutual security based on mutual benefit on interdependent economies and on respect for each other's identity and national character.

Already growth has enabled the East Asian states to reduce dramatically the mass poverty which had immemorially oppressed their peoples. By World Bank definition, an individual who is absolutely poor consumes less than 2,150 calories or subsists on an income equivalent to less than one U.S. dollar a day. In East Asia overall, "absolute poverty" by this definition declined — according to World Bank statistics — from 35 percent to only 10 percent, despite a 40 percent increase in the region's population, over the twenty years between 1970 and 1990. China and Indonesia have had the best record in reducing poverty. In China, the rate dropped from 33 percent to 10 percent; in Indonesia, from 60 percent to only 15 percent. In South Korea, the incidence of poverty diminished from 23 percent to 5 percent; in Thailand, from 26 percent to 16 percent; and in Malaysia, from 18 percent to 2 percent.

The equivalent figures for the Philippines are 35 percent in 1970 and 21 percent in 1990. This means our country has the largest relative number of poor people in East Asia. And this is why my government has focused both its domestic and foreign policy on economic growth. At home, we have sensitized economic policy to the well-being of those Filipinos who are without the means to lead decent and useful lives. Abroad, we are renewing and expanding our contacts and friendships — in East Asia, in the United States, in Western Europe — so that we can once again attract foreign investment, trade, and tourism.

We have committed our country wholeheartedly to ASEAN and its ideal of open regionalism. And we are redefining our concept of nationalism, which has, for too long, been introspective and unsure of itself. In the postwar period, we mistakenly equated nationalism with economic self-sufficiency and shut our doors against foreign investment and multinational industry. Meanwhile, our vigorous neighbors were measuring themselves against the best in the world. Only now have we regained our faith in our capabilities as a people.

Over these past twenty-four months of my presidency, we have painstakingly prepared the ground for economic takeoff. We have restored political stability. We have agreed on a social and economic vision for our country; and we have reached a consensus on the structural reforms that will make that vision of "Philippines 2000" a reality. Best of all, we Filipinos have regained our sense of purpose. We have arrested the decline of the national spirit that had so demoralized our people. The way ahead is clear. In our time, political stability, social cohesion, and economic growth that is equitable and unforced are a country's best guarantee of its security.

A Nation Renewed

The Philippines today is veritably a nation reborn. A long period of political-economic crises coinciding with natural calamities has tested our fortitude as a people. But even crisis has its uses. Our time of troubles has created the consensus that we must replace the old accustomed ways that no longer work. And so, hardened in the fire of adversity, we Filipinos can look to the future confidently. We have put our house in order; and we're back in business in the heart of the world's fastest-growing region. Once again we're ready to pull our weight in regional cooperation and to account for ourselves in the world.

That the economy is poised for takeoff we can see from the heights reached by our equity market (up by 155 percent in 1993); the dramatic rise in foreign investments (49.6 percent) and export receipts (12.8 percent); our successful return to the capital markets, the stability of prices, and the decline of interest rates. During the first quarter of 1994, the economy expanded by 4.8 percent, modest by East Asian standards but respectable in world terms, and to us gratifying after years of minimal growth. The growth projected by our economic managers for 1995—6.0 percent to 7.0 percent—should be closer to the regional norm.

We are steadily opening the economy to foreign investment and leveling the playing field of competition by dismantling cartels and monopolies injurious to the public interest. In this spirit, we have opened up strategic industries like telecommunications, shipping, and insurance to newcomers and have allowed foreign banks easier entry into our financial system.

In our quest for internal stability, we have broken through every barrier. With local secessionists, military rebels, and communist insurgents, we are negotiating a just and enduring peace. A new spirit of cooperation between the Legislature and the presidency prevents the gridlock that has obstructed policymaking in our far-from-perfect democracy. Cooperatively we are trying to build the effective government that is the primary requisite for successful modernization in East Asia.

Establishing Effective Government

Everywhere in the region, modernization began when strong, nationalistic states united their peoples behind their economic goals and generated unprecedented, as well as egalitarian, growth. This is a role the Philippine state must eventually fulfill, because it still remains vulnerable to the importunings of elite and vested-interest groups. Sharply focused interest groups had, until recently, competed successfully against the broad public interest in the making of public policy. Before the formulation of "Philippines 2000," our representative system had become a democracy of pressure groups: the economy was governed by politics instead of by markets.

To prescribe social discipline and authoritarianism for such a so-called soft state, as so many well-meaning outsiders have done, is to misdiagnose the illness. As we saw during our period of strongman rule (from the early 1970s up to the mid-1980s), authoritarianism in a weak state merely produces more corruption, more abuse, more injustice. Reform must begin by establishing effective government, and this is what we are putting in place in the Philippines today.

Our strategic framework for putting our house in order, so that our drive for development can begin, we call "Philippines 2000." This framework I set up as soon as I became president on June 30, 1992. Its goal is to bring us to the threshold of new industrializing country (NIC) status by the end of this century. To achieve this goal, we need to accomplish three things. The first is to restore political and civic stability. The second is to open the economy to competition. And the third is to deal, once and for all, with the endemic problem of corruption in office.

These three tasks, once completed, should secure the environment for self-sustaining growth and enable government to act consistently in the national interest.

Developing as a Democracy

What we have set out to do — to develop as a democracy — goes against the grain of the conventional wisdom in East Asia. The dominant view is that democracy and economic growth cannot go together because the exuberance of unrestrained democracy leads to undisciplined and disorderly conditions harmful to development. But I myself believe that political democracy, social discipline, and sustained development are not necessarily incompatible. And I do not agree that democracy can work only in a western context. The time for authoritarianism has passed, in our country and in the world. Instead of the discipline of command, governments must increasingly invoke the self-discipline of civic responsibility.

We have no illusions about the hardships that lie ahead of us in the Philippines. We accept as a given both the shortcomings of our democracy as practiced and the ordinary Filipino's attachment to the democratic ideal. Experience has taught us we cannot safely dismantle, even for the briefest period, our constitutional checks and balances, for suspending these mechanisms makes public administration no more efficient but only more corrupt. But we agree democracy should not mean government's following passively wherever the electoral majority inclines. Democracy should not mean public policies perpetually pitched at the least common denominator of agreement among conflicting interest groups.

Our democracy is far from perfect — that we all know. There is much we need to do before we can fully enjoy its potential. But we need not sell ourselves short. Imperfect as it is, Philippine democracy works. It works sufficiently for us to improve our situation incrementally. Not only does it keep us free; it enables us to organize our economy for self-sustaining growth.

Today we accept that developing as a democracy means reconciling interest groups and broadening consensus. It means coping with dissent, delays, and filibusters, sacrificing instant gratification in exchange for deliberate speed and dialogue. Developing as a democracy also means balancing reform between two extremes. On the one hand, we need to ensure that the steps we take do not go beyond constitutional and legal limits. On the other hand, we must also ensure that those steps are not too short, too tentative, too timid, so as to exhaust people's patience and their trust in the process of reform itself.

Today we know freedom does not by itself bring about progress. We know how easily political power without accountability can lead to despotism and plunder. We know how freedom without responsibility can result in a noisy minority overwhelming the silent majority.

We see our salvation not in curtailing our democracy but in enlarging it — by devolving political authority from the center in Manila to local governments throughout the archipelago and by encouraging ordinary Filipinos to use their votes and their organizational strength to ensure that their needs, desires, and hopes are heard in the making of public policy.

Instilling Civic Responsibility

The Philippine state has historically required extraordinarily little of its citizens. And, as individuals, we Filipinos have acknowledged few obligations to the national community. But this mutual indifference between state and citizen cannot go on. If we are to develop as a nation, the benefits of citizenship must be repaid by civic responsibility. Moral claims are not a one-way street. Only with civic commitment does sustained development become possible in a democratic society. One of our most urgent tasks is to see to it that citizens' sense of their civic responsibility become as well developed as their sense of their civic entitlements. And this includes changing the civic character of the Philippine elite to infuse a stronger sense of nationality in the only social class equipped with the education and technological expertise to lead our country's democratic development.

Beyond Economic Growth

Even as we consolidate our economic gains and carry out our agenda of sociopolitical reform, we can now begin to look beyond economic growth to the complete modernization of our country. Modernization, of course, is not only about expanding the economy. Being modern should not merely mean accumulating material goods, chasing after personal success, and seeking instant self-gratification. In fact, there are many countries where the pursuit of a policy of "every man for himself" has merely produced recurring crises in the workings of the state, in family relationships, and in civil society.

We acknowledge the power of self-interest in generating development. But we also insist that self-interest be mitigated by a sense of community. "Free enterprise" should not mean enterprise free of public accountability. Free enterprise should not mean free exploitation of the environment. Free enterprise should not mean the poor and powerless paying the human costs of development.

Modernization properly means people sharing a belief and commitment in how society should be ordered — for what purposes and for whose benefit. The modern Filipino society we envision is one that continues to care for the family, for the poor, the old, the weak, and the vulnerable, while ensuring the cohesion, competitiveness, and strength of the nation as a whole. Tradition and modernity do not necessarily contradict each other. There are continuities no less than ruptures in every society undergoing social change. We can change and develop in harmony with our history and our cultural values.

Modernization also means raising the political capabilities of the state: to free it once and all from the influence of self-seeking economic oligarchies and political dynasties. It also means the elected leaders becoming fully accountable to the governed. It means empowering ordinary Filipinos and awakening the well-to-do to their social conscience. Finally, modernization also means civic responsibility and democratization. It means the country's business becoming the business of every citizen.

Our Exemplary Role in East Asia

For a brief period in the early 1950s, the Philippines was second only to Japan in the vigor of its economy. And at an earlier time — now almost exactly a hundred years ago — we Filipinos had also proclaimed East Asia's first free republic. Today we are struggling to catch up with our dynamic neighbors in the race for economic growth and technological change. But perhaps we are more than abreast of them in one key component of modernization: we Filipinos have won our democratic revolution. History has made our political culture proof against tyranny; certainly the tradition of electoral politics as a source of political legitimacy has a continuing vitality in our country. Of course, freedom by itself does not bring about progress. But it makes the best foundation stone for the good society we are trying to build — for ourselves and for those who will come after us.

To my mind, there can be no grander vision than this for a Filipino patriot: that the Philippines can ultimately nourish, educate, and shelter the majority of its people and still preserve its best traditions of democracy and popular participation; that we can sustain respectable rates of economic growth, not by treading on people's rights or leaving behind the poor and the disadvantaged, but by supporting and empowering them to lead in their own liberation.

To lay the foundations for this vision is the goal — the only goal — of my government. And we face this challenge with optimism, confident we can bring the economy to takeoff and complete a profound reform of the Philippine state, raising its political capacity and strengthening its social commitments, before the dawn of the twenty-first century. Developing in freedom will be our own unique contribution to the history of East Asia, our part in building the new world order — a global civil society founded no longer on force and power but on concern for human welfare and respect for human dignity.

His Excellency

Alberto Fujimori

President of Peru

Peru and Latin America in the Post–Cold War World

An Unpredictable and Unstable International Context

It is becoming increasingly difficult to predict the future. In a world full of surprises, the reasonable capacity to predict the future has diminished considerably. During the last ten years, approximately, a series of transcendental international events completely altered the international landscape, making it completely unpredictable.

During the sixties and seventies no one could have imagined a Republican U.S. president addressing the Polish or Hungarian parliament. The disappearance of the Soviet Union was impossible to conceive and even more unimaginable, as a consequence, the emergence of Ukraine as a nuclear power.

Likewise, no one could have imagined the religious and cultural background of the Yugoslavian war between Christian Serbs and Bosnian Muslims. In Latin America, no one could have suspected the awakening of a political movement so radical as the Zapatista insurgency in Mexico, apparently one of the most stable countries of the region. And, of course, no one anticipated that Peru would come up with an atypical response to and solution for one of the most severe social crises of the century.

After World War II, a new order was built based on agreements, but also disagreements, among the winners of the war: the United States, the Soviet Union, France, and Great Britain. Nevertheless, there was still a margin of predictability at the end of that war. On the other hand, at present, almost no one foresaw the abrupt termination of this era of enormous universal tension between the two great nuclear powers known as the Cold War.

The "Cold War" and the "Hot War": Different Ends and Consequences

What is going to be the outcome of the disintegration of the gigantic multinational state that was the Soviet Union? The events that we are witnessing today are not providing any lesson. Once again, narrow-minded nationalism serves as a platform for demagogy and closes the doors to the civilized cohabitation of peoples that until a short time ago shared something in common.

We hear again long-forgotten language voicing collective frustrations. Such is the case of some Russian leaders and political forces that have recently gained strength in the last elections.

The Yugoslavian case is the best example of the consequences of extremism. However, we still harbor the hope that this will only be a difficult stage on the way toward a final understanding and not the birth of sources of military tension such as the ones already known to humanity during the course of this century.

Unfortunately, the scenes of the First and Second World Wars come to mind again because long-buried hatreds and misunderstandings are being born there all over again. And, more than anything else, because of the awareness of the suffering caused by the barbaric show of annihilating and homicidal power that marked the wars of 1914 and 1939.

The death of the Soviet state leaves the United States as the only first-rank power. The communist world does not possess the great forums anymore. Nevertheless, we now find that, in spite of everything, the bipolar equilibrium had its advantages. It was the limit that the United States and the Soviet Union reciprocally imposed on their interference in matters of other nations. Even so, that limit was overbalanced on many occasions. As examples we have Vietnam and Afghanistan. Nevertheless, there was a limit. Today we are worried to find ourselves in a world where only one superpower acts as the arbitrator in international matters. And it becomes directly involved only when its own vital interests and priorities are on the line. When that is not the case, it makes a graceful exit, arguing that "we cannot solve everything." Thus the bloodbath in Rwanda, where collapse and social crisis can produce a million deaths in only a few months.

The United Nations seems to be subordinated by the existence of this unipolar logic, just as in the past it was subordinated to the bipolar logic.

What Will Come after This?

Today, after the so-called post–Cold War, we are in a transition period when, together with the signs of an evident deterioration of the pre-1985 political world, we confront the appearance of new national and regional realities. This cannot as yet be called a "new international order." It is a political magma.

On the one hand, there are still some realities compatible with the Cold War's political atmosphere: the surviving communist societies, the countries that still carry on populist economies, and the nations where the state has collapsed. This is a world in decomposition, fast disappearing under the impetus of free economy and the vertiginous development of communications.

But, likewise, new realities are emerging at national and regional levels on the political, cultural, and commercial fields. These are the emancipated nations of the former USSR and those trying to assert themselves as independent states in what was Yugoslavia. The active presence of a community of Arab countries is increasingly noticeable. A European Union has already been formed, and the profile of pan-Slavism is taking shape, just to cite some examples.

On the commercial field, there are many grand agreements and pacts to liberalize exchanges, NAFTA being perhaps the most ambitious among them. Others with far-reaching projections are being formulated around the Pacific Basin.

All these realities have to coexist in a civilized manner until a new and more just and democratic world order is generated. The great powers have a big responsibility during this transition period. They can either rebuild power politics, once again dividing the world into zones of influence and thus becoming privileged nations and societies in front of the rest of the world, or they can abide by what they preach.

Let us not forget that the great powers preach democracy as a form of government and daily culture. Well, in international relations too there has to be democracy. Bigger nations should act through the United Nations, listening to and appraising the voices of all nations when addressing world or regional problems.

This surely sounds utopian, but the United Nations was created as the seed of a future world government; today it is very far away from that vision, barely acting as a real arbitrator for international conflicts.

The Revaluation and Reconstruction of Democracy

Even though it is true that the fall of communism brought as a logical consequence the immediate revaluation of representative democracy, in many parts of the world — from Russia to Italy and from Venezuela to Peru — little time passed before the people were able to compare reality with the forms and the promises. Just as the socialism that existed — and still exists — was no more than a dictatorship of the bureaucracy and not the almost perfect egalitarian society that Marx and Engels dreamt of, today in many countries democracy is just a word. The government of the people, for the people, and by the people has turned into the government of elites and "particratic" leaders in the "existing traditional democracy."

Today we can already speak of a traditional democracy in crisis, not only in the developing nations but also in the fully developed ones. In the former, the political system called "democratic" has not only failed to overcome backwardness, poverty, and institutional violence, but in many cases it has also served to delay national development. In Latin America, Peru is an example of how an apparently democratic political system has condemned the majority of its population to live under inhuman conditions for decades.

This formal democracy has always favored the interests and rights of a very small fraction of society and has ignored the great majorities, whose passivity they took for granted.

The political parties in Peru were not searching for a more just and rational order but for power for power's sake, and they represented the interests of elites and people in power. The political context was reduced to this. A revolutionary party like APRA, which far beyond the boundaries of Peru, from the thirties to the fifties, constituted a political model for Latin America, became an efficient electoral machinery to capture power; Acción Popular, another nationalist and populist party, was born to change the Peruvian reality, but it only managed to initiate the enormous crisis of 1967–1990. Mercantilism and clientilism undermined "particracy" and prevented the great social and democratic revolution in this part of the world.

During the last fifty years, in Peru and other countries of the region, urban marginality—a consequence of the agrarian crisis and the absence of a developed economy—has turned cities into showcases of underdevelopment: hunger, sickness, unemployment, promiscuity, delinquency, terrorism, and drug trafficking.

This social, economic, and human disaster was not produced overnight. It was the consequence of the irrational use of power for decades. This is the calling card of traditional democracy in Peru.

In some developed countries, democracy also faces serious problems like corruption. This undermines the ruling leader's moral authority. Nevertheless, new people are emerging on the political horizon—as in Peru's case—from outside the traditional political class.

The Road to Latin American Integration

Today, like yesterday, we are countries without capital and technology. But, unlike yesterday, we are countries that possess a wealth of experience and lessons from historic frustrations and never-ending delays. It would be foolish to go back to anti-imperialism, and naive to become simple satellites of the great powers all over again. This time we have to think in terms of national collectivities that can develop, thanks to our own energies, rationally using all our own resources and valuing the time factor. There is a lot of this in the Latin America of the nineties.

A developed Latin America is not to be disdained. We are talking about over 500 million inhabitants and one of the biggest economic potentials of this planet. But then I am talking about Latin America, and this is unavoidable.

None of our countries has by itself the power or the sufficient capacity to be heard. Maybe the bigger and more developed ones incite more concern, but they do not decide the destiny of the world. Besides the reality of a single superpower and the assumption of a "fragmented multipolarity," another reality has emerged — that of regional blocs.

Latin America is a regional bloc in terms of history, culture, geography, and trade. It is a region that has neither participated in nor been the scene of the great military calamities that have afflicted humanity during this century.

Latin American unity, too, has been a utopia. It has to stop being so. The unity and integration of Latin America runs through unsuspected paths. What political will could not achieve in the past now seems possible because of the impact of world changes.

These changes aim to generate such a fluid economic, commercial, and cultural exchange among the nations of the world that it has been called, accurately so, globalization.

And if this phenomenon emerges between countries separated by oceans, as well as by political and cultural traditions, how will it not occur between countries like ours that share a common geography, a common culture, a common language, and, what is more important, a history in which the biggest dream and aspiration is regional unity?

The dream of integration was a task that a man with the genius of the *libertador* Simon Bolivar formulated in the last century and entrusted to coming generations. If it has not materialized, it is due to the evolution of each of our republics, which have remained confined within a narrow nationalism and are slowly coming to the realization that national development without the context of regional development is an unsolvable contradiction.

This narrow nationalism has not only led to wasteful arms spending — which could have been directed to production, education, and health — but to incoherent economic policies.

We are leaving behind the infancy and adolescence of our societies to assume more realistic perspectives, committed to historic projects that are already at work in other latitudes. This is the kind of maturity on which viable integration can be built — a maturity that we are all coming to almost simultaneously because each of our countries has suffered, in its own way, frustrating experiences in its search of development and progress; and because each of our countries is conscious of the enormous social and economic liabilities in terms of extreme poverty, unemployment, institutional crisis, and other ailments.

But as the saying goes, "There is no illness that lasts for a hundred years and nobody who can endure it!" And today we see the Andean nations, with nuances, opting for realistic policies to confront the challenge of national development.

Thus, it is not political will, even though important, that has led to integration but rather the evolution that ushered in economic realism. This economic realism arises from the people's pressure on their leaders to change politics so that it serves society and not the other way around — that is, self-serving politics using society.

In Peru we have carried out, not without obstacles and resistance, a modernizing revolution that can sum up some of the greatest regional aspirations. Our reform of the Peruvian state and our profound structural reforms are aimed at unraveling an economic and social development based on the citizen's initiative, on the liberation of the energy of men and women who, in the past, were prevented by a monstrous state from fulfilling their aspirations as economic agents and human beings.

The Peruvian Case

The perception of the new geopolitical reality cannot be unique and universal. We, Peruvians and Latin Americans, have seen and, what is more important, lived the meaning of a world order from a very singular perspective. We have been — and still are — the periphery of that order.

For us, the Cold War meant alignment and economic, cultural, and ideological dependence. That is why I never understood the term "nonalignment." All the nonaligned countries gathered at regular intervals to proclaim their independence from capitalism and communism while, in fact, each one of them was profoundly linked to one bloc or the other, East or West.

After the collapse of socialist planification, market economy and free trade have indeed acquired universal recognition. But this economic order is frequently at loggerheads with the unipolar world.

During the Cold War era an economy based on free trade was interpreted as being aligned with the western democracies. A socialist economic model was predictably associated with the so-called popular democracies. Both models were repeatedly and alternately tried out by the Latin American countries.

Regardless of the model used, none of our countries ever achieved the much desired development. Dependent capitalism and socialism both proved to be utopian and left us with a bitter flavor. The third option, which proclaimed itself to be neither like Washington nor like Moscow, also proved a frustrating experience.

For Latin America, always hopeful, the post–Cold War era meant yet another opportunity to look for the ideal path to integral development. In Peru, we are adopting a market economy that is not fanatically ultraliberal. Personally, I do not consider myself to be a liberal: I believe that liberal economy should be an instrument to be used in a pragmatic manner and not simply as a recipe, as in the past. Dependency has always required recipes and, of course, somebody to apply them with total disregard for national realities.

Creating economies that could only function under the assumptions of either developed capitalism or authoritarian communism was a big mistake.

The search for the right path also means avoiding past political errors. The common background, the scenario that accompanied all economic models, was the lack of continuity, stability, coherence, and consistency.

The bitter and irresponsible strife of political elites and all the economic interests they represented frequently impinged upon the continuity and stability necessary for the application of economic policies. It prevented these policies from being coherent because the people who implemented them did not really believe in them.

The fundamental reason for the exceptional measures adopted by the Peruvian government on April 5, 1992, was precisely to guarantee the minimum continuity and stability necessary for the economic reforms to attain the expected results. They were likewise needed to defend the state against totalitarian threats like the terrorist group Shining Path.

The fact that Peru now has a coherent handling of its economy and a firm disposition to maintain the necessary order to allow civilized social coexistence, productive activity, and investment has brought about the steady recovery of the country from a severe crisis highlighted by the worst inflation in Latin America's history well as by the presence in its territory of two criminal forces bent on destroying the state: Polpotian terrorism and international drug trafficking.

I do not mean to present myself as a model for anybody, but I firmly defend common sense. If Latin America had managed to follow at the same time an efficient economic model along with a sustained political model for a given period, the consequence would have been development. But this did not happen. And it was precisely during the Cold War that the disagreement between political stability and economic efficiency became more evident.

It would be possible to think, as some tend to do, that all this is the consequence of an unequal relationship, consciously nourished by the rich North to continue to exploit the poor South. I do not entirely agree with this view because it is an affront to our dignity as rational beings.

It has been our social malformation and national immaturity that has generated underdevelopment and backwardness. We were never condemned to live entirely subordinated during the Cold War. We could have opted for the path to development.

Evidently, the fault is not that of the people but of the rulers who, while calling themselves democratic and representatives of the majorities, turned their back on them and the countries. It was the minorities and their interests that prevailed.

In Peru, people are completely free to act, to produce, and to express themselves. We are still reconstructing the country, but the majority of the 22 million Peruvians who have lived through the worst crisis in national history—the sum of historic hyperinflation and almost unlimited violence—know that today Peru is a viable country according to the opinion of national and international observers. And this is enough.

Her Excellency

Benazir Bhutto

Prime Minister of Pakistan

Pakistan's Foreign Policy

Challenges and Responses in the Post–Cold War Era

The formulation and conduct of foreign policy is vital for any country. As two eminent scholars, S. M. Burke and Lawrence Ziring, have observed, "Pakistan's foreign policy is an extension of its national security requirements. Threats to the country's existence are real and significant and its foreign relations have been fashioned to maximize the chances of survival."

Pakistan was born in 1947 in a condition of conflict with its neighbor India, particularly over Kashmir. This confrontation determined, to a large extent, the contours of Pakistan's foreign policy in the period following our independence. At that time, the Cold War between the alliances led by the United States and the Soviet Union was beginning.

The Cold War Period

The Cold War accentuated the political and religious divisions in South Asia. Pakistan allied itself—in SEATO, CENTO, and bilaterally—with the United States. India, notwithstanding the halo of nonalignment, was the Soviet Union's most valued Third World ally. The Cold War was fought vigorously if not violently in South Asia, especially at the end. When the Soviets launched their final thrust into Afghanistan, Pakistan stood its ground. Our neighbor India warned us repeatedly against defying the "realities" created by the Soviet presence in Afghanistan. Together, with the cooperation and support of our friends and allies — the Muslim world, the West, and China — Pakistan helped the Afghan people to roll back the Soviet intervention.

The Post–Cold War Era

In charting our foreign policy today, we take cognizance of new global transformations. The chapter of superpower rivalry has come to a close. Gone are the ideological factors as a source of conflict. The threat of nuclear holocaust has diminished.

The end of the Cold War has released positive and negative forces. The drive for power, the policies of domination and hegemony, the massive and persistent violations of the fundamental rights of peoples, and the long-suppressed animosities between nationalities and ethnic groups have emerged as the new threat to world peace and security.

The bipolar world has disappeared. It has not yet been replaced by alternative structures for maintaining a viable peace. There is now a single superpower. But its limitations and constraints are evident by recent events. Nor has the U.N. Security Council assumed the anticipated role of imposing, uniformly, the collective writ of the world community.

It is perhaps not surprising that with the restraints of the Cold War structures lifted, conflicts and disputes have erupted. What is surprising — and worrying — is that the world community has shown an inability and apathy in confronting the dark forces of aggression, racism, fascism, and bigotry that have again raised their heads in many parts of the world.

Implications for Pakistan

The changes taking place in international relations have multiple implications for Pakistan's security and national interests. Given the complexity and rapid evolution of the external environment, Pakistan now faces formidable challenges in promoting its strategic, political, and economic objectives. For the first time since its creation, Pakistan is obliged to evolve a multidirectional foreign policy, dictated by its geographical position at the juncture of South Asia, Central Asia, Southwest Asia, and the Gulf.

Objectives and Priorities of
Pakistan's Foreign Policy

Pakistan wishes to establish close links with the West, enhance existing brotherly ties with the Islamic world, and improve its relations with China, Japan, and Russia. At the same time, it cannot ignore the continuing difficulties in relations with its neighbor, India, and the threat to Pakistan's security.

In the recent past, two factors have remained dominant in the formulation and implementation of Pakistan's foreign policy, impinging upon every other facet of our external relations:

1. Differences with the United States stemming from the Pakistan-specific Pressler Amendment, which inhibits the process of regional nonproliferation.

2. Our political, diplomatic, and moral support for the struggle of the Kashmiri people.

Pakistan–U.S. Relations

Pakistan attaches the highest priority to its long-standing friendship with the United States. Both countries have been military allies for the last forty years. There is a sufficiently large convergence of interests between the two countries to enable them to build a new and mature relationship not dependent on transitory considerations or tactical objectives.

The Pressler Amendment has become a structural impediment in Pakistani–U.S. relations that was not rectified during the halcyon days of the Afghan war. It has blocked U.S. military and economic assistance to Pakistan but not to India, although India has a demonstrated nuclear capability.

The Pressler Amendment is the companion of equally discriminatory laws that remain on the U.S. statute books — the Symington Amendment, the Glenn Amendment, and the Solarz Amendment, all of which imposed discriminatory restrictions against the U.S. ally Pakistan and not the Soviet ally India, although that country exploded a nuclear device in 1974 and thus demonstrated a nuclear weapons capability.

The Pressler Amendment provides India with a virtual veto over the development of Pakistani–U.S. relations. According to U.S. officials, it is "bad law and worse policy."

However, the U.S. administration has not found it possible to challenge the proponents of this law in Congress. The early moves made in this direction by the administration came to naught. It is difficult to envisage a meaningful defense relationship between Pakistan and the United States so long as it is prevented from even delivering the F-16s and other defense equipment for which we have already paid.

Nevertheless, we are in the process of building a new and mature relationship with the United States focused on the promotion of economic and commercial cooperation. U.S. investment is flowing into Pakistan despite the constraints of the Pressler Amendment. As Willy Brandt once said, economics will determine the future of the world.

We do, however, have a legitimate expectation that the United States will not adopt policies toward South Asia that condone India's brutal denial of the rights of the Kashmiri people or encourage its pursuit of unequal relations with the other countries of South Asia.

Positive and Negative Trends in South Asia

Like many other parts of the world, South Asia is today in transition. The strife in the region poses a serious threat to international peace and stability. Its settlement enables South Asia to become an engine for world economic growth. The United States — the sole superpower — enjoys considerable influence today in all the states of South Asia. It can help them to make the right and rational choice.

Favorable Trends

There are several favorable trends in South Asia today. Most important, all the South Asian states are now functioning democracies. This is a healthy augury, especially if it is true that democracies do not make war against each other. Second, all the South Asian states have committed themselves to fundamental economic reforms and liberalization. This offers the hope that South Asia may be able to join the Asian "economic miracle." The initial signs, at least in Pakistan, are cause for considerable optimism.

Negative Developments

At the same time, no one can camouflage the dangerous developments in South Asia, particularly in relations between India and Pakistan. These developments have three dimensions: the confrontation over Kashmir, the Indian arms buildup, and the threat of a nuclear and missile arms race.

Kashmir

The Jammu and Kashmir dispute is the most intractable and dangerous of South Asia's problems. Kashmir is a dispute about the destiny of a people. India refuses to implement the resolutions of the Security Council calling for the Kashmiri people to decide — through a free, U.N.-supervised plebiscite — whether they wish to join India or Pakistan.

Since January 1990, over half a million Indian troops have been engaged in a campaign to suppress the freedom movement of the Kashmiri people. Forty thousand Kashmiris are estimated to have been killed; thousands are in jails; death in custody is common; torture is routine; arbitrary arrest is standard practice; rape is an instrument of occupation policy; massacres take place with numbing regularity.

India's strategy is to break the will of the Kashmiri people by massive force and, thereafter, promote a "political process" in Kashmir. But after almost five years of repression, three realities of the Kashmir situation are evident. First, the Kashmiri freedom struggle will not be crushed; the Indian army is bogged down in Kashmir. Second, despite India's assertions about Pakistan's interference, the Kashmiri struggle is obviously indigenous; it will continue, even if Pakistan wishes otherwise. Third, no credible Kashmiri group or leader will agree to a "solution" within the Indian Union.

For twenty-three years, Pakistan sought a bilateral dialogue with India to resolve the Jammu and Kashmir dispute in accordance with the Simla agreement. India persisted in resisting such a dialogue. It agreed in November 1993 to discuss "all aspects of the Jammu and Kashmir dispute," but only under the pressure of our initiative in the U.N. General Assembly to censure India's violations of human rights in Kashmir.

In the negotiations, India's position on Jammu and Kashmir has remained totally inflexible. It continues to claim Kashmir as an "integral part of India." It asserts the right to suppress, by massive force, the struggle of the Kashmiri people for the right to self-determination.

Since early 1994, India has adopted an inflexible and belligerent posture on Kashmir because it believes that the major powers are unwilling to censure India's human rights violations in Kashmir. The repression and killing has escalated, as have Indian violations of the cease-fire line.

The Indian Military Threat

India has attacked us thrice. It was responsible for dismembering our country in 1971. India fields the third-largest army in the world. Almost all of it was deployed against Pakistan. India enjoys a three-to-one advantage over Pakistan in the conventional field. Today, while it pursues its campaign of repression in Kashmir, the Indian government has openly threatened Pakistan with the use of force.

Contrary to its professions of nonviolence, India has been involved in seventeen wars since 1947—the highest number for any U.N. member state. India has disputes and problems with every one of its neighbors.

During the past decade, India was the world's largest arms importer. Between 1980 and 1992, India is estimated to have purchased arms worth around U.S.$30 billion, mostly from the Soviet Union. The Indian defense budget was increased in 1994 by 20 percent and is likely to grow further in the coming years.

By way of contrast, Pakistan's purchases, over the same period, have amounted to around U.S.$2.5 billion only. This includes the assistance provided to us by the United States during the Afghan war. Last year, Pakistan's defense spending actually declined in real terms.

A Nuclear and Missile Race

The threat of nuclear proliferation was brought to South Asia by India when that country exploded a nuclear bomb—ironically called "Smiling Buddha"—on May 17, 1974. Pakistan sought to counter the nuclear danger by proposing the creation of a Nuclear Weapons-Free Zone in South Asia. It is most unfortunate that this and numerous subsequent proposals made by Pakistan—such as simultaneous signature of the Nuclear Nonproliferation Treaty (NPT) or acceptance of full-scope safeguards—have all been spurned. India has also rejected the proposals made by the United States for a five-nation conference or, more recently, for multilateral talks on South Asian security.

Twenty years after exploding its nuclear bomb, India is about to take another fateful step toward proliferation of weapons of mass destruction: the production and deployment of its nuclear-capable short-range missile, the Prithvi. India is also continuing the development of its medium-range AGNI missile and intercontinental ballistic missiles as well. The Prithvi is a mobile missile. Once it is produced, we must presume that it has been deployed.

Pakistan wishes to avoid a missile and nuclear arms race. We have advanced the concept of a Zero Missile Zone in South Asia. India must be persuaded to refrain from producing and deploying the Prithvi and other missiles.

South Asia's Problems and the Need for Outside Help

In reality, India and Pakistan have never succeeded in solving any dispute through bilateral negotiations. Agreements reached on two major problems — the Indus Waters Treaty and the Rann of Kutch Indus Accord — were made possible by the intercession of a third party. External intercession is essential to overcome the political impasse in South Asia. The world community should not accept India's Brezhnev doctrine of "bilateralism" in South Asia.

Pakistan believes that the United States and its western allies, as well as China, Russia, and Japan, can play a critical role in promoting peace and security in South Asia. The United States enjoys considerable influence with both India and Pakistan. This can be used in resolving the Kashmir dispute and in evolving solutions to other problems that afflict the South Asian region.

We are convinced that it would be worthwhile for the U.S. administration to invest the political capital required to promote peace and cooperation in South Asia.

What Role Can the United States Play in South Asia?

We believe there are three areas where the United States can play a most helpful role in promoting security and progress in South Asia — Kashmir, arms control, and nuclear missile nonproliferation.

Kashmir is the core issue in South Asia. It can neither be pushed under the rug or put on the back burner. A peaceful resolution of the Kashmir problem will enhance the prospects of both conventional arms control and nonproliferation in South Asia; a failure to resolve the dispute will heighten the danger of conflict between India and Pakistan.

Pakistan is prepared for talks with India on Kashmir. It was Pakistan that initiated the foreign-secretary-level talks. In several rounds of talks, India remained totally inflexible on Kashmir. India's desire for negotiations with Pakistan carries little credibility while it continues the killing in Kashmir.

The United States should help to develop a framework for a sustained dialogue between India and Pakistan. A renewed dialogue should cover the proposals made by both sides, including Pakistan's two "nonpapers" on Kashmir.

Bold steps are also called for to promote nonproliferation and arms control in our region. Pakistan has displayed responsibility and restraint. While we have acquired a certain technological capability, we have not manufactured or exploded a nuclear device, deployed nuclear weapons, or transferred sensitive technologies to third states. This self-restraint has yet to be acknowledged by the United States and the world community.

Obtaining India's adherence to a comprehensive test ban treaty or fissile material cutoff convention will not, in itself, prevent it from eventually deploying a nuclear weapons arsenal. Two specific steps are now required to prevent nuclear weapons proliferation in South Asia. The first is an agreement by India and Pakistan not to develop or deploy ballistic missiles. India's production and deployment of the Prithvi will invite a matching response from Pakistan. The second is an agreement by India and Pakistan not to manufacture and deploy nuclear weapons. We have proposed this to India. It should respond positively.

A South Asian nonproliferation regime will not be durable until the threat of Indian conventional attack has been removed. Every effort should be made to prevent a renewed conventional arms buildup by India.

Pakistan has made several proposals to India for conventional arms control: negotiations on a mutually agreed ratio of forces; measures to prevent the possibility of surprise attack; and adoption of agreed principles for conventional arms control in South Asia. We hope that these proposals will be addressed in any future talks on South Asian security. We urge the United States not to give up its proposal for "multilateral talks" on South Asian security and nonproliferation. Kashmir, arms control, and nonproliferation are all interrelated issues. They must be addressed in an integrated way within an umbrella forum, as envisioned by the United States.

Pakistan-China Relations

China has played a vital role in preserving peace and stability in South Asia for the past four decades. China is a tested and trusted friend. It has extended support to Pakistan in many ways and at many critical times in our history. We look to China for our crucial needs to promote Pakistan's modernization, especially in view of the inequitable restrictions we face elsewhere.

China has now emerged as the world's most dynamic economy. According to certain estimates, China is likely to have the world's biggest economy well within the first quarter of the next century. The imperatives of economic restructuring make it necessary for China to have a peaceful, stable, and benign environment around its borders as well as at the regional and global levels. It will, therefore, have a strong interest in the maintenance of peace and stability of South Asia and the development of equitable and nonhegemonic relations between the countries of that region.

Japan

Japan is another Asian giant. In recent years, Japan has become Pakistan's largest trading partner. Pakistan looks forward to Japan's contribution to peace and stability in South Asia on the basis of equity and nondiscrimination. We hope Japan will retain its primacy in supporting Pakistan's economic and social development program. We seek further expansion of trade with Japan, which needs to be balanced by greater access to the Japanese market for Pakistan's exports.

Pakistan and the Muslim World

Pakistan has provided abiding, unequivocal, and unreserved support to Islamic causes around the world. Of particular concern to it lately has been the return to peace and normality in Afghanistan, right of self-determination of the Kashmiris, promotion of a comprehensive Middle East peace settlement, and struggle of the Bosnian Muslims against Serbian aggression.

Afghanistan

In Afghanistan, the fruits of a heroic victory have been lost to parochial ambition. Instability in Afghanistan has direct implications for Pakistan, among other things, in the shape of drug smuggling and banditry on our borders. Pakistan is making sincere and active efforts to promote peace and reconciliation between the warring Afghan factions. We have no favorites. Our priority is peace. We have a vested interest only in the unity and territorial integrity of Afghanistan.

Iran and Turkey

Pakistan enjoys exceptionally close and warm relations with Iran and Turkey. The quality of relationship is reflected in the frequency of high-level visits. Both Iran and Turkey have traditionally extended their full support to Pakistan on the Kashmir dispute. Iran and Pakistan have decided to pursue a number of projects for economic cooperation, including construction of oil and gas pipelines from Iran to Pakistan. With Turkey, we are cooperating in various areas, including Bosnia Herzegovina, the Caucasus, and Central Asia. We have always supported Turkey fully on the Cyprus question.

Gulf Countries

Pakistan has traditionally enjoyed close and cordial ties with the Gulf countries based on geographical proximity, historical affinities, and religious and cultural ties. Pakistan remains vitally concerned with the maintenance of peace and security in the Gulf, a region that remains strategically and politically sensitive. Pakistan has initiated several steps to enhance its relations with the Gulf states, particularly with Saudi Arabia, the United Arab Emirates, and Oman, in the field of commerce, investment, manpower exchanges, and defense.

Central Asia

Central Asia is a new dimension for our foreign policy. The independence of the Central Asian states offers new opportunities for them through Pakistan and its warm waters. Shortly after they became independent, the

Central Asian republics joined the Economic Cooperation Organization (ECO). ECO's founding members are Iran, Turkey, and Pakistan. For its part, Pakistan has offered the use of its port facilities. Pakistan and the Central Asian states are actively exploring the possibilities of developing land routes and railways linking us with Central Asia as well as constructing oil and gas pipelines from the region to the Pakistani coast.

Pakistan-Africa

Pakistan attaches great importance to its relations with the African countries. Comprising fifty-three countries, Africa is the only Muslim-majority continent in the world. It is important both in religious and political terms as well as in the context of economic possibilities. Pakistan has close and friendly relations with all African countries. It enjoys brotherly relations with the Arabic-speaking northern African countries of Libya, Tunisia, Algeria, and Morocco. Our relations with Comoros, Djibouti, Niger, Mauritania, and Senegal can be described as special. We have endeavored to provide the required technical and other assistance to the African countries.

Russia

Despite its current difficulties, Russia remains a major power and will continue to play an important role in world affairs. It also wields considerable influence in our region. Pakistan's relations with the Russian Federation have recently entered a new phase. We are engaged in building new links with Russia in the political, economic, commercial, cultural, and defense areas. The two countries have taken steps to overcome the legacy of mistrust dating back to the Cold War era.

Western Europe

Pakistan's relations with the Western European countries are based on such pragmatic considerations as cooperation in the economic, technical, and defense fields and a shared desire for peace, stability, and development in our region. As a region, Western Europe constitutes Pakistan's largest trading partner, but the balance remains consistently adverse to Pakistan.

United Nations

Pakistan has a vital stake in strengthening the United Nations. It is in the world organization that smaller states can collectively seek equity and justice in a world that continues to be characterized by power politics and the desire for domination and hegemony. It is in the United Nations that Pakistan must seek the implementation of the U.N. resolutions regarding self-determination for Kashmir and for the protection of the human rights of the Kashmiri people.

U.N. peacekeepers must continue to play a vital role in preventing conflicts and, where these take place, in ensuring that they are contained and do not lead to extreme human suffering. Pakistan is host to the oldest peacekeeping operation, the U.N. Military Observer Group in India and Pakistan (UNMOGIP). Today, with contingents in Somalia, Bosnia, and elsewhere, Pakistan is the largest contributor to U.N. peacekeeping operations. It has also sustained the highest number of casualties of any peace-keeping nation.

Global Economic Perspective

A new world has dawned. Or should we say "the old world" has returned. Once again trading routes and emerging markets influence the course of interstate relations as strategic compulsions fade into the past.

This is a more pragmatic world, marching to the tune of market forces rather than responding to the winds of the Cold War. However, free markets and open economies do not imply a disregard for the plight of the poor and disadvantaged. This principle must be applied as much among nations as within nations. Our collective objective should be to maximize economic growth and minimize human suffering.

Pakistan's Developmental Strategies

Pakistan has embarked upon a new path of socioeconomic revival and growth. We have created an economic climate most hospitable to domestic and foreign investment. In just over a year, agreements for foreign investment of over U.S.$12 billion have been concluded with investors from the United States, Great Britain, and Hong Kong in the energy sector.

Pakistan's Place in the
New World Order

Pakistan lies at the crossroads of historical trading routes: South Asia, the Gulf, and Central Asia. Our unique geostrategic and geoeconomic location can enable Pakistan to serve as a linchpin for political, economic, and commercial cooperation between these three emerging regions of Asia, bringing unprecedented growth and prosperity to all their peoples. We remain committed to the transformation of Pakistan into a democratic Muslim state upholding the rule of law and human rights and giving equal opportunities to all our citizens — men and women.

His Excellency

Olusegun Obasanjo

Former President of Nigeria

The African Region in the Post–Cold War Global System

Introduction

War and peace are basic contradictions of human experience. The history of mankind at the global level is a study of crisis, wars, and the search for peaceful coexistence. The history of global evolution is a variegated picture of crises. In essence, one form of global crisis after the other has for a long time dominated international relations. In the same vein at the end of every major global crisis or war, humanity has usually tarried a while to learn lessons from the processes and mistakes of the past and to seek new modalities for tackling and confronting new developments and for ordering human interaction for a foreseeable future.

In recent times, however, two major events have brought the issue of arrangement or re-arrangement of international interaction and relationships in the world sharply to the fore. These two major events are, first, the end of the Cold War between the East and the West, at least as it was waged between 1945 and 1989, and, second, the dramatic political events in Eastern Europe in 1989–1990, which culminated in the collapse of the Berlin Wall and the eventful reunification of the two Germanies, symbolically marking the end of the Cold War era. Of the two events, the Cold War remains the progenitor. It was essentially a period of uneasy peace and tension, with rival nuclear superpowers and ideological and economic blocs, which the world lived through from the end of the Second World War in 1945 until very recently.

The Cold War was also characterized by political and strategic confrontation between the superpowers. The main fissure was essentially between the Soviet Union and the United States, symbolizing the East and the West. In the West, allied with the United States were the industrialized capitalist countries of Europe as well as Canada and Japan. In the East, all the countries of Eastern Europe, except perhaps Yugoslavia, were ranged on the side of the Soviet Union. Most characteristic of this period was superpower hegemony and rivalry structured on opposing political ideology, threats of military confrontation, an arms race, and strategic balance of terror. The existence of the North Atlantic Treaty Organization (NATO) and the Warsaw Pact, or the Western Alliance and the Eastern bloc respectively, dramatized the global confrontation of that period.

Economically, while the Soviet Union and the socialist bloc vigorously promoted socialism, the United States and its western allies promoted capitalism and the market economy. But as the Cold War years advanced, growing inequalities between the industrialized nations of Europe and America, on the one hand, and the underdeveloped countries of the Third World, on the other, introduced new tensions and new fears and added another dimension to the already tense international atmosphere of the Cold War.

Ironically, however, the end of the Cold War order came about as a result of the crisis of one of its ideological pillars — that is, the crisis of communism. The end of the Cold War has a lot of strategic implications. Gone are the days when national liberation wars and armed conflicts were seen as opportunities for the realignment of ideological and military balance of power. The East and the West competed with each other and confused reality in such a way that the closer cooperation in various fields of mutual interests to humankind, such as arms control, economic cooperation, and social development, could not be fully realized. Repressive and corrupt governments were favored in order to gain or preserve spheres of influence as human rights values were sacrificed on the altar of the Cold War.

Africa in the Cold War Era

Of all the regions of the world, Africa fared worst in the political and economic arrangements that characterized the Cold War era. Most of the countries of Africa attained their independence in the 1960s, a phenomenon aided by postwar universal recognition of the right of independence for all colonized peoples. By the 1970s the euphoria of independence had yielded to disillusion, despondency, and a sense of inadequate performance on the part of the new nations. The 1980s were very bad for the continent, with chronic manifestations of political instability and insecurity, crushing debt and virtual economic collapse, a falling and degrading standard of living, and an endangered environment.

Under these conditions, it is therefore no surprise that the 1990s do not appear to be bringing cheering news of increased economic and political stability as part of Africa's preparation for the twenty-first century. In effect, although the change from the Cold War psyche to a relaxed international environment promises a welcome alternative to the tension and confrontation of the past, it should not give room for unnecessary euphoria because of the many uncertainties in the present situation. In fact, the future appears to harbor many unanswered questions.

Like the other parts of the Third World, Africa too became a victim of the ideological division between East and West. Although the Soviet Union was not a colonial power in the classical sense and consequently had no formal colonies in Africa, it succeeded to a very large extent in carving for itself areas of influence by virtue of the preponderant role it played ideologically and militarily in Africa's liberation struggles in the 1950s and the 1960s. The continued economic and military assistance of the Soviet Union to the newly independent countries helped to strengthen the ideological position of the East in Africa.

The effects of Cold War politics on Africa are mixed—and in the main negative. In a positive sense, Cold War politics encouraged and assisted the course of political emancipation from what is perceived as western colonial domination. Apart from the fact that the declarations of the U.N. Charter accorded legitimacy to the right of colonized peoples to independence, liberation struggles in Africa received considerable military and moral support from the Eastern bloc. Furthermore, Cold War rivalry impelled the superpowers and their allies into some competitive economic assistance to the newly independent African states in the 1960s.

On the other hand, the involvement of the new states in superpower ideological politics aggravated their internal conflict and encouraged instability. Besides, the readiness of the superpowers and their allies to supply arms to Africa encouraged unnecessary arms buildup in the new states and diverted resources meant for development to unproductive and wasteful ends.

At the continental level, every issue was seen through the prism of the Cold War. Consequently, African states could not make objective decisions or reach consensus on issues vital to their interests. The division of African states into Casablanca and Monrovia groups in the early 1960s, for instance, was a result of the ideological polarization of African leaders at that time along the West-East divide. Even when the Organization of African Unity (OAU) was eventually created in 1963, this congenital discord among the two groups hindered the successful pursuit of such objectives as common and collective security and economic and political union of the continent. To cite another example, the crisis of the Congo, now Zaire, in the 1960s and the tragic aftermath were externalized as the unfortunate consequences of the Cold War in Africa. If, at the political level, the foregoing represents examples of the effects of Cold War politics on the continent, the picture is more depressing on the social and economic platform.

By the 1970s, the euphoria that accompanied Africa's political independence had virtually disappeared. The 1980s were worse years in economic and social terms and were rightly referred to as the lost decade. The list of Africa's social, economic, and human problems is long.

Whatever statistics we cite, the picture is one of a continent that can be described as derelict, despondent, disillusioned, and detached from the mainstream of the rest of the world. Most socioeconomic indicators depict the continent as losing its share in world trade and manufacturing while such negative indices as poverty, infant and maternal mortality, and illiteracy are increasing. The most visible indices of Africa's increasing nationalization are its sharply declining shares in worlds exports, imports, foreign direct investment, and official development assistance. The persistent deterioration of Africa's terms of trade is also an index of relative regional deterioration. Unbearable external debt burden is another graphic measure of Africa's deteriorating global position. This is indeed a hapless picture and represents the situation on the continent as the Cold War ends and the world order changes.

Africa and the "New World Order"

The emergence of a somewhat unipolar world — characterized by a pyramidal power structure, with the United States at the apex, the shift of priorities in the industrial nations from military to economic issues, and the rise of multilateral economic alliances — seems to suggest that economic self-interest may become the ideology in the post–Cold War era and may be aggressively pursued within the context of economic groupings. This era may be strategically unipolar, but in the realms of economics, it would be multipolar in the most intense and competitive manner. Against this background, the weak, unorganized, inefficient, unstable, and ill prepared will simply become irrelevant.

A main feature of the Cold War was the military rivalry between the Soviet Union and the West, led by the United States; this culminated in awesome nuclear arsenals with their attendant threat to international peace and security. To some extent, the thaw in the superpower rivalry has doused the possibility of a nuclear confrontation. However, this danger is not completely averted. In fact, the international system formerly based on deterrence has been succeeded by a highly volatile and unstable constellation, making room for other kinds of acute or latent conflicts.

The political and economic restructuring that took place in the former Soviet Union and the subsequent changes that swept through Eastern Europe have produced far-reaching political implications worldwide, among which we have noted, most significantly, the end of the Cold War, the end of superpower ideological and strategic confrontation, the dissolution of the socialist bloc of Eastern Europe, the drastic slowing down of the arms race, and the high tide of pro-democracy and liberalization movements globally. For Africa, the implications are manifest in the domain of conflict resolution, a renewed surge of pro-democracy agitations, and the general effects on the economic relations and prospects of African countries in the emerging world order.

The decision of Russia to reorder its global priorities and redefine its commitments to its allies also affected its satellite socialist states in Africa. In practical terms, this redefinition involved the withdrawal of both economic and military assistance to these countries that had hitherto relied heavily on the Soviet Union for support.

The withdrawal of Russian military aid coupled with the spirit of cooperation and understanding between Russia and the United States facilitated the resolution of a number of conflict situations in Africa. For instance, the withdrawal of military aid and the evacuation of Cuban soldiers from Angola speeded up the independence process in Namibia. Of course, this process was also encouraged by the political acumen and foresight of Namibia's leading political figures who had opted for the country's adoption of a constitution that embodied, among other principles, a multiparty system, justiciable bill of rights, free press, limited presidential tenure, and so forth. A favorable international and domestic environment was thus provided for Namibia's independence.

Even in South Africa itself, the winds of change blowing through the apartheid enclave and the move toward a resolution of major political problems are also partly attributable to the withdrawal of the Soviet threat in that region. The "Mandela factor," which has now become a living reality, is a result of new thinking in South Africa, a fact reflecting the global liberalization mood of the times and emanating from the events in the Soviet Union and Eastern Europe. The experience in Ethiopia is also indicative of the hollow base on which many dictatorial regimes in Africa rest. The end of the protracted armed conflict in that country was abruptly brought about by the withdrawal of Soviet aid to the dictatorial Marxist government.

The undisputable conclusion from these examples is that the end of the Cold War encouraged the process of conflict resolution in Africa. One other significant implication of the impact of recent world events on developments in Africa is the encouragement given to pro-democracy movements on the continent. The winds that swept away corrupt dictatorships, autocratic one-party systems and state structures, inefficient systems, and unresponsive social institutions in Eastern Europe are not unfamiliar to Africa. But their success provided moral encouragement to their counterparts in Africa which were smoldering or dormant. Hitherto, pro-democracy movements in Africa were either suppressed or tagged subversive in the eyes of the outside world. The withdrawal of Soviet support from those regimes in Africa that camouflaged dictatorship under the banner of socialism strengthened the ranks of existing pro-democracy movements on the continent and increased their chances of success.

Furthermore, the demise of communism helped to expose those right-wing dictators in Africa who firmed up their repressive rule on the premise of containing the spread of communism and made their further existence unjustifiable. The result is that, in Africa today, both the left-wing and the right-wing dictators are being forced by popular pressure to accept a policy of democratization based on pluralism.

The factor of conflict resolution and political liberalization in Africa described above is indeed a welcome trend on the continent. It is a phenomenon that relates to governance and political leadership in Africa. We may be entering a new era on the continent in which the leaders will no longer choose to ignore the voices and the votes of their people and trample upon their fundamental human rights. The present situation, if managed and harnessed properly, may open the way to security and stability, which are indispensable for social and economic development.

Attractive as this trend may be, the vacuum created by the collapse of communism and consequently of Soviet and subsequent Russian influence in Africa predicates inherent dangers for future developments in the region. With the socioeconomic inequalities characteristic of the capitalist system, the question arises of whether, in the long term, a democratic welfarist model would not provide a better and more sustainable solution to the development problems of Africa.

An obvious cause of unease in the region is what is seen in some quarters as an attempt to impose western democratic models lock, stock, and barrel on African countries as a condition for economic assistance for development. For democracy to endure, it must be home-induced, home-grown, and home-sustained. Africa has a tradition of some form of democracy that should not be completely discarded but rather allowed to evolve and develop, and a single model of democracy may not be applicable to all societies. Moreover, the democratization process might take more time in some countries than in others.

To make democracy grow and flourish, it will be necessary to exercise patience and tolerance and make allowance for cultural peculiarities. It should also be realized that under the present African situation, "while good government is a necessary condition for development, it will not be sufficient by itself, in the light of crushing debt burdens, falling commodity prices, inadequate flow of resources, to meet the social demands that will invariably accompany free speech and pluralist democracy."

In other words, how durable will the resolution of conflicts on the continent be or how will popular democratic processes endure if the chronic developmental problems are not tackled and solved? The swapping of ideologies is just not sufficient to provide relief for Africa. Democracy and poverty are strange bedfellows. Conflict resolution and democratic reform will be fragile and inconclusive unless they are matched by resources to accelerate economic growth and enhance human development in Africa.

Africa's Economic Prospects in a "New World Order"

Present socioeconomic indicators underscore the marginalized status to which Africa has been reduced, particularly within the last decade. The nondemocratic and autocratic nature of most regimes in Africa has, more than any other factor, undermined the continent's potential and opportunity for sustainable economic development and growth.

Among all the regions, Africa and its people have suffered most in history and have continued to be the greatest sufferers. Africa was a passive actor in the Cold War and became its victim. Four years into the decade of the 1990s, the economic performance of most African countries remains dismal. Africa's economy grew by 3.0 percent in 1990, 1.9 percent in 1991, 2.4 percent in 1992, and about 3 percent in 1993. Most of these economic growth rates are of course far below the population rate, implying continuing decline in per capita income. Efforts both at the level of African countries and the international community have to be intensified if economic growth and development momentum is to be restored and accelerated, hopefully reversing Africa's poor development record of the 1980s and 1990s.

In the area of aid, the post–Cold War era has witnessed a dramatic increase in claimants of aid as well as a change in the concerns of donors. The immediate concern for now appears to be assisting in the transformation of the socialist economies of Eastern Europe and the former Soviet Union. During 1981–1991 the real growth of aid from the Organization for Economic Cooperation and Development (OECD), the Council for Mutual Economic Assistance (CMEA), and Arab donors averaged 4 percent according to a World Bank report of April 1993. From the 1990s right to the opening decades of the twenty-first century, the world economy is going to become more and more competitive, with the emergence of economic blocs and trade zones. The European Community promises to provide additional opportunities for increased trade between Africa and Europe. The whole of Europe is going to become a great economic market, and exchanges between East and West will increase considerably. But the opportunities are not going to be offered to Africa on a platter of gold. African states must brace themselves to face the challenges because the competition is not going to be easy. To be able to partake in the expanding trade environment emerging in the world and in Europe especially, they must carry out radical reforms in their economies in tune with the politico-economic mood of the times. The new political thinking, the objective of which is the complete dismantling of all authoritarian regimes in Africa, must be accompanied by a similar thoroughgoing restructuring of the economy. The released energies from the political and economic renewal process on the continent must be channeled into productive forces at all levels in order to revive and sustain the present tottering economy.

To appreciate the magnitude of the challenges that African states face under the emerging world economic system, it must be realized that for a number of reasons, internal and external, the dynamics of global economic permutations tend to operate negatively against Africa's development calculations. This situation is by no means improved by current political events in Europe.

The impact of the Soviet Union's policy of global disengagement and the subsequent political changes in Eastern Europe had far-reaching political, military, and economic effects in the Third World, particularly in Africa. Apart from the cessation of military aid, this policy brought about a drastic reduction in the volume of economic assistance from the Soviet bloc to African countries. Right now, it is hoped that the evolution of events in Eastern Europe will not diminish or erode the understanding and cooperation that have developed between these countries and Africa for over thirty years.

Official Development Assistance (ODA) has remained Africa's financial lifeline for quite a while now. It in fact represents an important non-debt-creating source of financing growth and development in Africa, more so when viewed against the context of Africa's low credit worthiness. This in itself is a function of its weak economic structures. Although the United States is the largest ODA donor, in absolute terms Africa is the beneficiary of the least U.S. aid in the world. Sub-Saharan Africa's annual aid share of U.S. ODA aid was 13.7 percent in 1989, 14 percent in 1990, and 11.8 percent in 1991. In dollar value, the amounts have averaged around $800 million. As a percentage of donor gross domestic product, U.S. aid to sub-Saharan

Africa in these respective years represented between 0.01 percent and 0.02 percent, or an average of $3.20 by every U.S. citizen a year, or $1.65 to every sub-Saharan African. Compare this to the situation in Egypt and Israel, where each recipient citizen receives between $25 and $1,000 of U.S. aid. Projections for 1993 stipulate that aid must grow by 4–6 percent per annum if per capita incomes are to rise. However, African countries are now confronted with the stark reality of a severe cutback of aid from donor countries. Sweden, in fact, a traditionally generous donor, has embarked on a 10 percent reduction in aid while the United Kingdom has cut back aid by at least 15 percent. In addition to this, IDA-10, a source of concessional funding, would have to be reduced from the initial projection of $23 billion. The import of this is, of course, self-evident. The situation for 1994 is worse.

The dissolution of Eastern Europe as a socialist bloc and the attendant radical political transformation that followed has attracted the attention and the economic interest of the West and has opened the way for massive investment opportunities in those countries, seemingly at the expense of the poorer and needier countries of Africa. It is true that Eastern European countries provide a more favorable investment environment for the West than Africa in terms of infrastructure, proximity, cultural affinity, and so on. It is equally true that these countries have put forward a host of incentives to attract foreign investors, of a type the African states are not in a position to offer. Besides, from the point of view of political sympathy and self-interest, massive resource flows from the West could be justified on the grounds of the need to rescue Eastern Europe from communist domination. But it is common knowledge that the marginalization and the precarious socioeconomic conditions of Africa predate events in Europe. Yet Africa has never enjoyed similar relief packages from the West.

One could not have thought it possible that the complacency of the consumer and increasingly inward-oriented societies in the North would ever again be capable of bringing about such an outpouring of political and humanist interest at the highest levels, leading to the offer of substantial official and private-resource flows, the proliferation of blueprints and development plans, as well as the marshaling of talent and public goodwill and understanding. The intensity of political will and commitment, the widespread enthusiasm and idealism apparent in the industrialized countries, similar to what many African countries enjoyed some thirty years ago, generally betrayed the hollow arguments of aid fatigue among donors, unavailability of resources, and lack of public awareness and understanding, increasingly heard during the last decade.

One can only hope that the changes in Eastern Europe will consolidate the understanding and solidarity between Africa and Eastern Europe that has developed throughout the last thirty-five years.

Not only is the near-spontaneous increase of resource flow from the West to Eastern Europe remarkable and almost unprecedented; the magnitude of it is unparalleled since the Marshall Plan. The establishment of the European Reconstruction and Development Bank "with a pledged capital for the Bank of $126 billion is more than twice the total of the net ODA disbursements to developing countries and multinational agencies in 1989, i.e. $52.5 billion." The future direction of development finance appears institutionalized. Eastern Europe must receive attention and assistance from the West because an economically improved and politically stable Eastern Europe is an advantage to the economy of the world from which Africa should eventually benefit.

But that is in the long run. Between Africa and Eastern Europe there should be a feeling of empathy, understanding, and accommodation, not recrimination, fear, suspicion, and antagonism. There is enough for both regions to have adequate resources and attention to make a difference to their economic situations, consequently leading to the revitalization and improved health of the world economy. Both regions should be calling for adequacy of resources and attention to them separately and collectively.

The European Community, embracing the enormous economic potential of a united Germany, risks diverting the attention of big investors of North America, Europe, and Asia from Africa to Europe, which promises to be the biggest market yet. What is more, an enlarged, strong, and integrated Europe could give rise to a Eurocentrism and lead to a protectionist Europe which, in terms of trade relations, may create problems and prove unhelpful for Africa, the Caribbean, and the Pacific region—the ACP countries. Even right now, the ACP countries face declining trade possibilities as a result of ad hoc preferences granted to products from Eastern European countries irrespective of any preferences that may have been expressed in the context of the Lome agreements between the European Community and ACP countries. To compete successfully in the market of the emerging Europe, the ACP countries, particularly Africa, will have to put their house in order, understand the rules of the game, and give aggressive pursuit.

Africa stands to lose in several other ways relative to Eastern Europe. Future ODA flows commensurate to the challenges of Africa are unlikely to be provided. The volume of resources available for rescheduling, reduction, or outright debt forgiveness for African countries will shrink. The best brains and talents in government and in multinational and medium-size corporations and banks in the West will be assigned to programs and projects in Eastern Europe. Political and media attention and concern will be diverted from the Third World, particularly Africa, to Eastern Europe.

Notwithstanding, the increase in foreign direct investment (FDI) flow for developing countries has increased in absolute terms, with the United States and Japan accounting for nearly 70 percent of the entire FDI flow to developing countries. In consequence, a triad pattern of FDI flow with regional associations appears to be growing: U.S. multinationals favor Latin America; the Japanese and the high-performing economies of East Asia are going the way of Asia; and the European Community is the major source of FDI in Eastern Europe.

Even at the global level, African countries face the threat of economic isolation. The emergence of regional economic blocs in many parts of the world risks leaving Africa isolated in the present emerging global economic configuration. The following groupings have already emerged or are likely to emerge: Europe; North and South America; a North American zone embracing the United States, Canada, and Mexico; Japan and Southeast Asia; a Pacific economic cooperation zone; the Middle East (because of its oil and strategic location). Under the circumstances, self-reliance and rapid physical and economic integration of the African continent are indispensable for Africa's economic survival in the 1990s if it is to experience socioeconomic transformation and competitiveness with the rest of the world. A crushing external debt burden is another indicator of Africa's deteriorating global position. Obviously, African countries cannot successfully embark on the road to economic recovery and sustainable development unless the chronic problem of debt burden is resolved in Africa's favor. Boutros Ghali captured it succinctly when he observed rather pithily that "external debt is a millstone around the neck of Africa. . . . It is a major obstacle to the return of private investment to Africa. Easing the continent's debt burden must be a priority for the international community." In a similar tone, President Abdou Diouf, while addressing the U.N. General Assembly in September 1992, also observed that "Africa is confronted by old problems, some of which have even become worse. Such is the case with Africa's external debt payment, to which the continent devotes the bulk of the meager financial resources left by the deteriorating terms of trade." Of course, this stands to reason because Africa's debt multiplies at an average annual growth rate of 10 percent. Estimated at $48.3 billion in 1978, it had risen to $230 billion by 1988 and $250 billion by 1989; and in 1990 it was $281 billion, in 1992 it was $288 billion, and over $300 billion in 1993. Unfavorable lending conditions have aggravated the burden. With interest rates rising from about 6 percent in the 1970s to over 10 percent in the 1980s, rising interest rates now constitute over $100 billion of the total stock of debt. According to the World Bank's debt tables for 1992–1993, only four African countries could claim to be current on payment of both interest and principal.

With the outbreak of the debt crisis and a number of countries no longer able to make repayments when due, a series of measures have been proposed in the recent past to deal with the situation, but none has proved adequate or satisfactory so far. Measures such as the Baker plan, Brady plan, Toronto guideline, and Trinidad approach have their inadequacies. While accepting the principle of joint responsibility and joint solution by creditors and debtors, each of these measures does not provide modalities to ensure discipline with development and growth in the debtor nations. At the same time, while creditor nations are worried about the danger of a one-year debt write-off, they want to see a genuine change of attitude, improved discipline, accountability, adoption of a market economy, and democratization by the debtor countries.

An adequate solution must take cognizance of the fears and aspirations of creditor nations without sacrificing the developmental aspirations and capacity of debtor nations. In the first place, the debtor nations should embark on a policy of self-induced or self-imposed sacrifice or conditionality, such as would elicit relief from creditor nations and institutions. These self-imposed conditions would be based on, among other considerations, political reform, economic discipline, social equity, commitment to the rule of law, limitation of military expenditure, and environmental development.

As a second step, with these self-imposed conditions as guarantee, the terms of a new debt-relief package should be based on the freezing of the debt principal for a period of twenty years or more and on the cancellation on an annual basis of the debt interest, thus relieving debtor nations of current debt-servicing burdens.

This should be a compact between the debtor nation and the creditor nation on the basis of an agreed-upon program and openness. Defaulting on an agreed program should lead to a one-year period of grace to change, failing which payment of interest should be reimposed. The International Monetary Fund should supervise the program and monitor defaults on commitments.

Sincere commitment to and execution of this strategy, based on these contractual programs, would encourage creditor countries and multinational agencies and, at the same time, release local resources for high-priority development programs for Africa.

The debt problem in Africa is not only a financial problem; it is also a developmental and management problem. The solution must be all-embracing. It must involve debt relief, capacity building, democratization, accountability, and instituting sound, sustainable policies committedly executed. The African situation is not a basket case. It is not a calabash case either, and its reversal is essentially the challenge of leadership on the part of Africans and the international community. If President Boris Yeltsin of Russia, a superpower of yesterday, could demand cancellation of interest on loans owed by his country after the generous U.S.$24 billion special arrangement for that country by the industrialized countries, debt cancellation for Africa should not be a matter of why but how and when.

It is conclusive from the scenario presented above that the international economic environment, which has hitherto not been favorably disposed toward African initiatives for development and survival, has not changed, even with the euphoria of a new world order. In fact, it appears that African countries are finding themselves pushed more and more to the periphery by evolving world events. The entire experience of African states for the past three decades is a cheerless picture.

But should we throw up our hands in despair? Of course not. The trend is reversible. History is replete with the rise and fall of peoples, of nations, of kingdoms, of empires. What Africa needs is to make conscious efforts to redress the distressing and depressing situation of the present and outlive its handicaps. New initiatives are needed to achieve effective political and economic restructuring of society. Responsive and effective governance is required to motivate economic growth, promote human development, and, at the same time, revive the dwindling interest of the international community in Africa's development efforts. This can only be achieved, in sum, in an atmosphere of peace, security, stability, cooperation, and development.

A Framework for Progress

In search of a meaningful solution to their problems, African states now fortunately have at their disposal a set of interrelated preconditions that must be instituted and institutionalized to meet the aspirations of their people for responsive governance and for development and, at the same time, to elicit the cooperation and support of the international community.

In May 1991, participants from Africa converged in Kampala, Uganda, to deliberate issues of security, stability, development, and cooperation in Africa. The Conference on Security, Stability, Development, and Cooperation in Africa (CSSDCA) was modeled on the Helsinki process but with African realism. The Kampala Document, which was the outcome of the deliberations, stipulated that peace, security, and stability are the preconditions for development and cooperation in Africa. The security, stability, and development of African states are inseparably interlinked; the erosion of security and stability is one of the major causes of the continuing crises and one of the principal impediments to economic growth and human development on the continent.

The Kampala Document further noted that peace constitutes the basis of all wholesome human interaction and that with peace should go security. Lack of democracy, denial of personal liberty, and abuse of human rights are the causes of insecurity. The concept of security transcends military considerations. On the one hand, it includes conflict prevention, containment, and resolution, and derives from common and collective continental security. On the other hand, it embraces all aspects of the society, including economic, political, and social dimensions of the individual, family, community, local, and national life. By this, it is understood that the security of a nation must be construed in terms of the security of the individual citizen not only to live in peace but to have access to the basic necessities of life, participate in freedom in the affairs of society, and enjoy fundamental human rights.

The issue of stability is just as important to development. Promoting political and social stability in individual African countries is, therefore, a key component of the CSSDCA process. Under the stability guidelines, all African states are to be guided by strict adherence to the rule of law, popular participation in governance, respect for human rights and fundamental freedoms; political organizations should not be based on religious, ethnic, regional, or racial considerations; there should be transparency in public policymaking and an absence of fundamentalism in religious practice.

In like manner, for the purpose of economic development, African states are to subscribe to certain fundamental principles under the CSSDCA process. Development based on self-reliance is the only viable basis for Africa's self-sustaining economic development and growth. Rapid physical and economic integration of the continent is indispensable for Africa's socioeconomic transformation and survival as well as for its competitiveness with the rest of the world in the twenty-first century.

One of the major causes of its present economic crisis is Africa's absolute reliance and dependence on commodity production solely for export. A time has come for effective diversification, both horizontally in terms of broadening the production base and vertically in terms of processing and marketing for rapid social and economic transformation.

Popular participation and equal opportunity and access must be promoted and sustained as a crucial basis for the realization of Africa's development objectives. Domestic partnership in development should be promoted. Leaders and the governed should assume responsibilities for various aspects of development. Leaders should provide the vision that guides development. This development process is to create a truly people-centered development. Out of pragmatic necessity the CSSDCA process addresses limited but key development issues to ensure a realistic chance of success.

The Kampala Document also provides a framework for collective action and for cooperation on a continental, regional, and international basis. It provides for cooperation between African states, between South and South, and between North and South; economic integration of African states in the African Economic Community; joint development of common natural resources; interdependence based on beneficial cooperative relations with other developing and industrialized nations; and supranationality based on the need to devolve certain key responsibilities to continental institutions.

The CSSDCA process has thus charted an invaluable course for Africa's development, creating a framework based on self-reliance, effective and responsive governance, regional integration, and international cooperation.

Integration and cooperation are to be guided by some basic common policy measure. If orthodox technical cooperation has not yielded satisfactory results for both donors and recipients and if projects like the U.N. program of action for Africa's economic recovery and development have had very little impact due to lack of support for Africa's reform efforts, a new attitude and a new approach to technical cooperation should be adopted. It should be based on a compact that can challenge and satisfy both sides through target and objective setting and through results that can be monitored, involving not only donor agencies and the private sector in the donor countries but also the nongovernmental organizations and the government in the recipient countries.

At the same time, efforts should be made to enhance endogenous institutional capacity, beginning with cooperation in ensuring communal efforts, peace and security at the local, national, subregional, and regional levels, and incentives for development and increased assistance.

In an independent world we cannot develop in isolation, and throughout history development has come to any region or any nation principally through its own sweat and the collaborative efforts of others in the form of labor, capital, technology, or market.

As an endnote, I make bold to say that the current neglect of Africa predicated on the collapse of communism may not in the long run augur well for the West. I say this because it is not impossible for a new era of Cold War superpower rivalry and confrontation still to resurface; if it does, the soft underbelly that Africa may turn out to be may be the weak link in the emergent tug of war.

Part 5

The Nonaligned Movement and the View from the South

His Excellency

Ali Alatas

Minister for Foreign Affairs of the
Republic of Indonesia

The Nonaligned Movement in the Post–Cold War Order

An Indonesian View

The end of the Cold War brought about global changes so profound and massive that today we are just beginning to understand some of their consequences and implications. Some of the benign aspects of the post–Cold War era, however, were immediately apparent: the dismantling of the bipolar structure of international politics, the dissipation of East-West tensions that brought humanity a few steps back from the abyss of nuclear war, and a resurgence of faith in the value and role of the United Nations. At the same time, deepening interdependence and globalization of the world economy has prompted nations to seek more equitable and mutually beneficial patterns of economic cooperation through multilateralism. Nations have found it wise to assume greater collective responsibility for their common security, not only in military terms but also in economic and social terms such as humanitarian action, sustainable development, democratization, and promotion and protection of human rights.

Although these positive aspects are now overcast by the dark clouds of new and unprecedented challenges and problems, by pervasive uncertainties and profound contrasts and contradictions, they nevertheless remain a source of hope for a better world.

Indeed, hope is still the dominant feeling in the world today. The past five decades have seen the emancipation and empowerment of many peoples, and many more were emancipated with the end of the Cold War. Now they feel they have the power to shape their own destinies by working with others within the framework of mutual respect, common responsibility, and shared benefits. The need to exercise that power has become compelling. An increasing number of emerging voices and institutions are actively promoting political, social, economic, cultural, and environmental causes with considerable global impact. If states and, indeed, the world community can respond wisely to these new actors, selecting out those that are negative and injurious and engaging those that are positive and constructive, these would contribute greatly to the making of better global governance.

For global governance, as the continuing process through which conflicting or diverse interests may be accommodated and cooperative action taken, now involves not only intergovernmental institutions but also nongovernmental organizations (NGOs), citizens' movements, transnational corporations, academia, and the mass media. Reflecting that need of people to exercise the power to take control of their own lives, a global civil society, with many movements reinforcing a sense of human solidarity, is emerging. States remain primary actors but have to work with others. The United Nations must continue to play a vital role, but it must also share its burden. All through the global neighborhood, peoples and institutions, public and private, must achieve higher levels of cooperation in areas of common concern and shared destiny. This will require a collaborative ethos based on the principles of consultation, transparency, and accountability as well as a commitment to common values that all humanity could uphold: respect for life, liberty, justice and equity, mutual respect, caring, and integrity.

That the positive changes ushered in by the post–Cold War era are intimately linked with the causes for which the Nonaligned Movement has striven during the past three and a half decades, to my mind, is no coincidence at all. After all, the movement served consistently as a counterpoint to the bipolar structure and confrontational orientation of world politics all during that time.

It would, of course, be impossible to set an exact measure of the movement's contributions to far-reaching reforms in international relationships. It is undeniable, however, that the unrelenting drive that it imparted to the worldwide decolonization process and to the struggle against apartheid has hastened the demise of colonial empires, the rise of newly independent states, and the retreat of institutionalized racism. The movement pushed hard for the long-overdue process of disarmament, which today is finally under way. The end of the Cold War itself is a vindication of the Non-aligned Movement's basic philosophy and principal policies. Had the philosophy of nonalignment been adopted by the great powers themselves, there would have been no need for the debilitating balance of terror that was the only source of global security during the Cold War.

The Seedbed of Nonalignment

Indonesia is privileged to have been associated with this great movement since its very birth. As a matter of fact, even long before nonalignment found its institutional shape at the first summit in Belgrade in 1961, Indonesia had already committed itself to nonalignment. Some forty-six years ago, the prime minister of Indonesia, Mohamad Hatta, first proclaimed Indonesia's active and independent or nonaligned policy as the central tenet of our external relationships and outlook on the world. This was but a logical consequence of our struggle for independence and freedom from foreign domination or great-power entanglement.

Indonesia subsequently had the honor of serving as the seedbed for the full germination of the concept of nonalignment. The 1955 Asia African Conference in Bandung is acknowledged as the conceptual precursor of nonalignment. Its Dasasila, or Ten Principles of International Relations, have remained as valid and as relevant today as they were thirty-nine years ago. Further elaborated and expanded by the Nonaligned Movement at its first summit in Belgrade and in subsequent summit meetings, these remain the unchanged values by which we live today.

And yet it was not too long ago that this question was raised: with the Cold War already behind us and the bipolar structure of world politics relegated to the past, is the Nonaligned Movement still relevant? By the time the movement was preparing for its tenth summit in Jakarta, it had already articulated the definitive answer to that question.

And the answer was that the basic principles and purposes as well as the essential values and ideals of the movement remained relevant, even with the dismantling of the bipolar structure of world politics. So long as world peace was endangered, the freedom of nations abridged, the fundamental aspirations of peoples curtailed, and economic injustice perpetuated, so long must the movement be in the forefront of the struggle to oppose them. It was, of course, up to the members themselves whether the movement would recede into irrelevance or rise to the challenges and the opportunities of the changing times, thus not only remaining relevant but becoming an even more active and crucial player on the international scene.

Faced with such a complex global reality, the Nonaligned Movement had the choice of whether to allow the ongoing changes to proceed under their own momentum, without coherence and direction but with all attendant risks of instability and upheaval, or to engage the international community in jointly directing these changes rationally and equitably — toward a new order that is more in harmony with the ideals and principles of nonalignment.

The Nonaligned Movement Reoriented

At the Tenth Nonaligned Movement Summit in Jakarta, the leaders of the movement made their choice. They declared that, as a political coalition representing more sovereign states than any other grouping in history, the movement should not be a mere spectator and should not resign itself to being sidelined in the currents of historic change. The movement, they stressed, must dynamically adapt to these currents by setting new priorities and reordering old ones, by devising new approaches and new strategies.

Knowing that stereotyped responses would fall short of the demands of the time and that the mere cataloguing of grievances, anxieties, and hopes would be an exercise in futility, the movement proceeded to craft the concepts and modalities that would be the basis and the framework of the concrete programs to which the members would commit themselves. At the same time, it girded itself for a vigorous advocacy that would place the views and concrete proposals of the movement into the mainstream of international thought and action. And, finally, without neglecting to address the political concerns that had gripped the world, the leaders of the Nonaligned Movement decided to restore the issue of economic cooperation to the top of the movement's agenda.

Thus, from that summit, the movement came out reinvigorated, strengthened in its resolve and clear in its purposes. All lingering doubts about the relevance of the movement in the post–Cold War era had been banished. International observers who were habitually skeptical of the movement must have been pleasantly surprised that for the first time a Non-aligned Movement summit did not dwell on grievances but instead sought a constructive dialogue and offered to engage the developed world in cooperation in all fields. And thus the movement discarded its old approach, which was dogmatic and adversarial, and adopted a new orientation, a new strategy to solving the interlinked global problems of our time.

That new orientation has turned out to be no mean contribution to the relaunching of a more earnest and effective global dialogue. Soon after a meeting of the Standing Ministerial Committee for Economic Cooperation in Bali in May 1993, which threshed out ways and means of moving the North-South and South-South processes forward, President Suharto, as the movement's chairman, seized the opportunity to extend its "Invitation to Dialogue" to the leaders of the Group of Seven on the eve of their summit meeting in Tokyo. The positive response of the G-7 leaders to the movement's offer of cooperation and constructive dialogue, which they articulated at the conclusion of the Tokyo summit and then again after the G-7 summit in Napoli the following year, has since been carried further by the movement. Working with the Group of 77 and other like-minded countries, including developed countries, the Nonaligned Movement initiated a draft resolution entitled "Renewal of the Dialogue on Strengthening International Cooperation for Development through Partnership." That the resolution was adopted by consensus clearly indicates that the international community supports the movement's basic strategy for achieving a new and more just international economic order based on the mutual interest, common benefit, and equitably shared responsibility of all nations.

An important aspect of the resolution was a request to the secretary-general to present the forty-ninth session of the U.N. General Assembly with recommendations on how the envisioned North-South dialogue could be promoted in a way that would reflect ongoing work on an Agenda for Development. In this regard, the secretary-general has issued his report on an Agenda for Development that we hope will bolster the prospects for balanced global economic growth. The movement's Coordinating Bureau, working with the Group of 77, is playing an active role in the deliberations on that agenda.

Even in their dealings with international financial institutions today, the members of the movement have shown remarkable realism and flexibility and have accordingly begun to redefine their relationship with these institutions. In the forthcoming review of Bretton Woods institutions, the nonaligned countries have a chance to build on the good start they have made in relating with these institutions. They should take an active part in that review and propose practical approaches for improving the efficacy and efficiency of these institutions, which, after all, have a special role to play in the South-South process. The Nonaligned Movement is mindful of the fact that many projects of great merit within the framework of South-South cooperation could have withered on the vine had not a third party, often an international financial institution, come to the rescue.

One group that the Nonaligned Movement, as an advocate of dialogue on international economic issues, must also consult with is that of the countries of central and eastern Europe, a number of them newly independent from the former Soviet Union and all of them in the process of political and economic transformation. Described today as "countries in transition," they have had a profound impact on the developing world, for they compete with other developing countries for scarce international resources for development. To the nonaligned countries, this is a matter of concern. But the political importance of these countries and their potential contributions cannot be overemphasized. For if there is a deterioration in the situation of these countries, the whole international community will be affected. From a historical perspective, even while they were within the exclusive sphere of Soviet influence, these countries have always been sympathetic to the developing world. After the breakdown of the Soviet Union, these countries have had to contend with the reality that political reforms do not necessarily bring about immediate relief from economic woes. These countries need help, and the international community should provide that help — without, however, sacrificing the aspirations of the rest of the developing world.

South-South Cooperation

Meanwhile, South-South cooperation within the Nonaligned Movement has indeed broadened and intensified since the tenth summit. The movement addressed the problem of food security through an Ad Hoc Advisory Group of Experts, which has submitted a proposed Action Program that was adopted by the Conference of the Ministers of Food and Agriculture of the Nonaligned Movement and Other Developing Countries in Jakarta in October 1994.

Also implemented within the framework of South-South cooperation is the Nonaligned Movement's initiative on the issue of population. A group of experts has likewise been put to work making in-depth studies on this issue, and their recommendations have been submitted. One of the results of this effort is a report entitled "Nonaligned Movement Support for South-South Collaboration in the Field of Population and Family Planning," which was based on Indonesia's experience.

Another major burden that the developing countries have to bear is the external debt crisis, which constitutes a major drain on the resources of developing countries and has often frustrated their endeavors at development in spite of various strategies tried by the international community to alleviate this crisis. As the movement's chairman, Indonesia has hosted three meetings of experts on external debt, resulting in a "Memorandum on Urgent Actions on Bilateral, Multilateral, and Commercial Debt of the Developing Countries," which was subsequently presented to the G-7 leaders through their chairman on the eve of their Tokyo summit.

In pursuing South-South cooperation, the movement has found most effective for ensuring sustainable development the action-oriented strategy of self-propelling growth. Founded on self-reliance, this strategy promotes community-based economic growth as well as the right of the poor to participate in and benefit from development. To further propagate this grassroots approach, Indonesia this year hosts the Open-Ended Joint Meeting of Experts and Decision-Makers of Developing Countries on Development Schemes.

Perhaps the South-South initiative that has had the greatest impact is the Asia-Africa Forum, which was held in late 1994 in, most appropriately, Bandung. In this forum, a follow-up to the Tokyo International Conference on African Development (TICAD), the developing countries of the Far East, which have impressed the world with their dynamic growth, shared their experiences, observations, and insights with the developing countries of Africa. A solid foundation was thereby established for promotion of development cooperation between Asian and African countries. Now also known as the Bandung Forum, it could serve as a model for future South-South cooperation efforts.

Positive Global Developments

As to the North-South partnership, tremendous opportunities are being offered through several recent positive developments. The successful conclusion of the Uruguay Round, for instance, has opened up new areas of trade and given impetus to the liberalization of the international trade system. The spirit of transparency and liberalization embodied in the Uruguay Round could provide a fresh impetus for all countries, especially the nonaligned countries, to work for a more liberalized trade and investment regime. For even with the expected far-reaching benefits of the Uruguay Round, we cannot afford to consider trade liberalization as a given in the global economic equation. We will still have to work for it and, with the developed countries, work to maintain the gains thus far achieved. We hope that developed countries will now take effective steps toward a reduction in the protective support and subsidies for agriculture. Particularly in the field of primary commodities, the countries of the North should immediately join the countries of the South in addressing the issue of declining prices — an issue that affects the livelihood of millions of farmers in the developing countries.

Another major positive development is in the area of environmental protection, which has now become intimately linked with social and economic development. The U.N. Conference on Environment and Development, held at Rio de Janeiro in June 1992, confirmed the Nonaligned Movement's long-held conviction that environmental and developmental issues cannot be separated from each other but should be addressed integrally and simultaneously on the basis of equitably shared responsibility of all countries. And for the developing countries, efforts to overcome the problems of poverty and population pressures will be essential if they are to pursue environmentally sound and sustainable development.

The documents that came out of the Earth Summit indeed constitute a remarkable breakthrough. But their effective implementation to a large extent depends on the formation of a new global partnership for sustainable development — and that further breakthrough, I believe, is possible only after a successful North-South dialogue. This is because effective implementation requires that developed countries and multilateral financial institutions provide to the developing countries commensurate additional financial resources and access to environmentally sound technologies.

With the North-South dialogue already begun and with South-South cooperation being broadened and intensified, there is greater need for coordination among developing countries. The Nonaligned Movement (NAM), therefore, through its Coordinating Bureau and working with the Group of 77, expedited the operationalization of the Joint Coordinating Committee (JCC) early last year. A few months later, the terms of reference of the committee were put into practice soon after the NAM Ministerial Meeting in Cairo. Thus the two major bodies of developing countries are now able to harness their collective strength to effectively and efficiently pursue various South-South development projects as well as dialogue with their counterparts in the developed North.

Realizing that social and economic development can be secure only in a regime of peace, the Nonaligned Movement continues to be seized with political issues as well as the tensions and conflicts that attend these issues. During the past two years, the movement has grown increasingly active in the search for solutions to international political disputes or conflicts. The movement's chairman has regularly sent his special emissaries to the countries in conflict, where they worked behind the scenes to advance the movement's advocacy for peaceful solutions to conflicts.

A Trend in the Nonaligned Movement's Chairmanship

It is clear from the Nonaligned Movement's many initiatives and involvements that the decisions taken at its Jakarta summit have not remained decisions on paper — they have been given concrete reality and have assumed a life of their own. Indonesia, as chairman of the movement, has taken pains to ensure that, whenever possible, these decisions should be translated into action. It has also made it a point to remind members of the movement to speak and to act in international forums in accordance with the intention and the spirit of these summit decisions. At the United Nations in New York, the movement's Coordinating Bureau has been meeting regularly to discuss not only the implementation of the decisions of the tenth summit but also to actively coordinate the movement's positions on various issues of importance to the nonaligned and other developing countries.

In this manner, Indonesia may have been able to set a trend in the conduct of the chairmanship of the movement. Many more initiatives have to be launched in order to help bring about the movement's envisioned new international order, and in each of these the chairmanship plays a central role. While the chairmanship of the movement is already provided with a mechanism for seeking assistance at the highest political level from the appropriate members whenever a common concern becomes urgent or critical, the movement's leaders may well consider further enhancing the capability of the chairmanship to take special initiatives when they meet at the eleventh summit in Bogota, Colombia. They could also consider establishing mechanisms for settling disputes among members.

In sum, the Nonaligned Movement has been able to change with the changing times. It has not only managed to preserve its relevance but also increased its involvement in worthy international causes that are consistent with its principles and ideals for world peace and justice. Where once it was the champion of national independence movements, it is now a leading advocate of genuine global interdependence. And where once it served as a counterpoint to bipolarism, it is now the ardent advocate of a global dialogue between North and South.

The Vital Role of the United Nations

Where and how will the North-South dialogue take place? On this, the Nonaligned Movement has once again shown realism and flexibility by making it clear that it is ready and willing to dialogue on matters of common interest with the developed countries of the North in any forum that is mutually acceptable. The dialogue does not require the creation of a new institution, for we could rely on the various existing international forums, especially within the context of the U.N. system. Should it be truly needed, however, and if indicated by a broad consensus, a suitable and special forum can always be created, as we created the Earth Summit in Rio de Janeiro to discuss urgent environmental issues.

The most appropriate setting for that dialogue, however, can only be the United Nations. The Nonaligned Movement is, in the first place, pledged to seek a new international order through the central and irreplaceable instrumentality of the United Nations. Being the singular forum where nonaligned and other developing countries are in a unique position to influence global issues and the direction of world developments, the United Nations should play a pivotal role in the North-South dialogue and in the subsequent forging of a broad partnership for development.

This is one more reason why the Nonaligned Movement is now more than ever determined to contribute actively to the revitalization, restructuring, and democratization of the United Nations. For this purpose, the leaders of the movement, during the Jakarta summit, established a High-Level Working Group for the Restructuring of the United Nations. Composed of twenty-nine country members, the group has since played an important role in the United Nations in the discussions on the question of the revitalization of the work of the General Assembly and in coordinating the views of the movement on the question of equitable representation on and increase of the membership of the U.N. Security Council.

We in the movement believe that a balanced relationship among the General Assembly, the Security Council, the Economic and Social Council, and the office of the secretary-general is imperative. There should be greater accountability of the Security Council to the General Assembly on decisions and actions affecting the interests of the entire international community. The role of the General Assembly as a forum for deliberation, negotiation, and decision making must be enhanced. The capacity of the United Nations for enhancing international development and cooperation should be strengthened by revitalizing the Economic and Social Council. The office of the secretary-general should be provided with resources commensurate to its tasks, which have vastly expanded as a result of recent world events. The secretary-general's mandate should be enlarged so as to enable him to take the necessary initiatives in the pursuit of preventive diplomacy and in enhancing the efficacy of U.N. peacemaking, peace-keeping, and peace-building operations.

Reviewing the Security Council

We believe also that it is time to address the matter of the size and composition of the Security Council. This, we realize, should be done with circumspection, for it involves a fundamental aspect of the organization's purposes and functions.

When the U.N. Charter was framed and its organs established in 1945, the main preoccupation of its founding members, and rightly so, was that never again should the scourge of war be allowed to devastate humankind. They therefore envisioned a collective security system that they thought would be capable of preventing another world war.

Since then, however, the world has changed in a most profound way. In five decades, numerous nations achieved independence and joined the

United Nations as sovereign member states, thus giving the organization near universality in its composition. Their entry reflected the universal drive of peoples to liberate themselves from colonial bondage. But that was not their ultimate purpose: they fought for political independence not because it was an end unto itself but because it was the necessary condition for the attainment of a larger goal — development. Freedom fighters were invariably inspired by a vision of their own people attaining the blessings and the dignity of economic and social progress, which is never possible in a state of political subjugation.

In a very real sense, true freedom is attained only through development, and the formal trappings of political independence are empty until they are substantiated with economic and social progress. While it may be true that colonialism in its classical form has virtually come to an end, the process of decolonization is never finished until economic independence is achieved.

Thus, if in the past the major preoccupation of the United Nations was rightly preventing another world conflagration and liberating peoples from political bondage, today the world and therefore the United Nations should be seized with the struggle of all countries for national development. This preoccupation should be reflected in the work of the United Nations and in the composition and dynamics of its organs, particularly the Security Council.

We live in an age of development where economic power has become more decisive than ever. We live in a world where billions of people in the developing countries of the South are beginning to assert their right to realize their economic and social potential.

We believe therefore that it is a matter of urgency that the Security Council be expanded. Such a move should take into account the principle of equitable geographic representation and accommodate the interests and concerns of developing countries, which comprise the overwhelming majority in the organization. We also believe that the number of permanent members on the Security Council should be increased. In this respect, it is our view that while the principle of geographic representation is important, it should not be the only criterion for determining eligibility for new permanent members. We believe that other objective criteria are equally important, such as political, economic, and demographic realities and a country's capability and record of contributing to the promotion of peace, security, and economic development, both regionally and globally, as well as the commitment of states to assume the responsibilities inherent in such a status. We further believe that it may also be timely and pertinent that the manner in which the veto powers are presently exercised should be subjected to a constructive review. In these endeavors, our goal must remain the promotion of transparency, legitimacy, accountability, and efficiency.

Democracy is Dynamic, not Static

In the same way that the United Nations and its organs should be further democratized, there should also be further democratization in the relationships between nations. It is ironic that the advanced countries of the West have lately been vocal in calling for democracy and "good governance" as an integral part of the development process, especially in the developing countries. Some are even inclined to make it a new condition in development cooperation. The call for democratization and democratic reform in all countries is indeed valid, for it relates directly to the basic aspirations of individuals and nations. But democracy is not a static concept limited to certain established forms and practices. Its basic principles and tenets are indeed of universal and immutable validity. But no single model of democracy can be assumed to be of universal applicability, given the diversity of cultural values and historical experiences of the nations of the world. Moreover, it is a denial of the basic tenets of democracy if its values are to be strictly observed within nations while they are being ignored among nations. Hence democracy and democratization are dynamic processes that should be in conformity with the fundamental values of each nation and constantly adapted to evolving realities in order to remain relevant and, more important, democratic.

Human Rights and the Human Potential

As to human rights, we in the Nonaligned Movement have always affirmed that basic human rights and fundamental freedoms are of universal validity. We welcome the growing trend toward democracy. We are committed to cooperating in the protection of human rights as we believe that economic and social progress facilitates the achievement of these objectives.

No country, however, should use its power to dictate its concept of democracy and of human rights or to impose conditionalities on others. In the promotion and protection of these rights, we maintain that the various categories of these rights are interrelated, that there should be a balance between individual and community rights, and we uphold the competence and responsibility of national governments in their implementation.

The nonaligned countries coordinated their positions on this issue and worked together during the second World Conference on Human Rights in June 1993 to ensure that the conference addressed all aspects of human rights on the basis of universality, indivisibility, impartiality, and nonselectivity.

It is also our firm conviction that the objective of human rights is the realization of the full potential of the human being and that human potential is not confined to the political. The fundamental right to economic and social development, for example, cannot be separated, and cannot be treated separately, from the other categories of human rights. And these rights apply to nations as well as to individuals. That is why we in the Nonaligned Movement firmly believe that social development is no less vital than political and economic development and that the social needs of people should be placed at the heart of U.N. endeavors. The full and equal integration of women into the development process has also always been a goal of the Nonaligned Movement. We believe that all children should be nurtured at a standard of living that is adequate for their health and well-being. We shall work for this as a matter of moral imperative and commit ourselves to the full and effective implementation of the Declaration and Plan of Action of the World Summit for Children.

The Nonmilitary Factors of Security

Nonmilitary security factors are important global concerns, for it has become clear in recent years that peace and security depend as much on socioeconomic as on military factors. Sharply reduced prospects for economic and social advancement, large-scale unemployment, abject poverty, massive cross-border migrations, and severe environmental degradation also endanger peace. We cannot hope to attain comprehensive security and stable peace without making substantive progress in the war against poverty, underdevelopment, disease, and social injustice.

Even without such factors weighing against the struggle to achieve stability in peace, and in spite of the end of the Cold War and the collapse of confrontational bipolar world politics, there is already too much turbulence in the world today. Simmering disputes, violent conflicts, aggression and foreign occupation, interference in the internal affairs of states, policies of hegemony and domination, ethnic strife, religious intolerance, new forms of racism, and narrowly conceived nationalism continue to obstruct the building of harmonious coexistence among states and societies. A profoundly anguishing example is the breakup of the former Socialist Federal Republic of Yugoslavia, which precipitated the tragedy of Bosnia and Herzegovina.

The Disarmament Agenda

In the face of so much violence and conflict in the world, disarmament efforts should be intensified. While it is true that there has been encouraging progress in limiting nuclear and conventional armaments, the disarmament agenda is still largely unfinished. Until a nuclear-weapons-free world is finally achieved, the threat to human survival will continue to cast its shadow over all our other endeavors and aspirations. Indonesia has therefore constantly urged accelerated efforts on other priority disarmament issues, particularly the prohibition of all weapons of mass destruction.

Besides posing an acute danger to world peace and security, a continuing global arms race and unbridled military spending also constitute a huge drain on national economies and on the world economy. We have consistently maintained that resources released through disarmament and arms reductions should be redirected to the social and economic development of all countries, especially the developing countries. The establishment of such a productive linkage between disarmament and development will also make it possible to attain security at lower levels of armament.

It is our hope that the new global security constellation, which will result from the swift and fundamental changes taking place in the world, will allow such a linkage. Indeed, we believe that the changing relationship patterns among the major powers will inevitably lead us toward a new global security environment. But precisely because it will no longer be anchored in the bipolarity of East-West contention, it will be an environment that is much more complex in its internal dynamics and, for some time to come, less predictable in its evolution. The transitional period can therefore be expected to be marked by inherent fluidity and instability.

In this situation of transition and flux, it is imperative that a developing and nonaligned country like Indonesia correctly assess the new challenges, as well as the new opportunities inherent in them, to develop a clear perception of the strategic implications of global developments and to adapt its security policies and approaches accordingly. Fortunately for Indonesia, though this has been and will always be a delicate task, it has not been an entirely lonely one.

The ASEAN Security Assessment

As early as 1971, at a meeting in Kuala Lumpur of foreign ministers from the countries that would soon become the founding members of the Association of Southeast Asian Nations (ASEAN), Indonesia among them, these foreign ministers had the foresight to discuss and plan for a post–Vietnam War Southeast Asia. Their prognosis then was that before long the war would end with the inevitable victory of North Vietnam over South Vietnam (as actually happened in 1975) and that a reunited Vietnam — together with the other former Indochinese states, Cambodia and Laos — should be counted in as new and important players in a more peaceful Southeast Asia. They resolved that ASEAN should seize the advent of peace as an opportunity to build a new pattern of relationships in Southeast Asia, within a framework of greater harmony and stability, rather than be drawn into new polarizations and relapse into new intraregional strife. In other words, their vision was to build one Southeast Asia and to try to develop intraregional relations on the basis of a set of agreed-upon conditions and modalities for mutually beneficial cooperation and common progress.

At that time, the common perception of the ASEAN member countries was that the most likely threats against their security would either take the form of internal subversion, whether or not aided and abetted by infiltration from the outside or destabilization, or would result from their being dragged once again into the conflicts and proxy wars among the major powers in the region. Of late, a third possible security threat has come to the fore — that of ASEAN countries getting embroiled in low-level yet quite destabilizing conflicts arising from overlapping sovereignty claims or unresolved maritime boundary issues, such as those involving certain areas in the South China Sea.

The ASEAN Response
to Security Threats

In the face of these perceived threats, the ASEAN countries evolved and endeavored to realize two complementary concepts, one directed internally to each of its own members, the other projected for wider regional acceptance and application.

The first is subsumed in the policy of enhancing national resilience leading toward regional resilience, which is a concept of security that goes beyond military considerations alone. It is premised on the belief that, given the nature of the perceived threats, ASEAN security for some time to come will not solely, or even primarily, be a military problem.

Therefore, apart from a basic military capacity, what is required is the development of the political, economic, and sociocultural strengths that together constitute a nation's real capacity to endure and to withstand threats to its integrity, viability, and security. That is why ASEAN countries have placed so much stress on nation-building and economic and social development—to deny subversion the troughs of poverty and social inequities that are its fertile spawning grounds. That is also why mutually beneficial socioeconomic cooperation, through ASEAN, constitutes such a vital ingredient for national and regional security.

The second concept is contained in the proposal to establish a Zone of Peace, Freedom, and Neutrality (ZOPFAN), which would encompass all states in the Southeast Asia subregion. In essence, it is a blueprint for a new framework for peace and peaceful cooperation, for greater stability and security covering the wider region of East Asia and the Pacific. It contains a set of principles and guidelines that would constitute a code of conduct governing relations of the states within the zone among themselves as well as with those outside it. It lists the measures and the voluntary restraints to be commonly agreed upon and undertaken by the zonal states as well as by the external powers, especially the major powers. Thus, it contains suggested policy guidelines and policy adjustments which, if undertaken and implemented by all sides, could reduce the need for direct military intervention by the major powers and, conversely, discourage the regional powers from again inviting or provoking unwarranted, major-power involvement in their bilateral affairs and problems. On the part of the regional countries, this will require, among other things, commensurate political determination and enhanced capacity for peaceful conflict resolution and active efforts to resolve the actual or potential conflict situations in the region, such as Cambodia, the Korean peninsula, and possibly the South China Sea. On the part of the major powers, it will require a commensurate change in their policies and perceptions of basic interests toward the regional countries and a conscious adjustment of their security doctrines and strategies. They will have to discard the bipolar adversarial relationships of the past and aim at greater stability and security within a multipolar setting of diverse security interests and concerns.

Inclusion of Major Powers

Thus, ZOPFAN is by no means designed to exclude any or all of the major powers, but precisely to keep them constructively engaged in the region. ZOPFAN is an evolutionary process. Since the concept was launched in 1972, the ASEAN states have steadily developed and elaborated on it. Its full realization has unfortunately been retarded by the outbreak and persistence of the Cambodia conflict. Nevertheless, some of its major elements have already been incorporated in the 1976 Treaty of Amity and Cooperation, to which the ASEAN countries as well as Papua New Guinea, Vietnam, and Laos have now subscribed and which remains open for accession by all other Southeast Asian states.

It is also in this context that ASEAN is working toward the establishment of a Southeast Asia nuclear-weapons-free zone (SEA-NWFZ) as an essential component of ZOPFAN. In line with the general parameters of the concept, it is envisioned that the zone would include the land areas and the maritime and air space under sovereignty of the Southeast Asian countries, the boundaries and limits of which would be determined in accordance with generally recognized principles of international law, including those of the U.N. Convention on the Law of the Sea.

None of the countries in Southeast Asia has any intention of acquiring or manufacturing nuclear weapons, all being parties to the Nuclear Nonproliferation Treaty. This common denominator augurs well for the SEA-NWFZ initiative. Such a zone is particularly desirable in this region with its long history of endemic conflict and instability.

ASEAN's proposed zone has encountered opposition from some nuclear powers that perceive it as undermining their doctrine of nuclear deterrence and as establishing an unacceptable precedent for other regions.

It is a view that we do not share. In a post–Cold War political setting, such a view has become untenable and irrelevant, particularly because in the regime envisioned for the region, transit rights will remain unaffected. Indonesia, therefore, is hopeful that the proposed Southeast Asian zone will become a reality in the near future.

Constant Consultation

In this spirit, the leaders of ASEAN, at the recent Singapore summit, issued a declaration that ASEAN will now seek to realize ZOPFAN and SEA-NWFZ in "consultation with friendly countries, taking into account changing circumstances."

On the potential conflicts in the South China Sea, ASEAN has issued a Declaration on the South China Sea that calls on all parties concerned to apply the principles contained in the Treaty of Amity and Cooperation in Southeast Asia as the basis for establishing a code of international conduct over the area. ASEAN has also decided to explore various avenues of cooperation in the South China Sea, without prejudicing the sovereignty and jurisdiction of countries interested in it. If this endeavor is successful, it could veritably transform the South China Sea from an area of potential conflict into an area of cooperation among its littoral states without in any way prejudicing their various territorial and jurisdictional claims.

The attainment of these objectives — early realization of both ZOPFAN and SEA-NWFZ combined with national reconciliation and rehabilitation in Cambodia and the successful management of potential conflict in the South China Sea — will definitely constitute a breakthrough toward a durable and stable peace in the region. We in ASEAN are therefore intensifying our consultations, not only with the regional countries but also with the major powers in order to build understanding of each other's position and eventually trust in each other's intentions.

This is the main idea and the hope behind the launching of the ASEAN Regional Forum (ARF) in Bangkok last year. The ARF is the first and only regionwide and high-level political and security consultative forum in the Asia-Pacific region. It brings together the five major powers — the United States, Russia, China, Japan, and the European Union — as well as ASEAN, Australia, Canada, New Zealand, South Korea, Laos, Vietnam, and Papua New Guinea. Discussions are informal and in a relaxed atmosphere. ASEAN has emphasized that the ARF will not become a forum modeled on the Conference for Security and Cooperation in Europe (CSCE) type; it will remain a forum for conflict prevention rather than conflict settlement.

ASEAN Economic Cooperation

True to its advocacy for national and regional resilience based on stability, economic growth, and the equitable distribution of the fruits of economic growth, ASEAN has in more recent times begun to pay closer attention to the need for cooperation in all fields, especially sustained economic cooperation, not only within the organization but also with other regions and with nonregional economic partners.

It is heartening to note that ASEAN nations, individually and as a group, are moving from a position of economic weakness and dependence to positions of greater economic strength and independence. ASEAN countries have managed to sustain growth in spite of market constraints, historically low primary commodity prices, mounting external debt burdens, and diminishing financial flows for development. This growth can be sustained if the ASEAN countries manage to broaden and intensify economic cooperation with various bilateral and multilateral dialogue partners as well as international organizations, but first and primarily among themselves. It was in this spirit that the fourth ASEAN summit established the ASEAN Free Trade Area (AFTA), which is targeted for implementation in ten years through the Common Effective Preferential Tariff (CEPT) scheme, proposed by Indonesia. The CEPT scheme will enlarge and integrate the ASEAN market, allow ASEAN businesses to capitalize on comparative advantages, achieve economies of scale, and ensure that their economies remain competitive. With CEPT in place, then AFTA would be able to develop into an instrument for the enhancement and invigoration of intra-ASEAN economic cooperation.

Having become one of the most effective and successful subregional organizations in the world, ASEAN has confidently begun to enlarge its membership, with Vietnam becoming its seventh member in July 1995. Both Laos and Cambodia have expressed strong interest in joining ASEAN in the near future. Laos has been an observer country since 1992, as Cambodia will be in July 1995. Expansion of ASEAN to eventually include all Southeast Asian countries will no doubt strengthen the organization and boost regional resilience.

It should be emphasized, however, that ASEAN will never be an inward-looking organization. As a matter of fact, the pattern of its internal cooperation could well be applied to its relationships with other regions and other countries. For example, it is Indonesia's sincere belief that ASEAN, which now occupies a vanguard position in the developing world, could serve as the engine for the acceleration of South-South cooperation. In this context, ASEAN countries could pool together their technological resources for development and offer these to the other developing countries so that more of them would be able to benefit from the Technical Cooperation among Developing Countries (TCDC) program.

The Common Resolve of Asia Pacific Economic Cooperation

The ASEAN countries also have contributions to make as dynamic economies in the most dynamic region in the world today, the Asia Pacific region. One factor that will help ensure the continued dynamism of the region is the Asia Pacific Economic Cooperation (APEC) forum, which was organized a few years ago to add impetus to the trend of trade liberalization and promote cooperation among the economies in the region. Having issued a vision statement on its goal of forming a community of Asia-Pacific economies at the first APEC Economic Leaders Meeting in Seattle in November 1993, APEC achieved another breakthrough during its second such meeting in November 1994 at Bogor, where the leaders of the eighteen member economies issued the APEC Leaders' Declaration of Common Resolve. Through this document, APEC members committed themselves to work to achieve free trade and investment liberalization in the region by the year 2020 on the part of the developing economies and by 2010 on the part of the developed economies. This will be done in a manner that will encourage trade and investment liberalization throughout the whole world in conformity with their GATT commitments.

In support of the liberalization process, APEC will expand and accelerate its trade and investment facilitation program. It therefore asked ministers and senior officials to submit proposals on APEC arrangements regarding customs, standards, investment principles, and administrative barriers to market access. They also agreed to continue consultations on economic growth strategies, regional capital flows, and other macroeconomic issues. By thus intensifying development cooperation, APEC hopes to develop more effectively the human and natural resources of the region to attain sustainable growth and equitable development of the member economies while reducing economic disparities among them.

This means an expansion of such human resources development efforts as education and training and the improvement of management and technical skills, the development of APEC study centers, and cooperation in science and technology, including technology transfer. These will be complemented with efforts aimed at promoting small- and medium-scale enterprises as well as improving such economic infrastructure as energy, transportation, information, telecommunication, and tourism. There will also be cooperation in environmental efforts.

In recognition of the contributions of the business sector in the economic growth of the region, the APEC leaders decided to integrate the business sector in its programs. And in recognition of the contributions of the Eminent Persons Group and the Pacific Business Forum in the articulation of issues that APEC must address, APEC leaders asked their ministers and officials to seriously consider the recommendations of the two groups. The APEC leaders then asked the two groups to continue to provide APEC with assessments of its progress and further recommendations to step up cooperation, to review the interrelationships between APEC and existing subregional arrangements, and to examine options for harmonizing these arrangements with APEC.

Indonesia is indeed honored to have been the host of the APEC Economic Leaders Meeting in which these far-reaching decisions were made. We are deeply pleased that the Bogor Declaration faithfully reflects Indonesia's philosophy of development as embodied in these words: "The approach will be coherent and comprehensive, embracing the three pillars: sustainable growth, equitable development and national stability." It also reflects Indonesia's philosophy of cooperation: ". . . as we approach the 21st century, APEC needs to reinforce economic cooperation in the Asia-Pacific region on the basis of equal partnership, shared responsibility, mutual respect, common interest and common benefit." Those are the very principles on which Indonesia has based its relationship with all other nations.

An Optimistic Outlook

More than any other group of economies in the world, the APEC members, including Indonesia, have reason to be optimistic about the new liberalizing trends on the economic horizon. But we must never lose sight of the tremendous diversity of our cultures and sociopolitical systems as well as in the stages of our development. For although this diversity could be the source of our unique collective strength, it is also a weight that constrains us in all our activities to make haste deliberately — lest we stumble into a situation of unequal competition and its attendant friction and tensions. In this context, APEC must not dilute the identity or restrict the role of the existing regional cooperative groupings in this region; on the contrary, it should go hand in hand with the activities of these regional cooperative forums. I sincerely believe that a stronger and more prosperous ASEAN and a functional East Asia Economic Caucus (EAEC) will strengthen APEC even further.

Indeed, we believe that the various forums in which Indonesia has been privileged to participate have all contributed substantially to allaying much of the disorder that now exists in the post–Cold War era. Indonesia will thus remain committed to a policy of cooperation with all like-minded partners, bilaterally as well as in the multilateral forums, which include the United Nations and its organs, the Nonaligned Movement, ASEAN, and APEC. Indeed, Indonesia is eager to work with all groups and institutions, both public and private, that share our core values in fashioning improved arrangements for international governance. In this post–Cold War era, the world is changing so swiftly that it has been said that the future has encroached on the present and developments have thus become increasingly unpredictable. But by working constructively with all actors on the international stage, with positive concerns for humanity and the planet it inhabits, we can help manage these changes so that within our time we may he able to develop adequate mechanisms for global governance and thus come closer to the world of greater peace, justice, and shared prosperity that the Indonesian people envisioned in our 1945 constitution.

The Honorable

Dr. Osama El-Baz

Director for Political Affairs,
Office of the President of Egypt

The Third World and the Post–Cold War Order

*Challenges and
Contributions*

The last decade of the twentieth century raised hopes for a new era in international politics. The legacy of the great success of the last ninety years in political, economic, and technological spheres, combined with dramatic failure in the issues of peace and war, taught the world community a lesson. The spirit of reconciliation and partnership building between East and West and North and South is inevitable. Our concepts and conduct in international affairs will be different. The great powers have moved away from the tension of conflict that has resulted in two major wars and a protracted Cold War into an era of partnership. The path of Third World countries in that difficult century has been mostly positive. The era of liberation has led to another era of pragmatic development and a quest for a North-South partnership.

The spirit that helped the United States rebuild after the Civil War of the last century, "malice toward none and charity for all," as Abraham Lincoln put it, should guide policies of the great powers and the developing countries alike.

In the 1990s, claims of the eventual marginalization of the Third World faded away. The new map of world economy shows great success in some countries of what used to be called the Third World. The industrial complex of the world is no longer limited to the West. The East Asian Tigers are competing effectively with Europe and the United States.

On the other hand, political accomplishment was more of a mixed bag. Certain spots of tension that suffered from turmoil during the Cold War moved toward settlement. Yet ethnic, racial, and other types of conflicts are tearing other countries apart.

But the 1990s confronted the Third World with three fundamental challenges that will heavily influence its future course.

The first is redefinition of its world political role in view of the radical changes in world politics following the end of the Cold War, the changing code of conduct, and the impact of new telecommunications and transportation technologies, which turned the world into a small village.

The second is the impact of the parallel trends toward regionalism and globalism. On the one hand, major trading blocs are being formed in Europe, North America, and East Asia. On the other hand, a vigorous new drive has been ushered toward the liberalization of international trade by the establishment of the World Trade Organization. Regionalism will have an impact on political, economic, and cultural spheres. The prospect of the exclusion of some parts of the Third World from these new regional blocs poses a serious challenge to the globalization trend.

The third is the challenge of cross-cultural understanding. It remains to be seen whether the future will be one of repeated clashes based on cultural differences and prejudices, or an era of a new human culture based on "unity in diversity" and tolerance — whether culture is destiny or whether human ability to absorb inventions and to live beyond cultural boundaries will prevail.

These three challenges will define the future course of the Third World in issues of security, economic development, and cooperation.

As the century draws to a close, the World Community faces a complex challenge; two competing trends are pulling the international system in opposing directions. At a time when the world is becoming increasingly integrated and globalized through unprecedented advances in telecommunications and transportation, the threat of fragmentation and discord, fueled by ethnic, religious, or social differences, lingers on in some corners. The spirit of reconciliation and interdependence has been threatened by attempts to fuel new clashes or resurrect old ones based on culture, religion, or civilization.

But the prophecy of disorder and anarchy is not inevitable. On the contrary, a new sense of shared destiny and collective responsibility has emerged. The end of the Cold War has led to the revival of the concept of East-West partnership. Old rivals are now becoming partners in security and trade. Political realism and reconciliation have come to dominate two major areas that have suffered from protracted conflict: the Middle East and South Africa. The new trend of international cooperation has raised expectations. The world is on the verge of realizing an era of reconciliation in which nations act in good faith toward fostering peace, security, and stability on the regional and global levels.

The new world order needs something more than good intentions and well-wishing; it needs a more concerted effort to promote and enhance global partnership throughout the entire world community. It also requires a universal commitment to the legitimate, time-honored aspirations of the entire human race. The haves and the have-nots should work together to realize collective security and global economic growth without compromising the noble values of tolerance and mutual understanding among all human cultures.

The quest for East-West partnership has altered the norms, concepts, and mechanisms of international relations. Enlargement of the franchise to encompass developing countries will have great impact on the world system and will diminish any probable misperceptions that may arise from replacing the East-West dichotomy with North-South relations. This need not be. The world community should look toward cases of international cooperation as harbingers for the future.

Building a North-South partnership to deal with problems of international security and to seize opportunities created by increasing globalization and interdependence is the new real challenge. On the economic front, there are parallel movements toward integration. Traditional insularity of national economies is diminishing with the reconstruction of an international economy under the World Trade Organization. However, it should also be noted that the simultaneous development of regional blocs may threaten possibilities of globalization. A world of distinct blocs would run counter to the expectations of a more integrated world economy and might possibly exclude developing countries from vital markets. Globalism and regionalism need not clash, for both can be incorporated in a worldwide partnership.

Politically, there is a growing concern over those regional conflicts that do not directly relate to the great powers' strategic interests. They may face benign neglect and apathy. A global village will not be safe if the world community fails to deal effectively with protracted regional disputes or civil conflicts. Nor will the world be safe if the commitment to curb proliferation of weapons of mass destruction is hindered by inconsistent standards or lack of resolve. This is the reason why we advocate, in both cases, a worldwide global partnership that will surely create the channels for more effective policy and stronger commitments.

Security as a Major Concern

The end of the Cold War has changed the overall view of international security. Global threats declined, but regional conflicts and fragmented societies resurfaced as the major new threat to international stability. On the three perspectives of international, regional, and national security, the Third World countries' policies will play an important role.

Global threats, in terms of potential confrontation between the two nuclear superpowers, have almost faded away, yet two problems remain of a global concern: the problem of proliferation of weapons of mass destruction and the spread of social unrest and terrorism.

Third World countries have supported the drive for the nonproliferation of weapons of mass destruction. In the Middle East, Egypt sponsored the first proposal to make the region a nuclear-free zone in 1974, reiterated by President Mubarak in 1981. Other attempts were initiated in Africa, Latin America, and East Asia. But the major issues of controversy have focused on how to avoid double standards and ensure universality. This was the core of the discussion in New York at the conference on the extension of Nonproliferation Treaty (NPT). It is also at the core of the discussion with regard to the Convention on the Prohibition of Chemical and Biological Weapons agreement. The Arab states have argued that the agreement should include Israel. It is indeed ironic that the world community exempts Israel from joining the NPT and enforces it on its neighbors. Furthermore, it will be a fundamental security dilemma for the Arab states that opted for signing the extension of the treaty. On the other hand, it was argued that NPT provisions, with regard to the responsibility of the nuclear powers, have not been fulfilled.

Terrorism has become a major concern for all countries. Cooperation in a worldwide antiterrorist campaign is acquiring wide support. But terrorism should not be isolated from the political and socioeconomic roots of conflict and social unrest. Cooperative efforts to deal with these roots, either with regard to regional or national conflicts, are needed as effective tools to curb terrorism.

Regional conflicts were prolonged and manipulated during the Cold War era. The new era requires a new outlook. It is high time we shied away from the Cold War legacy, which fomented strife as a means of superpower competition on regions of influence. Conflict-resolution mechanisms, on the international or on the regional level, should be consolidated. Both peacemaking and peacekeeping operations should be preceded by a vigorous preventive diplomacy aimed at containing disputes before they turn into full-fledged conflicts.

Conflicts in strife-torn societies have become a major concern of world security in Europe, Africa, the Middle East, Asia, and even in the Americas. The Bosnian tragedy has left an imprint on world consciousness. European passivity and U.N. inaction in the face of the ethnic-cleansing policies of the Serbian forces inflicted tremendous injustices on the Muslim community in Bosnia.

Equally disturbing was world passivity toward the tragic developments in Rwanda, Somalia, and Liberia. There is an urgent need for consolidating international and regional mechanisms to prevent the recurrence of such tragic events. There is also a need for a new approach to settle these conflicts, one that will not result in winners and losers but that creates a basis for a lasting equilibrium of interests and rights among the communities involved.

The current security environment is new and full of uncertainties. As Americans debate their future course of action, isolationists argue with interventionists, advocates of multilateralism argue with unilateralists, the world community debates the real meaning of national security and sovereignty — all in the new era of interdependence. Security is no longer a military problem alone, but a synthesis of military, economic, technological, and social strength. On the other hand, there are those in the Third World who fear that the arms race will recede in the North but be diverted to the South. Great powers are still seeking new outlets for their military hardware. Regional conflicts are still perceived as an arena of balance of power.

The new era should emphasize political settlements through conflict resolution rather than pure power calculation.

Multilateralism, based on a more democratic international decision-making process, should be the norm. The U.N. role should be enhanced. The decision-making process in the Security Council should be democratized. Wider participation in the process, one including nonpermanent members, should be the basis for any future action. Expansion of the Security Council, with permanent and nonpermanent membership, should be seriously considered to make the council more representative of the international community.

But until such expansion takes place, the Security Council should adhere to the spirit of the U.N. Charter, which provides for a wider informal consultation among the member states and a sense of international responsibility among the permanent members. That would consolidate the credibility and legitimacy of U.N. actions in both peacemaking and peacekeeping.

The new security environment makes it inevitable for all countries to reach out for a new code of ethics for international action, one that should reflect the traumatic experience of the twentieth century and the quest for peace and stability that it inspires. Arms trade, arms proliferation, and manipulation of regional conflicts are not only counterproductive in the long run but also detrimental to international peace and stability. But to deal effectively with these issues, a sense of justice and a commitment to principles of equality and fairness should prevail.

A North-South partnership would allow for a more effective management of the problems of peace and war in the twenty-first century.

The Dilemma of Development

In the 1960s, development experts were arguing that the only process of development will be a repetition of the process of industrialization in the western world. Thirty years later, these same experts argue that each country might establish a unique model of development. Several countries that were considered to be among the Third World in the 1960s achieved a gigantic jump in higher levels of economic growth. Models of growth in South Korea, Malaysia, Indonesia, Singapore, and Thailand are being studied by experts everywhere. They became a subject of research by the World Bank and the International Monetary Fund and are always seen as good examples to be followed by the developing countries. The old perception of an East-West balance of power that prevailed during the era of the Cold War has been replaced by a new perception of two competing industrial complexes, one in the West and the other emerging in the East.

Other areas have not fared badly. In the Middle East, West Asia, India, or Latin America other cases of success have emerged. Turkey, India, Pakistan, Brazil, and Chile are moving along this road. Even the countries that faced enormous political and economic pressures as a result of protracted wars and tremendous population growth have maintained a high level of economic growth, which enabled them to reduce the negative impact of population growth. Egypt is a case in point. Whereas population has doubled over the last three decades and the protracted Middle East conflict absorbed a sizable sum of its resources, Egypt was able to maintain its standard of living and to reform its economy to be ready for a takeoff similar to the Asian model. Other countries in the Arab world — Syria, Jordan, Morocco, and Tunisia — are also good examples.

Against these optimistic and promising cases, other parts of the Third World have not fared so well. Africa suffered heavily in the last three decades, which witnessed declining prices of raw materials, capital outflows, and a crippling burden of debt servicing. The standard of living has greatly declined. The dilemma of development confronting the developing countries, those which fared well and those which did not, is manifested in a number of difficult choices.

First, there is the problem of crafting a balanced policy of economic reform toward a market economy without sacrificing the requirements for social stability. Most of these countries followed a centrally planned economic system, which guaranteed a certain minimum of standard of living for the low-income classes — the majority. A market economy will have to remove these subsidies and other mechanisms that were built for this purpose and replace them with a more efficient, market-oriented allocation of resources. A sudden shift might lead to social upheaval. The search for the right mix has been a subject of intense debate between Third World reformers and experts from the World Bank and International Monetary Fund. There is a need to reach a better understanding between both sides to facilitate transition toward a market economy through structural adjustment programs with a human face.

Second, liberalization of international trade means opening the market of Third World countries to industrial goods and services from developed economies. In some cases, it will be detrimental to the national industries. On the other hand, protectionist policies have not led to the growth of these industries toward producing high-quality, competition-oriented products. It only led to supporting an undeveloping industry in closed markets. The delicate balance between the necessity of liberalizing trade and protecting national industries needs further careful consideration in view of the fact that some experts argue that governments in the industrial economies continually reorganize their markets to protect their industries.

Third, the old concept of development has encouraged the overpopulated countries to encourage labor-intensive projects, but the last decade proved that the East Asian economies have achieved a major jump through a policy that focused on few capital-intensive, export-oriented industries. How to find the right mix is still an issue of debate.

Fourth, it has become clear in the last three decades that investments in human resources—in education, health, and training—is basic to economic development. The question is how the developing countries would achieve the right policy in this fundamental area of development. The dilemma of development has both domestic and external dimensions. True, developing countries need to adopt the right policies, move along the right course, and make difficult choices. But the international economic environment should also be adjusted to be friendly to the developing countries. This could be achieved by building a North-South partnership for peace and development.

North-South Partnership

Over the last four decades, the demarcating line between the North and the South has changed. New political borders, integrated economic communities, and the emergence of new industrial centers have created new political and economic maps. These major developments have led both the North and South to reconsider their goals and policies. Whereas the North has been preoccupied with the problems of integrating Eastern Europe and Russia into the international economy and the European security system, the South has been reevaluating its strategies and future role in the emerging world order. Both have been moving toward a new concept of legitimacy and order to replace old concepts that prevailed during the Cold War.

The Nonaligned Movement remains the main umbrella for most of the developing world. The movement's Ministerial Meeting in Cairo in

1994 emphasized North-South partnership. The meeting reiterated the movement's commitment to international peace and stability, arms control, international cooperation for economic development, respect for human rights, and coexistence among different cultures and societies. It emphasized the need to promote an equitable international political and economic order, to ensure equal opportunity for developing countries to partake in the world market and to have a fair share in managing global affairs. In an unprecedented meeting of the Mediterranean community, proposed by Egypt and sponsored by ten major countries, the agendas of both North and South were presented. Concerns about security, immigration, political instability, and environmental degradation in the North were integrated with the South's concerns about economic development and growth, regional security, and cooperation in technology and scientific research. The meeting proved that a unified agenda could be worked out to build a new North-South partnership.

With regard to security, the new partnership must enhance the ability of the world community to address the two major threats to international stability: namely, regional disputes and proliferation of weapons of mass destruction.

In the post–Cold War era, regional disputes and civil disorders have become primary causes of instability. A major obstacle to international efforts in such cases has been the moral dilemma, which has been burdened by double standards in international action. International reluctance about Bosnia, Somalia, or Rwanda contrasts poorly with the quick action taken when strategic interests of the great powers were threatened. A more effective policy to address these conflicts will have to establish a code of conduct according to the U.N. Charter, allow for more participation of developing countries in the decision-making process, and emphasize the role of regional mechanisms for conflict resolution, in collaboration with the United Nations. Egypt has advocated these ideas and has taken an active role in U.N. efforts to address these conflicts, including sending troops to serve as part of U.N. peacekeeping forces.

A second threat to international security is the proliferation of weapons of mass destruction. The debate about the extension of the Nuclear Nonproliferation Treaty (NPT) and the ratification of the treaty on chemical and biological weapons reveals profound differences in perceptions and concerns between the North and the South. Whereas the North has been primarily concerned with threats of proliferation, the South, on the other hand, has been preoccupied with concerns about the transfer of peaceful nuclear technology and about the possibility of unequal treatment of non-nuclear states. A new agenda that combines both concerns will facilitate the establishment of legitimate new rules of conduct in this area. The new agenda must take into consideration the concerns expressed by the South regarding an imposition of inconsistent standards when dealing with nuclear proliferation, as well as the use of nonproliferation policies as a pretext for impeding economic and technological development of the South by imposing arbitrary restrictions on the transfer of technology and chemical materials. To build a solid North-South partnership that supports nonproliferation, these concerns have to be seriously addressed. In addition, the new arms control system has to include guarantees against the use or threat of use of nuclear weapons as well as all weapons of mass destruction.

Cooperation for development and economic growth is the core of the new international partnership. The trend toward economic liberalization and the successful conclusion of the Uruguay Round of the GATT creates a climate suitable for expansion of international trade and economic cooperation. However, several problems characterize this global trend.

The opportunities offered by the globalization of the economy are threatened by a rising trend toward regionalism, particularly as manifested by the establishment of regional economic blocs. A world of distinct blocs stimulates fears in developing countries and emerging states of the former socialist bloc that they will be excluded from, or frozen out of, international economic markets.

The widening gap between the developed and the developing countries also overshadows world economic performance. Various negative factors hinder development in the latter, such as declining commodity prices in real terms, the lack of capital flows, the slow transfer of technology, restrictive business practices in some industrialized countries, and new forms of exclusion under different pretexts. Foreign debt has haunted developing countries for more than two decades and needs effective and practical solutions. Meaningful debt relief would entail the reduction of this financial burden, with proportional sharing of losses among all creditors. Undoubtedly, economic progress and growth in industrialized countries will be augmented by increasing growth in developing countries. Industrialized countries should seriously consider greater partnerships with developing states. A global package, based on mutual interests, may be reached.

From Regionalism to Globalism

As the twenty-first century approaches, the pulse of the planet and the pace of change in the world have accelerated. Moral and power calculations point to the need to rebuild a global partnership that transcends national and regional boundaries to embrace all cultures and societies. The spirit of reconciliation that has changed the regional landscape in the Middle East, Europe, and South Africa should be extended to the global level.

On the global level, the United Nations has recaptured its vigorous spirit as originally prescribed in its charter. Apart from its political role, it has adopted a new function — to assist in development and build international consensus in dealing with global concerns, such as the environment, population growth, and social development. The International Conference on Population and Development, held in Cairo in September 1994, reflected this spirit. The heated debate between the Group of 77, the European Union, the Vatican, the Islamic World, the Chinese, and the Indians struck at the heart of cultural values in industrialized and developing countries. It also reflected diverse views and concepts on security, sovereignty, and development. President Mubarak's opening speech called for making the conference a point of convergence and reconciliation, between people and the environment and among cultures, religions, and civilizations, by avoiding dogmatism and fanaticism and exploring common ground and shared interests. The meeting not only offered glimpses of a new era of North-South partnership; it also mirrored the world community's quest for a new social and political order based on a shared code of behavior, norms, and values. The twenty-first century will not be a repetition of the past. The logic of interdependence and globalization will make it impossible to build new walls between economies. Even in the era of the Cold War, convergence and interdependence were growing despite ideological antagonism.

The Cairo conference revealed the difficulty of building partnerships as a result of changing perceptions, attitudes, and norms of conduct. It also underscored the benefits of cooperation in addressing global problems and paved the way for addressing central issues of security and development through a North-South coalition. The North-South discord will have a hazardous impact on weapons proliferation as well as on the global effort to halt environmental degradation.

The spirit of global partnership will help amass the political will, energy, and resources to address issues of security and development and to establish new rules of conduct. Democratization of the international system and global cooperation should be the main pillars of the new order. Linkages among regional communities should be a priority on the international agenda. First, North-South consultation and cooperation should be developed by conjoining the Group of 77, representing the South, and the Group of Seven, representing the North. Second, there should be linkages and consultations among the other regional communities in Latin America, Africa, and Asia.

There is also a need to strengthen the role of regional organizations in conflict resolution and economic cooperation. Thus, the world community should strengthen the Organization of African Unity (OAU), the Arab League, the Association of Southeast Asian Nations (ASEAN), and the Organization of American States (OAS). The success of these organizations in creating effective mechanisms for conflict resolution and in facilitating economic cooperation among their respective numbers and between their respective members and other regional groups will provide great support to the emerging world order.

The United Nations remains the primary focus of the new partnership. Informal mechanisms for coordination between the developed North and the developing South will reinforce the role and functions of the United Nations. Still, the United Nations needs to adjust to new trends and realities on the world scene, such as the increasing significance of the North-South partnership and the growth of regional cooperation.

In response to the new configuration in world polities, the structure and focus of the United Nations should be reconsidered. Reform of U.N. organizational performance and introduction of new ideas should be a continual process. U.N. policies should reflect the significance of the issues of the South. The Security Council should be expanded to allow for the participation of major geographical regions in the South. Overrepresentation of some regions on the council reflects an imbalance that could be addressed easily by its expanding membership. Incorporating new member states from Africa, Asia, and Latin America would greatly enhance the legitimacy of the Security Council's resolutions. The same principles of equitable representation of the South and transparency in decision making should guide reforms in the specialized agencies of the United Nations as well.

The Middle East as a Mirror

The Middle East ushered in the spirit of reconciliation long before the end of the Cold War. Egypt's peace initiatives in 1970 and Sadat's visit to Jerusalem in 1977 were turning points in the region's history. But the peace process has been derailed by failure to move forward on the Palestinian track after the Oslo Agreement and on the Syrian and Lebanese tracks thereafter. Comprehensive peace will usher in a new era in the Middle East. The real challenge, however, remains how to build a genuine and durable peace in the region.

Societies do not change overnight. Peaceful relations among nations are not just a result of agreements signed by leaders. Attitudes and perceptions must change in order to facilitate social and cultural reconciliation. To succeed, peace has to be based on principles of fairness and justice, and should reflect conceptual changes in national interest and security needs among the countries of the region. Egypt has emphasized the need for a new concept of regional security, based on mutual commitment and the development of common interests. These principles gained wide regional and international recognition and support.

The Middle East's transformation bears many similarities to the reconstruction of Europe after World War II. The same principles that allowed Europe to move from conflict to cooperation should be applied. Gradual transformation will establish solid grounds for regional cooperation. The region is predisposed for change, but it relies on the regional parties involved to make such change a successful experiment in building a regional order, setting new precedents for cooperation in the twenty-first century.

The new structure should be built on geopolitical, cultural, and national realities. Arab-Israeli reconciliation and the trend toward global cooperation are two major new factors. Thus, the new structure should be two-layered. The first layer is an Arab regional system comprising the Arab states and based on several institutional links. The second is a new regional system that would allow for coordination and cooperation among Arab states and their neighbors such as Israel, Turkey, and potentially Iran. At both levels, principles of fairness, mutual respect for sovereignty, and even distribution of the benefits of regional cooperation will guarantee the smooth transition into a new era.

Equally important is the steering of the right course between regionalism, as shown by building mechanisms for cooperation among Middle

Eastern countries, and globalism, which underscores the necessity of integration into the international system.

Collective security is central to the evolution of a new regional order. Egypt has advocated a new concept of security that is more conducive to regional stability and global peace. The new concept defines security not simply in military terms, but as the integration of multiple economic, technological, and cultural strengths and as the result of enlarging the scope of common interests among the parties concerned. Technological advances have made former perceptions of security obsolete. The occupation of territories or the suppression of peoples can never guarantee security in an era of missile technology and in the face of the current commonality of low-intensity conflicts that only drain the energy of opponents.

The underlying thrust of the new arrangement for regional security emphasizes cultivation of common interests, as opposed to increasing defense budgets. Cultivation of collective interests will generate a network among regional parties that will establish a solid framework for security. A high level of security can be achieved by reducing militarization trends and developing a regional security system. This regional system will include mechanisms for arms control, internal and external monitoring of military activities, and early-warning systems. It also has to adhere to the principles of transparency and regional consultation. The European experience during and after the Cold War in establishing regional security arrangements could serve as a model for a Middle Eastern plan. With appropriate adjustments, schemes such as the European Conference on Security and Cooperation could be examined and utilized.

However, an essential principle of regional security is parity of obligations and commitment to arms control. Inequality on either part will lead to implicit, or even explicit, arms stockpiling and renewed problems of security. Regional security cannot be safeguarded without addressing the problem of nuclear proliferation and the concurrent acquisition of alternative weapons of mass destruction.

Egypt has advocated the creation of a Middle East nuclear-free zone since 1974. Similarly, President Mubarak proposed in April 1990 establishment of a regional zone free from weapons of mass destruction. Egypt has also signed and ratified the NPT, which Israel, a nuclear threshold state, refused to sign. The Israeli position subsequently influenced Egypt's and other Arab states' decision not to sign an international treaty on chemical and biological weapons, pending a resolution of the NPT impasse. Regional security will be possible only when all states agree to equitable terms of arms control and arms reduction. Making the region free from weapons of mass destruction will promote the nonproliferation movement and consolidate the quest for international stability.

Economic cooperation is another element that will change the regional landscape. Between the expectations of regional integration and the legacy of discord and conflict, realistic grounds for regional cooperation should be established and expanded gradually. Already multilateral talks have examined areas of trade, industry, tourism, and the environment. The potential for cooperation is undeniable, although regional integration has never been an easy task. Concerns about uneven distribution of benefits sharpen the elements of discord. Adherence to principles of fairness and equality is central to the success of the current efforts.

On the one hand, concerns about possible effects of uneven economic development and unequal benefits in trade, investment, and technology that might arise between Arab states and Israel should be eliminated through cooperative regulations. On the other, industrial and technological progress should not be monopolized by one party, and multiple centers of technological capabilities must be developed to initiate cooperation among equals. The liberalization of trade should be in accordance with the requirements of national development policies in each country, in agreement with the rules of the World Trade Organization.

Toward Global Partnership

Fifty years after the end of World War II, the world finds itself in a different postwar era — one in which it is again presented with the opportunity to remodel the international system. The stakes, as before, are high and now, as ever, the forces of division, fragmentation, and tension must be overcome. The spirit of reconciliation that was ushered in at the end of the Cold War and that has manifested itself in the move toward peace in the Middle East and South Africa, toward partnership in Europe, and toward the extension of the NPT must now be translated into a global partnership. This is the responsibility of great powers and developing nations alike. The quest for a new code of conduct in international policies must reflect the great experiences of the world community in building peace after several debacles and wars in the last century. It must also reflect the new concepts of international security and development.

The core of the new partnership should be the quest for a new universal culture, based on diversity, where dialogue among western, Islamic, Chinese, or Indian civilizations will enhance humanity's understanding of its historical role. Building a partnership means changing perceptions and attitudes, integrating the agenda of the parties concerned, and developing a unified stand toward collective concerns in security, development, and global issues. It means reconciliation between man and the environment, between domestic aspirations and the requirements for regional order, between regional integration and global cooperation.

Part 6

Ideology in the
Post–Cold War Order

His Excellency

Eduardo Frei Ruiz-Tagle

President of the Republic of Chile

Liberty and Solidarity

Post–Cold War Challenges to Democracy

Introduction

I am writing this article from the perspective of Chile, an emerging nation seeking to participate actively in this new stage of human society.

In spite of our extreme southern location on the planet, we were not spared the effects of the Cold War, which engulfed the globe. Chile, in fact, was for some years one of the scenes of the dispute over hegemony between the great powers. This ideological confrontation divided the world into two opposing blocs, introducing dogmatism, polarization, and violence never before known to our political life.

Thus, for example, when an attempt was made to construct "the Chilean road to socialism," a socialist system within a democratic framework, the project's success or failure acquired an importance that went far beyond our frontiers. Politics in Chile came to be considered a decisive field of battle in the world political struggle; overtly or covertly, the great powers attempted to influence the development of domestic events. This extreme ideological dogmatism drowned our democratic traditions and suffocated our democracy, rendering it incapable of resolving the irreconcilable differences between the two sides with the proper instruments of the state of law, which finally resulted in a forceful outcome in 1973.

No wonder, then, that when the authoritarian regime came to power, its rhetoric proclaimed victory over international communism. The country, meanwhile, began to undergo the difficult practical consequences of the doctrine of "national security." Once again, an ideological construction, a product of the Cold War born in a distant land, became a frame of reference and an inspiration for those holding power.

But just as the most acute phases of the Cold War directly influenced our historical process, the years of relaxed tensions, particularly during the second half of the 1980s, were also accompanied in our country by a search for agreement among the forces of democracy. The 1980s were the years of gestation for decisive political alliances and instruments to articulate a peaceful strategy directed to the recovery of a state of law.

As the chain of events culminated in the fall of the Berlin Wall, symbol par excellence of the radical schism between East and West, Chileans reopened the road to democracy in December 1989. A president of the Republic was chosen in the first free, secret, and informed elections since 1970. As the world celebrated the end of a division that could have led to nuclear holocaust and as a period of peace and cooperation was inaugurated, the recovery of Chilean republican traditions began and prospects of reconciliation took on a certain reality.

In recent years our country has been able to live together harmoniously, on a foundation of economic, political, and social stability. We have been a part of the conflicts of humanity, but we also hope to contribute to the realization of humanity's greatest aspirations. The new world evolving affects us, and we want, on our modest scale, to contribute to giving it a positive outlook.

Security in the Framework of Relaxed Tensions

Perhaps the most evident manifestation of the new conditions is the transformation of the classic concept of security. That concept was the defining characteristic of the Cold War. The strategies of confrontation, negotiation, and the balance of power among the nations in contention were based on or revolved around security.

Now that we have left behind us the danger of a global nuclear conflict between states, the most notorious and obvious conditions of insecurity affecting communities, families, and individuals come again to the fore. The principal factors impacting the security of people today are unemployment, hunger, poverty, neglect, crime, and discrimination based on class, sex, religion, culture, and race. It is no longer possible to suppress these factors by invoking the pretext of external threat. People demand inclusion in a development process that allows equality of opportunity, and they ask that mutual progress ensure growing degrees of security for everyone. Today's societies know that social polarization becomes their principal source of uncertainty.

The world economy, too, recognizes that fact. Today we know that there are no stable investments in unstable societies and that economic security does not prosper in the midst of human insecurity. On the contrary, it becomes more and more obvious that one of the principal sources of future growth and development will be the incorporation, in all countries, of those excluded today from the worldwide productive system now under construction.

Processes now under way in the globalization and internationalization of the contemporary world have caused the emergence of a new set of security-related problems, which may only be addressed by joint international action. Such problems include the corrosive influence of drug production and consumption; the corruptive effect of the enormous volumes of money thus diverted; degradation of the environment, ranging from its global impact on the ozone layer to its local impact on the health of children and senior citizens; and the great international migratory flows resulting from insecurity in the countries of origin.

Such phenomena as the production, transportation, and storage of nuclear products and waste, the expansion of international terrorism, and the growth of such transmissible diseases as AIDS spread fear and concern that go beyond borders and affect relations among states.

We realize then that the nucleus of concerns of the Cold War agenda has been transformed and completely overcome by a new reality.

An Opportunity for Humanity

A broad framework of opportunities for the entire world and, of course, for the renascent democracy of Chile has been inaugurated. Released from the heavy clouds of ideological confrontation, we can look upon reality in a new way, discovering not only the new tendencies that determine tomorrow's world but the serious and urgent problems we must resolve. We can affirm our hope and faith in the possibility of a new international order which satisfies the requirements of all peoples, races, and nations.

This new scenario represents a particular challenge for the humanists of all religions and creeds. It obliges us to assume new outlooks in a calm and sober manner. We cannot fall into blind optimism, believing ingenuously that the spontaneous development of existing tendencies will suffice for a positive future. Neither can we be discouraged by the acute problems we see today more clearly than ever within our own societies.

What are the principal positive aspects of our new situation? The most relevant is that the peoples of the world have more freedom today to seek their own path to development. The broad and simultaneous upsurge in value of political and economic liberties, in conjunction with a strong globalization of different spheres of activity, opens more possibilities for every community to seek its own well-being on its own terms.

These positive aspects cannot be taken as a given reality for now and forever. They simply form a framework of opportunities that we, as humanists, must seize upon to construct a hopeful future. As political leaders we must learn the lessons of the Cold War and, on the basis of a common ethical framework, dedicate ourselves to a new schedule of work and struggle for a more just, free, and democratic world order.

The Value of Democracy and Human Rights

In various regions of the world, but particularly in Latin America and in Chile, we have learned a basic lesson through sacrifice and pain: the individual is above any ideology, and no citizen may be sacrificed to a theoretical concept of society and the economy.

It appears that the brutality and totalitarian genocide of World War II were not enough to seat that conviction firmly in the heart of our societies. In many countries of the world, it was still necessary to experience mass political assassinations, indiscriminate torture, and the disappearance of individuals for us to recognize the definitive value of a thoroughgoing respect for human life. As the century draws to a close, however, democracy and the primacy of human rights appear to have become inextricably linked in the universal conscience.

In the past, some neglected the formal requirements of democracy as a political regime. Experience, however, has shown that a breakdown in the state of law leaves the citizen defenseless. The essence of democracy consists of the separation of powers, checks and balances, adequate representation of the interests of the majority and of the minority, and free and periodic elections, all of which constitute the individual's first layer of protection. Today there is a broad consensus with regard to the value assigned to political liberties as the essential basis for consolidating and broadening human rights in the social and economic spheres.

Just as fissures in authoritarianism call for commitment, speaking out, and heroism, normality is an invitation to work unceasingly on the dissemination and promotion of respect for the human individual in the daily life of our peoples. Today we are more conscious of the fact that it is always possible to achieve more and better democracy and that its consolidation is a long process of perseverance that allows neither passivity nor indolence.

This fact implies that we must be alert to new requirements. The citizen of the post–Cold War world has many faces: the woman who seeks to legitimize her own sphere of existence and action, the senior citizen who demands his dignity, the children who demand a childhood without abuse and exploitation, various minorities that require space for diversity, and communities that seek to protect their environment.

This quiet work within each people must ensure respect in the heart of the culture of the future as a basic reflex that responds quickly to needs threatening the dignity of individuals and stimulates the expression of true civic virtues.

Along those lines, we value the fact that the task of limiting power vis-à-vis recognition of the value of the dignity of the human individual has been extended to the international sphere, particularly since the end of World War II. Testimony to that fact are the Universal Declaration of Human Rights (in the preparation of which Chile participated actively in the United Nations in the period 1946–1948), the Civil and Political Rights Treaties, the Economic, Social, and Cultural Rights Treaties, and a number of treaties establishing specific rights. Now that the Cold War is over, the fact that no state which violates any of these pacts can invoke ideological considerations to justify its actions is a big step forward.

The nations are no longer isolated entities but integral parts of the international community. To maintain that community they must put into practice a set of essential values, central to which is respect for the human individual. This ongoing task within each nation and in the world community will validate democracy and allow no corner of the planet to exist in which human dignity can be ignored.

A New Political Style

Today we note a certain perplexity in the political elites of various regions. This new phenomenon is very understandable. Politics has lost its heroic, messianic quality. Furthermore, social life is no longer ruled by the iron hand of political logic. Thus the voices of culture, science, and technology speak out more boldly. Nation-states find themselves questioned by the emergence of ancient cultures trying to define their own space. Old problems reappear with new vigor, new problems demand attention, and there are no old recipes or solutions for them. People are more centered on their own daily lives and on improving the quality of their lives. National problems, moreover, become more obvious and demand effective solutions.

The meaning itself of collective action has vanished. There is no longer an enemy to be overthrown or at least impeded in its strategic advance. How can the vacuum of a life without enemies be structured? For some, the solution is to invent a new enemy: a religion, a neighbor country, perhaps the nation itself. Others fall into apathy and criticize politics, already incapable of mobilizing the community in a great crusade to conquer evil. Faced with this new reality, to what end must we work?

The present moment requires our generation to hold and nurture the torch of liberty and pass it on to the next generation, bright enough to illuminate those corners which, until now, have been dark. Democracy has already perfected its quantitative principle as expressed in majority rule. In coming years democracy must find criteria to measure its own quality.

While parties may be of the most different types and characteristics, in all systems they require cohesion and coherence to facilitate citizen representation and participation. Parties are now subjected to demanding challenges. Ideological rhetoric and simplistic solutions are no longer sufficient for a political offering. Each party must demonstrate that it has a positive plan that articulates values and responses to multifaceted national realities. It must modernize its organization and function to adequately process new concerns ranging from the purely local and regional, usually quite concrete in nature, to those expressed in debates on ethics, such as concerns related to the value of human life in its various stages. Political organizations are also subject to tensions in the search for their own identity in a framework where political differences are not as great as before. These are some of the tasks they must resolve successfully to recreate politics in an inescapable period of demanding adaptations.

Participation, moreover, has become decisive in democracy. We need societies that are active and vital, masters of their own destiny, capable of changing their manner of reacting to ever-changing challenges. This means that citizens must not only perceive and defend their inalienable rights; they must also know and perform their inherent responsibilities.

Various intellectuals and statesmen have called for a charter outlining citizen duties. Such a statement becomes an urgent necessity in the contemporary world, particularly for those countries that have given short shrift to the development of civil society as the result of collective totalitarianism or the enshrinement of selfishness. I should like to mention just two fundamental citizen duties: respect for the hierarchy of talent, merit, and heroism, and a responsibility to the culture linking us inescapably to our concerns, whether they are the neighborhood, town, region, family, or work.

Citizen action is essential to strengthening civil society and making it easier for the state to dedicate itself to its unavoidable tasks.

In Latin America the lack of broader, more motivated, more intense, and longer-lasting citizen social action results in a vacuum of apathy and neglect. Small wonder, then, that antistate rhetoric is accompanied by gestures and behaviors evoking a past in which the state attempted to do everything.

In the coming years it is absolutely essential to demonstrate that strengthening civil society can mean greater social solidarity and cohesion. There are two immediate areas in which the leadership role of civil society is decisive in the context of public- and private-sector cooperation: greater leadership in voluntary actions to eradicate poverty and the generation of a society of consumers who require the free market to supply quality.

Today, more than ever, democracy requires accountability of its leaders and their dealings. The present active information networks no longer allow broad areas of secrecy in politics. In the past, explanations to citizens and the rendering of accounts were reduced by invoking security considerations. The Cold War justified styles and behaviors today more simply described as corruption. People call on their leaders to be coherent in their statements and actions, to demonstrate a career of true public service, and to make a clear separation between their role in the public sphere and their private business. A great part of the credibility of our system of representation depends upon the accountability of politicians.

At the present time, democracy must show its superiority over authoritarian regimes in making economic decisions derived from the international context. Democracy, in fact, can be more efficient in privatizing without corruption, in deregulating without discrimination, and in streamlining government administration without hidden pressures. Accountability is the source of confidence in authorities, and thus the source of their real legitimacy.

We must also assume the decisive role of information. The abundance of data and the facility of access make it feasible for all social space to become public. That possibility presupposes lucidity in regulating the generation of and access to information. The quality of these processes will undoubtedly have a decisive impact on the political culture.

Specifically, with advances in technology, citizens could potentially be visible in all their acts, with no privacy at all. We must find an adequate balance between the growing circulation of information, the demand for accountability, and adequate protection of personal privacy. It is necessary, therefore, to seek new institutions to ensure that a better-informed society is, in truth, a more democratic society.

A New Concept of Economic and Social Development

Any statement about a new world order not founded on a basic consensus with regard to cooperation, equity, and a common concept of social development is illusory and fallacious.

The poor and needy on earth today number more than 1.1 billion; by the end of the century, should this trend continue, poverty will engulf 1.3 billion people. A fifth of the world's population is indigent, with very little possibility of escaping from poverty. It is no longer possible to appeal to reasons beyond our control, or to factors that elude the comprehension of communities, to justify poverty. And poverty without future or possible escape, as history dramatically demonstrates, is the most formidable threat to the peace of nations and to peace in the world.

In order not to deceive ourselves on this subject, I think we must impose on the world a new concept of the state. In recent decades, it has become obvious that the welfare state — as a model — has shown a certain exhaustion and a growing inability to resolve people's concrete problems. No less certainly, on the other hand, during the ideological struggle against communist statism the virtues of the free market were exaggerated and promoted with a notable lack of criticism of its vacuum with regard to social development.

That is the reason I believe we must advance toward a state of equity. Such a state does not avoid the social implications of its task. As a matter of fact, it deepens that dimension on the foundation of basic justice and equal opportunity.

The first task of a state of equity is to foster sustainable growth that distributes wealth based upon such growth, without surrendering to populist zeal. Specifically, it concentrates on social investment—investments in health, in justice, and especially in education—to assure equal opportunity in practical terms. It must effectively address the needs of the most vulnerable groups, those not benefited directly by growth or immediately by education. In brief, it is a state that assures all its citizens the opportunity to express their capacities and obtain the tools to generate their own progress.

For that purpose, it is necessary to cast aside the weight of Cold War ideologies that made public- and private-sector action mutually exclusive, particularly in Latin America. Indeed, anything that approached public-sector involvement was understood by one of the two sides as synonymous with statism, inefficiency, and the lack of freedom. For the other, anything associated with the private sector was experienced as synonymous with greed, a wager on inequality and privilege, perpetuating poverty and inequity.

Today, this state of equity bases itself on the fact that progress and development can be attained only within the framework of close collaboration between the public and private sectors, particularly in the generation of more and better-quality jobs. Economic growth and the generation of wealth are no longer solely a matter of concern to the private sector, nor is the challenge of equity and the reduction of inequalities the public sector's exclusive responsibility. On the contrary, everyone working together, in close collaboration, can make the materialization of a nation's aspirations possible.

This state of equity will be possible only through the dissemination and internalization of a new style of cooperation. Cooperation has too frequently been an instrument of coercion or of affirmation of the hegemony of one bloc or another in a particular region or country. Today we can define cooperation on the basis of the sense of urgency and priority it has for the future of us all. All the developed nations, which have enormous historic responsibilities, as well as the emerging nations, which today find themselves in a position to contribute to the international community, must participate in this task. This is an essential gesture of retribution.

In most nations, human misery coexists with progress, the sectors that benefit from growth and development along with the ones that have no access to the minimum requirements of a decent life. But there are also territories and countries in which poverty is general and complete. These societies are on the verge of collapse, with no basic tools to confront the gravity of their problems. In those places the first and most decisive impulse must come from international cooperation. We cannot deceive ourselves with partial solutions or rhetorical pronouncements. In such cases, the international community must assume a responsibility as inescapable as it is urgent.

We live in an age that has available knowledge, technologies, and tools of analysis and strategic planning much superior to those of our forebears. That makes us morally much more responsible for the destiny of this earth. It is our generation which is responsible for the historic task of eliminating the age-old causes of poverty. For that reason alone, because of the magnitude of the challenges before us, we cannot waste those instruments of progress, no matter if they have served other interests before. It is of extreme importance to apply all the knowledge, all the mechanisms, and all the technology of the modern age to advance more rapidly in this struggle.

There is also a very concrete relationship between poverty and the protection and conservation of the environment. Only in recent decades has the conscience of humanity advanced to the point of noting the irreversible damage dealt to the world we inhabit. It is therefore urgent to adopt measures that allow for the exploitation of natural resources without destroying the environment and without exhausting those resources, now and forever. Environmental measures, nevertheless, are costly. Nations that have been building their present standard of living without regard to ecological balance for more than a century cannot be allowed today to call upon the poorer countries to assume those costs alone. Paradoxically, the underdeveloped nations are asked today to make adjustments in their economies, overcome poverty, and care for the environment, all at once.

Here, too, international cooperation is essential and peremptory, not only directly in the planning and provision of resources to avoid environmental damage, but also indirectly through technology transfers to allow these countries to escape their position as basic suppliers of raw materials.

The creation of a more just social and economic order is surrounded by pronouncements that are mere rhetoric. What is needed is ongoing, vigilant action to achieve continuity and success during this long crusade. Each government can show its political will to eradicate misery. Civil society must contribute with moral perseverance.

We must never forget that the struggle against poverty requires ethical support. Poverty is not an irremediable condemnation, written in the nature of the earth or of the cosmos, nor an unmodifiable datum with regard to the human condition. Poverty is not just a problem of resources. The contribution of funds to social expenditures is not enough to challenge it. Above all, a social and ethical movement supporting the measures adopted by governments is necessary — a movement to be the vigilant conscience and the moral enthusiasm of the efforts to eradicate misery.

International Free Trade

One of the principal characteristics of the post–Cold War era is the intensification of commercial exchange. In many cases it is trade that forges greater ties in the political and cultural environment. In others old friendships are renewed by a new commercial impulse. It is in this area that the potential for and the obstacles to the creation of a new world order become obvious. In addition to promoting the foundation of such a new world order based on cooperation and equity, we must therefore champion free trade and the opening of markets with equal fervor.

There is no doubt that a structural change is taking place in international trade. After the market-opening processes during the second half of the 1980s, world trade volume grew at rates in excess of 6 percent, with similar figures expected for the 1990s. Greater dynamism accrues to sectors that incorporate high added values. Several associated phenomena result. The first is a widening gap between raw-material-producing countries and those with a higher level of technology. The gulf separating them accents inequities that threaten the stability of national economies and the international economic system. The second is an outgrowth of the first: the road to development unfailingly requires adding value to production. Adding value, in turn, implies profound educational system reforms and the development of science and technology.

As a consequence of the growth of international trade, nations tend to cluster into regional associations that facilitate their collective bargaining capacity and assure the free circulation of goods and services within each group.

One central characteristic of this type of association is flexibility, not only with respect to its geographic coverage but also its range of topics. The most successful and innovative schemes are precisely those that adapt to the changing necessities of its members and leave room for the divergent situations of their most immediate neighbors. Differences with regard to processes of opening markets — in basic wealth, in productive structure, in conception of the role of the state, and in macroeconomic policies — do not constitute a motive for distance. On the contrary, such differences are factors that enrich international relations and make them more dynamic.

Moreover, our experience in Latin America clearly demonstrates the benefits of this type of integration. We have developed innovative forms of economic cooperation that generate greater mutual interdependence and may bring us closer to the ideals of unity that have motivated our nations throughout their history. During recent years we have made more real advances toward the integration of our economies than in the previous three decades. New highway, river, and pipeline networks unite the continent on an unprecedented scale. An intense network of regional, subregional, and bilateral agreements are achieving increasing liberalization of trade and growing economic and political cooperation. The picture is undoubtedly complex and sometimes confusing, but it is bringing concrete results. Beyond the options that become permanent, our experience is that integration is a process that improves our countries' entry into the world economy and intensifies our commercial, financial, and investment ties with the great international centers.

We believe that regionalization is an enormously positive process for the participating countries. But we are not partisans of regional blocs that become closed, protectionist spaces against the rest of the international community. Should that tendency crystallize, exacerbated economic rivalry would become a source of tensions and insecurity for the world community.

We are not referring to abstractions. In virtually all the great markets of the world, the growth of trade has sometimes been impeded by the persistence of selective and discriminatory protectionism, particularly in such sectors as agriculture, steel, textiles, automobiles, certain cutting-edge technologies, and some service sectors.

This true neoprotectionism, fed by the pressure of powerful interest groups in each country, makes it necessary to seek effective formulas of vigilance and collective response by the countries most affected.

In that sense, it is our position that regional organizations such as the Rio Group should assume their position as valid interlocutors with the great trading powers and redouble their efforts to coordinate opposition to protectionism. In that connection, the conclusion of the Uruguay Round represents an important advance in the liberalization of world trade. The Latin American nations made a significant contribution to making that achievement effective, and we will continue to work in the different world forums for a free trade system that requires full congruence of words and deeds.

Conclusion

Consideration has been given throughout this text to the larger aspirations present alongside the afflictions and hopes experienced by the peoples of the earth in the course of the century now ending — the search for greater liberty and effective solidarity among human beings.

Paradoxically, these values and their practical consequences have been perceived as mutually antagonistic and contradictory. With the experience accumulated, which contains an enormous amount of pain and suffering, we now know that liberty without solidarity leads to extreme individualism, with harmful, disintegrative effects for our societies. At the same time, we note that the search for solidarity without liberty dead-ends in an asphyxiating and inefficient collectivism. Thus the future we want and imagine embodies the union of the two great aspirations of liberty and solidarity. In this spirit, the democrats of the world are preparing to construct a future with a real human face.

His Excellency

Muammar Abu Minyar El-Qadhafi

Revolutionary Leader of the
Socialist People's Libyan Arab Jamahiriya

A Revolutionary Perspective on the New World Order

When we look at the world of today, analyze its reality and its prospects, and seek to know its concerns and aspirations, we should be very cautious, right from the start, in dealing with all the ideas and analysis produced by the western school of thought on the rapid developments that have engulfed the world since the announcement of Gorbachev's *perestroika* in 1985 up until now.

Regrettably, western propaganda has monitored these transformations from the perspective of the capitalist West, particularly the perspective of America, and not from a total human perspective. Western propaganda analyzed these transformations from the perspective of the West and its interests and not from the perspective of fact and reason.

This western propaganda made a habit of twisting facts, abstracting them in hasty ideas that it rapidly fed to its huge media apparatus to spread all over the world, in an apparently repetitive manner, through all mass communication media. The whole thing gave an impression that it was a deliberate attempt to think on behalf of the whole world, involve it in biased analysis, and overshadow any total independent and objective human thought that would shed light on the reality of the modern world and clearly project the future.

In this context, the western propaganda machine produced a self-contained system of ready-made ideas which are easily manufactured and easily spread. Its objectives were crystal clear. The West tried to impose all these ideas by force on truth and reality. The western propaganda machine promoted the idea that "the Collapse of Marxism means the crowning of capitalism as the one and only eternal system in the world" and that "the prevalence of the capitalist model is the end of history." It thus ignored the fact that the crisis of capitalism preceded that of Marxism and that the ailment has been eating at the body of both systems one and at the same time. The fact that one did come before the other does not mean that this other is healthy and sound and will live forever. However, the fact is that the whole thing is just a matter of different conditions and capabilities and the ability of each one to resist. As in boxing, the two fighters usually do not fall down at the same time.

Western propaganda wants us to believe that "the collapse of the totalitarian regimes means that the multiparty system is the only way to democracy," ignoring the fact that free choice by the people is the simplest and most natural condition of democracy. The West also ignores the fact that the larger part of the world's tragedies has been the result of a destructive power struggle. The worst dictatorships in history flourished under the visage of parliaments and multiparty systems, and the strongest protests and rebellions in today's world take place specifically against multiparty systems.

Western propaganda has forcefully promoted the idea that "the disappearance of the Soviet Union means that the time of the great revolutions is over, and that the fighters for freedom will be buried, pursued by the curse of the West and the disgrace of terrorism." But the architects of this propaganda seem to be blind to the fact that activities in the West these days, including demonstrations and rebellions, strikes, and low voter turnout, are the first precursors of a violent revolution that will definitely engulf and change the world.

The concept of the "New World Order," which they want to impose on governments and call on peoples to accept, is nothing more than another attempt at hiding the bitter truth of the way the world is being ruled these days — a world still languishing in the chains of the inherited world order, shackled by its old values, its barren ideas, and poor solutions. Maybe the only difference between the old and the new orders is that the old order has lost its balance and no longer has any resistance against desires, lusts, and evils.

War Is Not Over

Can we acknowledge that the Cold War is over? Can we agree that now wars have ended? That is what is being promoted by mass communication media, some politicians, and even some so-called thinkers.

We do not want to enter into a political controversy over the concept of "cold war" and how it was formulated, the circumstances that led to its creation, and its reflection and effects on small peoples and poor countries. However, we can decidedly state that wars — whatever the definition of the Cold War — have not ended. Regrettably wars will never end. War is going on now and is expected to erupt in the future. We cannot believe that war is over when we see it in all forms, be it direct invasion, intervention wars, regional conflicts, and civil wars that surround us everywhere. The smell of death shocks us every morning, in Bosnia-Herzegovina, Somalia, Haiti, Rwanda, Burundi, occupied Palestine, Chechnya, Armenia, Azerbaijan, Yemen, the Sudan, Afghanistan, South Lebanon, and other parts of the world.

We cannot accept that war is over while thousands of children in Iraq starve to death because of war. We cannot believe that war is over when North Korea is threatened with war, and when the Libyan Arab Jamahiriya is being threatened by applying Chapter VII of the U.N. Charter against it. We cannot believe that the war is over when clouds of war are accumulating in many parts of Africa, Asia, and even in the heart of Europe itself.

It seems that those who promote the idea that war is over are looking at a completely different picture, because armed conflicts in the world have dramatically increased, in an unprecedented manner, in the aftermath of the collapse of the Soviet Union. It is as if the globe has suddenly exploded, under the pressure of all that was hidden under the balance of the two superpowers. This includes religious, ethnic, and national conflict motivations, at a time when the new controlling superpower started to seek revenge against certain peoples. More than that, a great many armed conflicts these days take place under the banner of the United Nations, the organization that was established by the peoples of the world, after awesome world wars, in order to prevent a recurrence of these wars and put an end to their scourge.

The War Continues

War continues. It is the dominant fact in today's world. In addition to armed conflicts, it is embodied in the frightening figures of the world's military spending, which reached 75,000 [sic] billion dollars during the period 1987–1994, an annual average of 1,000 [sic] billion dollars. Of course, this is in addition to the fact that the larger part of weapons stockpiles have been used up in current conflicts. It is no secret that some poor countries spend on weapons more than what they spend on education and health services combined.

War will not end so long as its causes and motivations are there. Civil wars will not end so long as ethnic and religious conflicts continue. Nobody can prevent violence when hunger spreads and intensifies. And the potential for regional wars will always exist in areas where there are no well-established social security systems. Nobody would venture to predict that wars of intervention will cease so long as the United States of America can at any time get from the Security Council the required international war license whenever it wants to settle old scores, or solve a problem with a member in the international organization. Lastly, nobody believes that war will end at a time when the death industry — with its experts and specialists — has become available to a large number of the world's countries.

Those who see in the U.S.-Russian agreement to reduce their nuclear warheads to 3,500 each, or the minor reduction in international military spending over the last three years, a sign that the war is ending forget that a few nuclear warheads are sufficient to destroy the world, and that the progress achieved in weapons technologies now enables factories to produce more death at a lower cost.

Thus, wars are continuous, and explosive by virtue of their means and their attestations, and their causes and motivations, which now loom larger and more serious than at any time in the past.

War Is a Western Product

Wars — whether those that are going on now or ones that may erupt in the future — are a necessity for capitalism. War and capitalism go together. They are like identical twins who never separate. There is no life for capitalism without war, expansion, and control. And since capitalism means competition, monopoly, and rush to reap profits at any cost, in addition to pressures for opening more markets and acquiring more raw materials and investment opportunities, war will always be necessary as a tool to be used and as an integral part of capitalism's organic structure. The more the lust for profits intensifies, the greater the tendency toward the militarization of society and the deeper the motivation for war and exploitation.

The two largest world wars in humanity's history erupted because of competition in dividing markets. Lust for profit and expansion was behind the regional wars that the world has witnessed after World War II. It doesn't matter if the countries that manufacture weapons have participated in these wars themselves or just supported them. Irrespective of the size and duration of the war, its direct parties, or those behind them, capitalists will always be there following the war, collecting war spoils and accumulating profits.

What makes the relationship between capitalism and war strong is the fact that the war itself has turned into an industry, commerce and monopolies. The weapons industry is the most profitable in today's world. A great part of America's resources was channeled into the weapons industry during World War II, absorbing large numbers of the work force and accounting for a good part of national income. The weapons industry then entered into complex relations with other sectors, changing into capital that must be invested to create a return. Of course, this industry needs to dispose of its goods and get rid of its stockpiles and export them. It is well known that weapons markets are battlefields whose only sure harvest, for both victors and vanquished, is death. Thus capitalism cannot stop manufacturing death and exporting it and transforming it into huge profits.

On the other hand, weapons monopolies in capitalist societies are not alien to power. As a matter of fact, they are part of the power structure in the society. Sometimes they themselves control decision making in the capitalist society. At other times their surrogates do the job for them. In the absence of either the former or the latter, they resort to lobbying and exert tremendous pressures on governments. In all cases, weapons monopolies and weapons and war brokers are capable of exploiting governments that are capable of launching wars and governments that are weak, in order to create a climate favorable for trade in arms and the expansion of death fields.

Here, we cannot exonerate weapons traders, weapons monopolies, and weapons brokers for inciting the Korean war in order to dispose of America's weapons surplus following the end of World War II. Neither can we forgive them the series of Asian wars, the Vietnam war, and the successive wars of the Arab nation against the Hebrew state in 1948, 1956, 1967, and 1973. And who would exonerate them for inciting the wars that now engulf the world and rage everywhere you look?

I would like now to quote a paragraph from a report published by the

United Nations on human development in 1990, which supports and emphasizes this meaning: "It should be noted that industrialized countries and other main exporters of weapons are responsible for the increasing military spending in the Third World. In many cases money budgeted by the developed countries for defense assistance has increased, at a time when economic assistance has been reduced." Also, ministries of defense in the industrialized countries have, on many occasions, strongly sought to reach customers willing to buy weapons, offering them concessionary loans. They have even given them the weapons sometimes as a gift or through illegal means.

The same thing applies to other arms-producing countries, such as Russia, and other companies that manufacture these weapons. All of them need outlets for their goods. This, in turn, can be an impossible job without creating fields and opportunities for death and fighting. Since companies that produce goods usually look for markets for these goods, create the proper marketing tools, and sign contracts and deals to promote and publicize them, companies that manufacture weapons need to dispose of their products and need ways and methods to promote them and sell them everywhere. These companies may even give some of their products as a gift or a grant in order to promote and propagate these products. That is why these companies never cease to incite wars everywhere, using their governments and pushing their intelligence services to sow seeds of sedition and create chaos and pockets of tension all over the world.

At first sight, today's wars all over the world may seem to be political wars being fought for only political reasons or because of only the personal whims of rulers. The fact, however, is that these wars are no more than showrooms for selling weapons produced by the manufacturing companies and a kind of promotion for these weapons. These companies use and direct the governments capable of buying these weapons, exploiting and even blackmailing weak governments. Historical honesty and moral responsibility should prompt these rulers, who promote wars and flaunt their roles in waging them, to confess that they are no more than arms brokers and tools in the hands of companies that manufacture weapons.

The Cold War Will Never End

If "hot wars" are exploding and continuing, what about the Cold War? We cannot agree that it has ended. It is a situation that prevailed in the aftermath of World War II. It took the form of an arms race between the two world blocs that led to a balance of power between them and deterred any direct wars between them. However, it opened the door for surrogate wars, created pockets of tension affecting other countries, opened wide the door of economic competition, and exacerbated ideological conflicts. Faced with this picture, no reasonable person would claim that the Cold War is over or that conflict between human blocs and ethnic groups is over. All of this will continue as long as their causes continue. America may enjoy for a while the absence of direct Russian hostility, and Russia may avoid provoking America for some time. But a temporary armistice is something, and the end of the war is a completely different thing. Hostility between the two countries is old and deep-rooted, and has a historical background that goes back hundreds of years. It would be a grave mistake for anybody to think that a conference between the two countries, a treaty signed by the two parties, or the two presidents toasting each other will nullify an old conflict between two old cultures and end decades of hatred and resentment between them.

Even under Russia's submission and the absence of American provocation, we can easily detect symptoms of the Cold War between them. They are clear in the differing points of view of the two countries on attempts by America and Europe to expand NATO at the expense of the now defunct Warsaw Pact. Symptoms are also evident in the war in Bosnia-Herzegovina and in the stance over Cuba. This can also be seen in the embargo imposed against both the Jamahiriya and Iraq. All of these are clear pieces of evidence that the Cold War is still going on. Even in the absence of any evidence, the fact that Russia would keep a low profile for some time doesn't mean that it will remain pliant all the time. Once Russia is able to regain its balance and achieve internal stability, getting rid of the remaining inherited problems and its stifling economic crisis, and once the struggle for power between its conflicting parties is settled, the new goals will find expression in new positions and new criteria.

By the same token, nobody can state with certainty that the countries of Eastern Europe have raised the white flag before the capitalist system and thrown away all their past and their experience, especially since the results of the latest elections in a number of these countries signal the return of some socialists to power again. This time, they will be helped by the frustrations of the masses and the experience they gained from the crisis. They will be strongly pushed toward a renewed political and ideological struggle with capitalism.

Even if we assume, for the sake of argument, that the Cold War has ended between America and Russia and that the disputes between them have been forever buried, what would America do with other powers that started to get ready to enter the fields of the Cold War? And how can anyone explain the trade conflict between America and Japan, the nascent political and economic struggle that is gradually getting under way between America and Germany, and the ups and downs of relations between America and China? Also, how can we explain the GATT agreement and the economic bloc being built by America with the countries of Latin America and its attempts at getting around the seven Asian tigers? Isn't that a continuation of a cold war that could escalate and exacerbate with the rise in contradictions between the new powers and their interests? Also, what can anyone expect from the unjust relationship between the prosperous North and the extremely poor South and the hunger gap that keeps widening and deepening between them with every passing day? Couldn't this lead to a total revolt by the hungry and the onslaught of a new cold war or at least the seeds that would surprise the world by exploding into a cold war?

Cold war, like hot war, has not ended between the two powers. It is not expected to disappear in the near future. Most probably, it will spread to other centers and to the whole world. It can even change into a hot water at any time, threatening stability and preempting potential for growth and development.

America, Messenger of War

American policy, in particular, is the policy that is leading the world to war, tension, and conflict. America is seeking to transform the Cold War into a destructive hot war, at any time. America thought or was misled into thinking that it is the only power in control, and thus it can dictate to the world and impose on it whatever it wants. It thought that it could impose on the whole world its vision and its culture, using it according to its wishes and whims, and that the peoples and governments of the world have to obey it and be at its beck and call.

America formulated its strategy toward the world on an opportunistic basis, exploiting available opportunities and the conditions of confusion and dizziness that followed the earthquake that hit the Warsaw Pact, in order to take from the world everything in return for nothing. It provided that only it can harvest the gains in which nobody else should share. This opportunism has been clearly expressed in former president Nixon's book *Seize the Moment*, which is one of the pillars of strategic thinking in America. This has also been clearly embodied in the results of the Gulf war, when American companies also monopolized investment in and rebuilding of the region. Through this opportunistic conduct, America wants to eradicate the traditional role of Russia and to prevent it from ever regaining its previous position of strength. Thus, it is trying to prevent any other power from coming closer to the pinnacle of the New World Order, even among its allies.

By doing this, America wants to rearrange the situation in the world in a manner that would definitively safeguard its interests in all regions: in Central America, Europe, Asia, and the Arab region, even at the expense of millions of people and through the creation of an illusion of a false world peace. More dangerous still, America is seeking to impose its own concepts and understanding of peace and security, terrorism, human rights, development, and social peace on all countries and peoples. In doing this, it exploits the strength of its mass media, the weakness of international institutions, and the absence of the Soviet Union. As a result of this policy, there are now two concepts of things — the American concept and the true concept. For example, there is American peace and there is just peace. There is development the American way and there is independent development. There is an American definition of terrorism and there are movements that struggle for freedom and liberation. Also there is stability according to the American definition and its equivalent, which is the people's rejection of American hegemony and its wild behavior.

With these double concepts, there are double stances and double views of various questions. Relations between America and other countries of the North are governed by the balance of interests, and they are conducted in a climate characterized by freedom and dialogue. On the other hand, relations with the South are governed by the concept of power and characterized by dictation and orders, which leads to the disappearance of fair human values, under the pressures of power and American interests. Thus, America's policy has become tainted with excessive opportunism and glaring double standards, coupled with megalomania, the arrogance of power, and undisciplined and irresponsible thinking, which may be the product of psychological and historical reasons relating to the nature and structure of American society. This society created an arrogant spirit that prompted it to occupy small countries like Grenada, Panama, and Haiti. Maybe it is the same spirit that prompted the Americans to fight in Vietnam, occupy the Gulf, and impose a blockade against the Jamahiriya and Iraq.

However, we believe that this situation, in which America has become a policeman citing people for infringements, confiscating peoples' wills and property, and using international organizations in implementing its policies, will create accumulated layers of hatred and resentment against America and hostility toward its people. And when they can't bear it anymore, the persecuted and poor peoples will explode in a revolt against oppression. This will touch the American administration and its role in the world and will destroy its interests everywhere.

The World Is Unstable

We cannot accept, at face value, the claim that the world has stabilized and is now establishing a New World Order, and that humanity has reached final and drastic solutions for its problems. After two world wars, what we have seen is only palliatives and concocted solutions. The palliatives of World War I led us to World War II. The concocted solutions devised in the aftermath of World War II led to the collapse of the present.

If we try to pinpoint the reasons behind this collapse, we will first see a dramatic one-power system, in which America is alone at the top of the present world order. This is a fact nobody can deny, since the other power has totally or temporarily withdrawn from the arena. This exclusivity of power may explain America's behavior, but it can't explain the whole world. The fact that America is alone at the top of the world order is a transient and temporary condition, resulting from the absence of the other power, the Soviet Union, assisted by brutal American military power. However, we don't believe that America possesses now what it takes to stay at the top alone for a long period of time.

The relative weight of the American economy compared with other emerging economies is visibly receding to the extent that the American economy must choose between external adventures and internal reforms. It can no longer do both. Also, the relative strength of America's military power is gradually shrinking, at a time when the economy decides relative weights. Other powers with spheres of influence are inching their way up to the top of the world structure: such powers as Japan, China, Germany, and Europe, which is gradually uniting, now have the ability to challenge the American economy over the world markets and investment opportunities in these markets.

Some of these economies have cultural factors that would encourage them to exercise pressure on America and push it outside the cycle of leadership. Here we can refer to several documented futuristic studies, and even American reports, which are unanimous in saying that America is facing intractable internal problems, and that Japan, China, and Germany have advanced to the field of international competition. Moreover, the balance of payments between these countries are greatly favorable to these countries. Because America has realized the truth of its transient and temporary situation, it rushed, with all its power, to realize the greatest gains in the shortest possible time. Undoubtedly, this explains its hostile behavior in relation to the peoples of the world, the double standards it uses, and the selfishness that governs its positions. This transient and temporary factor, however, does not explain the current phase of our lives even if it uncovered one of its most salient features.

Then comes the idea that the conflict between East and West has changed into a North-South conflict. This is no doubt the most sterile idea, attempting to diagnose the reality of today's world. The fact is that the West, temporarily relieved of its conflict with Eastern Europe, began pressuring the South, which suffers from poverty, famine, the negative consequences of capitalist development, debt servicing, continued looting by transnational and multinational companies, cultural invasion, puppet regimes, and lastly an unbalanced population explosion pushing the South to below-poverty-line situations. As one of the salient features of the present world, the North-South conflict is embodied in the North's incessant attempts at marginalizing the South, although it is inhabited by 4.5 billion people, or close to 85 percent of the world's population. It is also reflected in the North's imposing choices on other peoples and the use of their agricultural lands to bury their waste. The South is also being used as an outlet for the North's economic crises.

The North resists any attempts at redistributing the resources of the world. Also, it collectively exercises pressure on the prices of the South's products, mainly raw materials, and taxes them. The North-South conflict is also reflected in all forms of discrimination against the sons of the South, and in monopolizing sources of technology and knowledge. However, this factor does not explain all aspects of the world's present crisis and does not reveal the reality of the current movement in the life of the world. Thus we can say that the so-called end of the Cold War is a trick, and that the unipolar system is transient and the North-South conflict is only an aspect of a deeper crisis. All of this does not explain or describe the present world.

There is also another observation related to some intellectual terms that have become popular in our time, such as "Capitalism is forever," "multiparty systems," "the end of the era of revolutions," and "New World Order." These are not, in any way, naive ideas. They are necessary for continued control and for justifying oppression.

World developments over the last two decades led, for the first time since the end of World War II, to the appearance of economic, military, and intellectual power centers from outside the West and away from its environment. These power centers started to threaten the West's total control of the globe. Japan, China, and other Asian countries emerged as economic powerhouses that gained importance on the international arena, at a time when America has been transformed into the largest city-state in the world. North Korea, China, and Pakistan also emerged as military centers that would threaten the West's superiority, at a time when American military strength has started to recede under the pressure of the arms race. New intellectual centers have emerged, and old lighthouses have been resurrected, thanks to the movements of peoples aimed at affirming and maintaining their own identity in the face of intellectual invasion and cultural conquest, at a time when intellectual conviction has collapsed and the glitter of faith has dimmed in western culture.

At a time when America's leading position and its exclusive presence at the top of the world is threatened, these ideas came to constitute intellectual pillars, used to help it continue its control of the world and preempt any attempt by any nonwestern power to threaten its leading role, take its share in the leadership of the world, or contribute to the determination of its march and its destination.

This World

The image of the world of today was drawn at the end of World War II, when the victors coercively rearranged the world to permanently safeguard their victories and be able to control the world. During that period, the world witnessed processes of disassembling, assembling, and annexation.

All this took place in a way that ignored reality and national and historical considerations.

The Berlin Wall was built to artificially separate two parts of one nation; the Hebrew state was established as a dagger in the heart of the Arab nation; a ninth article was added to the constitution of Japan against the will of the Japanese people, preventing it from military industrialization and the building of an independent army. Korea and Vietnam were divided into North and South. Europe was subjected to the Marshall Plan, which helped spread American bases in Europe, forcing countries of Eastern Europe to be satellites of the Soviet Union. The borders of Europe were redrawn in a manner that mingled nationalities and ethnic groups. Divisions in the Arab world were perpetuated and deepened. NATO was established in the Western Hemisphere, and the Warsaw Pact in the Eastern Hemisphere, to guard all these arrangements during the period of the balance of power between the two groups.

Thus, when Russia withdrew from the arena, leading to the collapse of the international balance that prevented the fall and delayed the breakdown, the coercive arrangements that followed World War II fell apart, together with the concocted measures imposed by force on the peoples of the world.

Era of Collapse

The present phase of the history of the world is not as they claim, the phase of the end of the Cold War. The Cold War is not over. The fact is that the present phase is the era of the collapse of the arrangements that followed World War II, having become obsolete, useless, and incapable of continuing.

Up until now, the Berlin Wall was demolished; Germany was reunified; the Warsaw Pact disappeared; the strong links between countries of Eastern Europe, forged during the war, dissolved; Yugoslavia fell apart on ethnic and nationalistic lines, leading to the emergence of a state for the Serbs, a state in Bosnia and Macedonia. Czechoslovakia was divided into a Czech Republic and a Slovak Republic. The apartheid regime in South Africa collapsed and was replaced by a new country where blocs prevailed, as the Green Book predicted.

Thus, this part of World War II arrangements have vanished. The rest of the arrangements and concocted solutions are on their way to disappearance, together with all the coercive measures. We anticipate a quick end to all countries artificially established and to all the borders coercively drawn. We anticipate the reunification of the countries forcefully divided by the victors. We anticipate the emergence of the Fourth Reich and the advance of Germany up the ladder of world power. Japan will regain its full independence, enter the military industrialization race, and build its own independent army. We anticipate that Russia will be expelled from all the islands it occupies. We anticipate the end of the Hebrew state, the fall of royal thrones, the disappearance of some Arab emirates, and the reunification of the Arab homeland from the ocean to the Gulf. We anticipate the reunification of Korea and Vietnam. We anticipate the end of American singularity. We anticipate changes in many maps and the collapse of old empires.

We anticipate the emergence of new problems in Europe where geography and demography interact. Thus, border problems might emerge between Italy and Hungary, Poland and Germany, Italy and Yugoslavia, Hungary and Poland. The Alsace and Lorraine dispute will erupt again between Germany and France. We also anticipate the disappearance of the state of Switzerland because it consists of several ethnic groups, each of which will recede and become integrated into its natural mother nation.

Thus it becomes clear that the movement of history is the movement of the masses, the movement of any group for its own self-interest. In this age and era, the world will witness nationalist conflicts, triggered by oppressed groups, because social struggle is the basis of the movement of history, since it is much stronger than all other factors. It is the origin. It is the nature of the human race, of man in general and even the nature of life itself. Nationalism in the realms of man and animal is the counterpart of gravity in the realms of matter and celestial bodies. In the absence of the gravity of the sun, the sun will lose its singleness and unity, and its unity is the reason for its existence. Existence is based on unity. The factor that unites any group is the social factor. That is why groups struggle for their national unity because this unity guarantees their existence.

Labor

The conflicts and tensions witnessed by the world these days are not difficult to understand or analyze. They are not without significance and they are not off the mark. They in no way prove that humanity has lost its compass. Behind this chaos and in it we see a very clear and consistent picture of a new and different future. What we have to do is to understand and comprehend the crisis of the present world, analyze it deeply, and reflect on its future based on a new mass vision.

Put simply, we believe that the world of today is a world in a crisis. We do not believe, as western propaganda would like us to believe, that Marxism has been behind the crisis. We know full well that Marxism and its social system and the powers it was built on constituted a real problem for the West and its social systems. However, for the rest of the world, Marxism was only one facet of a larger, deeper, and more comprehensive crisis. I do believe that Marxism was the least important and least dangerous of the facets of this crisis. Also, it was never a solution for the crisis as some would claim.

We see the crisis of the world in a very clear manner, in the glaring contradiction between government systems in today's world, their world embodiments and their living models, and humanity's need and hope for development, justice, democracy, and peace. It has become evident that the continuation of these government systems constitutes a real barrier before humanity's hopes. It even threatens humanity with annihilation.

Here it is a question of individual will or the will of the rulers themselves, but it relates mainly to the basic characteristics of these systems. All of them, including the present international political, economic, and monetary organization, carry the same basic characteristics. There is one thread that connects all of them together and touches their common essence, which supports the usurpation by the few of all tools of power. They are based on the principle of "representation" politically, on the "law of profit and the system of hiring" economically, and on "power, control, and expansion" militarily. In these monopolistic characteristics lies the real crisis of the world. These tyrannical systems destroyed the natural relationship between the masses, on one hand, and the power instruments and the means of accumulating wealth and weapons stockpiles, on the other hand, thus erecting a barrier between peoples and their aspirations at the international level and between the masses and their fate at the local level.

The advance and fate of the world in which we live depends on the contribution of every individual and the participation of all its peoples in defining its course, based on democracy, the fair redistribution of its wealth and means, and the establishment of an equal partnership in which everybody takes part, in order to solve the intractable problems facing it and achieve the prosperity and security it lacks. These conditions, however, clash with the current systems, which deprive peoples of exercising their natural role and enjoying their legitimate rights and which enable the minority to control decision making relating to the world and its fate, confiscating its wealth, and exploiting it for its own gain at the expense of the overwhelming majority of the peoples of the world who face famine, disease, and marginalization. Freedom in any land requires that the masses control their decisions and their fate and resources, exploiting these according to their will and interests. However, the movement of the masses clashes with systems of hegemony and exploitation, which usurp power, loot wealth, and monopolize arms. This, very simply, means that the world cannot rid itself of its crisis unless it works in a collective manner based on joint responsibility, equal participation, and cooperation among all its peoples. But the current systems will not permit that, by virtue of their composition, goals, and interests.

In view of this historical imbalance in the relation of the masses to factors of power and strength at the world level, an imbalance that prevails in the world of today and explains its crisis, we can pinpoint the facts of the world crisis. They consist in giving the minority a monopoly of international decisions, the means of accumulating wealth, and the sources of weapons while submitting the majority to control, monopoly, and starvation. Everything in today's world testifies to this and clearly embodies it. There is a minority that controls the course of events in the world and exploits all its wealth. In the Security Council, there are five permanent members that govern the world and control international decisions. There is also the Big Seven, which divide the wealth of the world among themselves, determine the course of international trade, and plan world investments. One member controls world financial flows and steers the world system of providing assistance. On the other hand, there are over 175 states that, in fact, can do nothing except to surrender and submit. A minority, which does not exceed 15 percent of the globe's population, lives in the North and controls 70 percent of the world's resources, supported by an enormous technological revolution. On the other hand, 85 percent of the world's population lives in the South. Their numbers increase daily, and they suffer from poverty and famine and creeping desertification everywhere. These two conflicting, contradictory poles live on one planet whose resources are shrinking daily, threatened by pollution, overexploitation, contagious diseases, and the likelihood of the eruption of a nuclear war at any time.

The people's awareness of the reality of the crisis is deepening and taking root with every passing day. The masses have started to reject palliatives and temporary reforms. They no longer trust governments and parties. These days, only naive and ignorant people stand in voting lines. Workers have started to seek partnerships and refuse being just hired. They seek to own the means of production. To do this, they strike and demonstrate, unafraid of police sticks or the hooves of horses. They aspire to a new age, an age that catches the eye and evokes strong emotions, while being created in the womb of reality, a reality filled with pain, conflict, and tension — the age of the masses.

This Is the Age of the Masses

This age cannot be defined as the age of the end of the Cold War since wars have not ended. Unfortunately, wars are increasing and expanding, thanks to arms companies and the arrogance of America and its attempt at controlling the world. But we can truly call it the age of the masses, which are leading the final and decisive battle against the forces of oppression that work against the masses, whether it be governments, which seek to control them, or parliaments, which seek to falsify their will and act on their behalf, or capitalist classes that seek to exploit them and the fruits of their sweat, or armies that seek to exercise fascism against these masses.

The age of the masses is not just a prophecy contained in the Green Book, or a dream of the oppressed, the suppressed, and the governed in the world. It is the result of a political and historical development and an accumulated knowledge that will definitely lead to an unprecedented march toward the disappearance of conventional governments and the establishment of the power of the people everywhere, based on a pragmatic system that will realize the idea of direct democracy called for by philosophers and thinkers, of which humanity has been dreaming throughout the ages. In this systems, a people would be divided into popular congresses. Each congress would select a secretariat. The masses of these popular congresses would then choose administrative committees to replace government departments. All utilities would be managed by popular committees. These popular committees that manage the utilities would be responsible before the popular congresses, which dictate to them their policies and monitor their implementation. Thus the administration becomes popular, and the monitoring becomes popular. This would end the obsolete definition of democracy that says "Democracy is the control and monitoring of the government by the people," replacing it with the correct definition, "Democracy means control of the people by the people." This would end the tools of dictatorial rule and make the people itself the tool and means of government, thus putting a final end to the problem of democracy that has occupied humanity over the ages.

Thus it becomes clear that direct democracy is the ideal method, which, if applied, will never be controversial. Maybe it was because people, irrespective of their number, are impossible to get together at one and the same time to discuss, study, and decide policy that nations did not adopt direct democracy, which remained an ideal remote from reality. It was replaced by several government theories such as parliaments, party blocs, and referendums, which led to depriving the people of administering their own affairs, the usurpation of their sovereignty, and the monopolization of policy and sovereignty by these successive and conflicting instruments that struggle for power, from the individual to the class to the tribe to the council and the party.

The current phase is not, then, the end of the Cold War, as they say, but a natural precursor of a new age when humanity gets rid of its chains and steadily pushes forward toward freedom. It is the phase of the struggle between the masses and their age, on one side, and the forces of oppression and their systems, on the other. It is a bitter struggle in which the masses are advancing on all fronts, amidst stubborn resistance by these conventional forces defending their positions and their interests. But the result is inevitable. It is the triumph of the age of the masses, its values, concepts, and relationships, and the disappearance of the governments that have usurped the power of the people, the end of elections that have falsified the will of the people and the parliaments that ruled on behalf of these people, the demobilization of the armies that brought defeat and destroyed peoples' capabilities. The world will be rebuilt on the basis of nationalist states, equal in value and prestige, which could be jointly responsible for the world and share fairly in world prosperity. All of them would cooperate together in order to save their planet from the effects of looting, waste, destruction, and pollution. All of them would equally share in the wealth of the world and keep for coming generations whatever is their due. Thus the world would get rid of impulses of aggression, threats, and hegemony and enjoy a natural, eternal peace, instead of illusions of peace based on terror and nuclear balance, where conditions of justice and democracy disappear and all impulses of aggression and control prevail. In the new world, no people would ever feel the urge to leave its land and occupy the land of others.

Thus our world is moving toward the future, guided by this objective and inevitable trend, which is being supported and enhanced by all the ongoing changes.

The end of World War II arrangements, the emergence and strengthening of nationalist movements, the call by most countries of the world for a new and more democratic world political order and a more just world economic system, constant pressures for a redistribution of the world's wealth in a manner that would regain the lost balance of this planet, the rising cries against the draining and pollution of the earth, the call for arms reduction and for nuclear, chemical, and biological disarmament by all countries without any discrimination, recognition of the failure of development based on the tenets of capitalism, seeking to change the lot of the oppressed groups, and liberation from the monopoly of knowledge and information — all of these forces push toward the new age, prepare for it, and open the road for it.

We can see the new age, in a clever way, in the squares and streets of the world, in the decreasing numbers of people in ballot lines year after year, and the increasing number who are seen daily on the streets protesting all forms of injustice. We see the new age in the destructive struggle for power in every corner of the world, in throngs of unemployed people in capitalist societies, in factories that are increasingly closing out, and in the companies laying off hundreds of thousands of its workers. We see it in the quick change in the feelings of the masses in Eastern Europe and their longing for the old order after their first experience with capitalism.

We see the new age, in a clearer manner, in new patterns of life that are beginning to take root and attract millions of people. We see it in peoples' tendency to form popular congresses and their attraction to self-management measures, in their seeking to build partnerships and producer cooperatives, in the spread of productive families, self-sufficiency, and free education, and in other patterns reflecting the end of the systems of disparity and injustice.

That is why we anticipate that people will seek better forms of struggle on the road to the new age. We anticipate that the masses will indefinitely abandon the road of party struggle. We expect the march of the masses to build the pillars of the power of the people (people's congresses and people's committees). We anticipate the spread of the model of the society of the masses, with its promising potentials for freedom, justice, and creativity. Then and only then will peace prevail, peace that is eternal, lasting, and natural.

Let Us March Forward

Since we are certain that the age of the masses is an inevitable and historical development and that its causes are stronger than the will of those who control today's world, we are enthusiastic about this age; we long for it; we will propagate it and draw the attention of the world to it. We are committed to constantly working for its realization in our country. We will continue to promote it, will encourage every initiative in its direction, and will support every symptom of this new age anywhere in the world.

Of course, we know the size of the pain, risks, and difficulties that separate us from this new age, for the road to the new age goes through bitter struggle — national, religious, and cultural — between the forces of the old world, which will not easily surrender and abandon their interests and will thus resort to palliatives and temporary solutions, and the forces of the new age, which come from among the people, who are now ruled by parliaments, elections, and parties and are exploited by the system of hiring, and from among oppressed groups and minorities threatened with integration or annihilation.

Although we appreciate the size of the conflict and the risks involved, we do not want to be deceived or misled. Also, we cannot deceive the world around us, nor do we want anybody to deceive the world in our presence. We are a people that loves freedom and fully respects the freedom of others. Our people know their capabilities and understand the capabilities of others. We belong to the future, without any hesitation, and work hard to reach it. We are a people that cannot go along with the world in falsehood. Our people embody a commitment to the future on our own land, by building a model for a new age of the masses to replace governments and parliaments, by doing without elections and referendums. The new model builds a world of partners to replace a world of laborers and hired people. It develops an armed people to replace conventional armies. Our people are determined to end on their territory this historical imbalance in the relationship of masses to power, wealth, and weapons, in order to get rid of all that is related to systems of injustice and control, and to be totally ready for a bright tomorrow.

We do not deceive the world and do not want any force to deceive it. We express that very clearly in our position vis-à-vis the world's questions and problems. We candidly talk to the world about its true crisis and the failure of its concocted solutions. We cannot go along with it, in actions or measures that we know in advance are futile. Our rejection of force as the tool of controlling the world — and the view we express on the inadequacy of the international political system, the world economic system, the unjust relationship between North and South, the monopoly of knowledge and culture, and the coercive education systems — reflects not only the fact that we are among the victims, but mainly the fact that we do not want to succumb to or accept these situations and do not want the world to be misled by them.

Our declared positions on the false concepts of peace, terrorism, stability, and human rights and our confrontation of them by real concepts do not emanate only from our own interests; this is also based on the fact that we do not want anyone to continue misleading and deceiving the world. The whole world knows that we have paid a high price for our faith in the future and our refusal to take part in deception and falsification. That is why we are always accused of standing outside the prevailing system. As a matter of fact, we are outside their system because, simply put, it is a false, fading, hopeless system with no future.

We declare our commitment to the new age and its propagation. We adopt its values and support its beginnings. However, we realize that its creation and early realization depends on the awareness of those who have goodwill in the world and their firm determination to realize this new age. It is a historical responsibility. It is the responsibility of all those who care for tomorrow — the victims of the current oppressive system, those who respond to the new concepts of the masses, nongovernmental organizations, and educated people who uncovered the falsehood of the prevailing exploitative system and the reality of societies of oppression. All of the above, with our support and urging, have to shoulder the responsibility of building the society of tomorrow and the dawn of the age of the masses.

The Honorable

Rachid Ghannouchi

Eminent Islamic Thinker and
Leader of the Tunisian Opposition
Party An-Nahdah

Islam and the West

Concord or Inevitable Conflict

Islam today occupies a leading position on the platform of intellectual and political arguments and within the realm of strategic planning, intelligence activity, and international relations, not as a salvation sought by a human community that is desperate for justice and tranquillity, but as a potential threat to the West, a danger to world peace, and a detriment to human heritage. It is viewed as a danger to peace and stability in the Middle East and to Israel, which, were it not for the fundamentalist nuisance, is about to be crowned leader of the new Middle East as the global leadership is transferred from Washington to Jerusalem, just as it moved before from London to Washington.

Thus, how real is this threat? In attempting to answer this question, I shall deal with a number of issues pertaining to the relationship between Islam and the West.

The Condition of the Muslim World

Around 1.5 billion Muslims (more than one-fifth of the world's population) inhabit approximately one-quarter of the total area of the globe. Two-thirds of them constitute majorities in fifty-five states that belong to the underdeveloped countries of the South. Most

Muslims are governed by autocratic and despotic regimes, whether monarchic or republican. Evidently, in the Arab world, the very heart of the Muslim world, not a single regime has been produced by free elections. The rate of illiteracy is above 60 percent, and the economy is afflicted with unemployment, foreign debts, subordination, and severe shortages in basic food materials. For the past fifty years, the Palestinian question has been a central point of interest for official and popular circles. However, due to the failure of the secular despotic governments in accomplishing anything worthwhile at the level of development or democracy or the liberation of Palestine, not to mention preserving the identity or the rights of the people, a return-to-Islam phenomenon has emerged and spread. The repeated defeats of the governments and their sheer failure to confront the Zionist challenge led to an escalation in popular opposition thrusting in the direction of a return to their roots, demanding civil liberties, popular representation, social justice, and the implementation of Shari'ah as a comprehensive charter for the restoration of the nation's edifice. But the nature of these autocratic regimes and their associations did not permit them to fulfill the minimum demands of the peoples. Consequently, the tide of popular protest gained momentum while the governments escalated their repressive measures against the people. Clashes between the people and the regimes have become one of the important features of the Arab world in particular. By virtue of the fact that the regimes acquired their intellectual authority and international support from the West and from the corrupt, inept, and despotic secular elites, it was only natural that the main opposition would be Islamic. The West, and particularly its leader, the United States of America, the arch Satan as referred to by Imam Khomeyni, emerged as the main obstacle occluding the aspirations and dreams of the *umma* (community of believers).

The Political Objectives
of the Muslim World

The talk about common political objectives for both governments and peoples in the Muslim world is irrelevant due to, first, the divisions separating states and, second, the ongoing conflict between nations and governments. As far as the rulers are concerned, remaining in power and enjoying its bounties for an indefinite period is the greatest objective, for whose sake all values and sanctities may be sacrificed and stepped upon.

The archives of international human rights organizations provide unequivocal proof of the corrupt nature of these regimes. Another proof is provided by the repeated successes of the regimes themselves in elections, the result of which is no less than 99.99 percent in favor of the ruling elite. No sensible person would imagine that any human being, no matter how popular, could attain such strong popular support. Undoubtedly, these rulers have been trying to achieve some development in order to maintain stability and deny the Islamic opposition the opportunity to exploit the degrading circumstances in order to enlighten the public.

The territorial integrity of the various countries of the Muslim world, which is groaning under the oppression of corrupt despotic secular regimes, is threatened by civil wars and invasion. As the crisis of development intensifies due to government corruption and lack of credibility and due to the growing rate of looting by the western center of the peripheries, the real policies of the majority of the Muslim countries, especially after having relinquished the objective of liberating Palestine, seem to be confined to a security-oriented function to suppress the aspirations of the people and guarantee the existence and stability of the regimes.

As for the peoples of the Muslim world, their objectives contradict those of their regimes. They aspire to regain their Islamic identity, to improve their financial, cultural, educational, and technological conditions on the basis of their faith, and to reorganize their domestic affairs in accordance with the teachings of their religion while benefiting from the legacy of humanity.[1] They are far from posing any threat of invading any other nation or intervening in its affairs. All they wish from the others is recognition of their sovereignty and respect for their religion and civilization in exchange for a similar recognition and respect in a relationship of mutual cooperation and coexistence.

The Islamic peoples aspire to complement their political independence with cultural, economic, and civilizational independence. They seek to accomplish a genuine democratic transition in their societies where the rule of the majority will replace the rule of the minority. They hope to accomplish true development by meeting the basic needs of humans, liberating their potential energies and resources within the framework of the Islamic code of conduct that encourages work and considers it to be a form of worship, and that respects private ownership, pursues justice, promotes cooperation and compassion, replaces usury by the principle of partnership, and combats all forms of corruption.

The peoples of the Muslim world are determined to perfect their national liberation, to support the banished people of Palestine until they return to their homeland, and to accomplish economic, cultural, and political integration.

The Crisis in the Relationship between the West and Islam

The relationship between the West and Islam is suffering a real crisis that has the potential to explode and cause massive damage. The crisis is self-evident in the exchange of accusations and in portraying the "other" as the source of evil and danger. Although the Muslim perception of the West has improved, thanks to the increase in the number of Muslims exposed to the culture and literature of the West, to the extent of admiration and imitation, the percentage of westerners who learn Arabic or study the Islamic culture, especially within the ranks of politicians, journalists, economists, and intellectuals, is still very small and is actually decreasing. Unlike their predecessors, diplomats who work in the Arab countries nowadays rarely master the Arabic language.[2] Islam is a misunderstood religion, and more people discover it through the attitude of Muslim extremists. Hence, a negative picture originating in the era of the Crusaders has been consolidated after having been reinforced through the ages by various forms of conflict. With the downfall of communism, Islam replaced communism as the source of fear.[3]

The western and the U.S. media have, deliberately or out of ignorance, exploited the public's ignorance regarding Islam and its history and have succeeded to a large extent in isolating Muslims and in portraying Islam as an antagonist of the West and its civilization. One may cite as an example the media coverage of the World Trade Center bombing in New York. The media focused on the identity of the defendants, and by virtue of their being Muslim, Islam became the main defendant in the whole issue.[4] The U.S. media turned the event into a trial for Islam and Muslims. Conversely, the Jewish Defense League previously perpetrated no less than seventy bombings in the United States. They were covered up, and no one accused the Jews or Judaism of anything.[5]

Although Muslims are to be held responsible for any irresponsible, terrorist, or hostile reactions or statements that distort the image of Islam, the western media has — since the eruption of the Iranian revolution — been feeding the public with distorted images that cause resentment and fear and that associates Islam with danger, as if it were opposed to sublime values and to the aspirations of humanity in accomplishing peace, freedom, progress, and equality.[6]

The Theory of the
Conflict between Civilizations

The negative attitude toward Islam has surpassed the stage of media propaganda, which might indeed be attributed to ignorance, to historical and philosophical analyses alleging the conflict with Islam to be a strategic and historical inevitability. Harvard University professor Samuel Huntington's theory, formulated in his Summer 1993 *Foreign Affairs* article, is a striking example.[7]

The Role of the Zionist Lobby

Although the Arabs and the Muslims have never been weaker, to the extent that their richest countries have become almost bankrupt, and although the primary beneficiary of post–Cold War transitions and the Gulf war aftermath is the Zionist entity, the Zionists have mobilized all their global resources in lobbying all the powers in the world against Islam under the pretext that it is now the threat. Consequently, Israel is once again portrayed as the West's strategic ally that ought to be supported and financed in order to confront the new threat. The Israelis were horrified to see the West accomplish its objectives in the Gulf without requiring the assistance of Israel, which appeared aged and dwarflike and seemed a dispensable subordinate. The danger has gone, and all parties now compete to attain the pleasure of the West. Therefore, in order to restore the traditional status and role and to guarantee the continuation of generous aid, it is necessary to invent an enemy for the West and its interests in the region and in the world. For historical and psychological reasons, Islam has been picked. The media machine and Jewish diplomacy have for the past three years been banging the drums of war against Islam, mobilizing powers and offering expertise to fight against it.[8] In 1992, the president of the Hebrew state addressed the European Parliament, instigating it against the "fundamentalist threat," belittling its members, and accusing them of ignorance with regard to the Middle East and insisting that fundamentalism posed the greatest threat to the world. Yitzhak Rabin was no less unequivocal in his instigation of enmity against Muslims when, in Washington, he stated that the United States had to support Israel so as to wage war against the Islamists, the enemies of peace, who threaten Algeria and the ruling regimes in Egypt, Tunisia, and other countries in the region. Shimon Peres was no less unequivocal in underlining this strategy and in provoking the West against Islam. In February 1993, he addressed U.S. officials at the White House saying, "The U.S. should increase its aid to Israel rather than reduce it since Israel is waging a ferocious war against Islamic extremism." Addressing the Federation of Jewish Organizations in Washington, Rabin said, "We are not sure that President Clinton and his team fully realize the threat of Islamic fundamentalism and the decisive role Israel plays in combating it."[9] The Israeli leader was not content with instigating the West but went further to provoke the Arab states, saying, "The Arab world and the whole world will pay dearly if this Islamic cancer is not stopped. . . . By fighting Muslim terrorists we aim to awaken the world that is sleeping unaware of an important fact, namely that this danger is serious, real and threatens world peace. Today, we the Israelis, truly stand in the firing line against fundamentalist Islam. We demand all states and nations to focus their attention on this huge threat inherent in Islamic fundamentalism."

The Zionist orchestra swiftly responded to the instructions of the maestro. In its conference, the American Israel Public Affairs Committee (AIPAC) called for the necessity of confronting the Islamic fundamentalist dangers and urged the United States to rely on its Israeli ally to accomplish this objective.[10] The American Zionist writer Paul Model was most unequivocal in expressing this strategy when he said, "The Americans must comprehend that Israel has served them for many years when it stood as a barrier preventing the spread of the communist threat in the Middle East. Now, following the disappearance of this threat, a new huge threat has emerged, namely Islamic fundamentalism, against which Israel stands because it threatens the Middle East and the entire Christian world. Hence, it is incumbent upon the Americans to fully support Israel so as to confront this new threat."[11]

Within this framework we find an abundance of writings by prominent journalists and academics such as Judie Miller, Bernard Lewis, his pupil Martin Kramer, and Yusef Budenski. In their promotion of the idea of the fundamentalist threat to the West and the Israeli role in confronting it, they do not differ from the leaders of Israel or the leaders of the Arab states that adopt the security option in confronting the Islamists.[12] It is worth noting that, just like partisan propaganda, this campaign against fundamentalism, in which respectable writers and academics take part, adopts the methods of exaggeration and generalization. It avoids any attempt to provide clear definitions for such vague and obscure concepts as fundamentalism, which has been applied to every worker in the field of Islamic *da'wah* (propagation), and perhaps every Muslim, without distinction in this wide arena between the mainstream, moderate trend within the Islamic movement, which endeavors to work within the system and resists any attempt to draw it into a violent confrontation with the regimes, and a minority trend that could not tolerate the oppression and tyranny of the rulers and opted to respond to the rulers' violence against their opponents, whether they were Islamists or non-Islamists, with counterviolence.

Daniel Pipes, the editor of the respectable specialized journal *Middle East Policy*, has no hesitation in describing those who work for Islam as fundamentalists: "Can we really distinguish between a bad fundamentalist and a good fundamentalist as the Clinton Administration claimed considering those fundamentalist who resort to terrorism and endanger our interests are our enemies and not those who are committed to political activity within the system? I disagree with this theory. They are all extremists and they all despise our civilization. They do not despise us because of what we do but because of what we are. A fundamentalist is one who seeks to establish a style of life that is incompatible with ours. The United States should not encourage or cooperate or communicate with such people. It should not work with the fundamentalist but should rather confront them. As we worked before with the right against the left, we are requested today, following the disappearance of the threat of the left, to cooperate with it against the right (the fundamentalists), that is cooperate with the FNL in Algeria and with Dostom in Afghanistan. I call for supporting these governments and groups in their fight against fundamentalists. Therefore, it is necessary to support the French position in siding with the existing government even though we know it is corrupt simply because it does not threaten our interests in North Africa and Egypt whereas the success of the fundamentalists will and may even harm our interests in Western Europe and the Middle East."[13]

The Propaganda Machine

Events in succession have provided the well-equipped western media machine with an opportunity to agitate against Islam and to mobilize public opinion against the Islamic awakening, stirring fears that the West's interests, lifestyle, and values are being threatened. To speak of fundamentalism is to speak of Islam and to speak of violence, hijacking, women's subjugation, and hostility to all the beautiful things invented by the West. The Iranian revolution, and the events that succeeded it, had the impact of an earthquake on the West. Concern about freedom of expression and criticism and the sense of threat created in western circles by Imam Khomeyni's *fatwa* against British writer Salman Rushdie, in contrast to the disappointment and resentment felt by the Muslims in response to the forms of honorific gestures accorded to Rushdie by western political and intellectual circles, augmented the tension between the two sides. Suspicion and apprehension are further heightened by the existence of large Muslim communities in major cities in the West, whose civilization has never before experienced what Muslim societies experienced of religious and ethnic pluralism. This phenomenon sustained the feelings of apprehension toward Islam, which was perceived as a threat to the western lifestyle. It even led to an escalation in xenophobia and boosted the popularity of the extreme right, which blames all social illnesses, unemployment, and crime on Muslim immigrants. The Islamic threat was, after all, transferred from abroad to home, where it became an issue for political campaigning, especially in France, whose wound of defeat in Algeria has not yet healed and which is known for its extreme secular heritage that is very hostile to Islam. Even the atheist pioneers of enlightenment, such as Voltaire, had no hesitation in flattering the religious and political establishments of his time by expressing hatred for Islam and instigating war against it. Voltaire, who had written a book of slander against Prophet Muhammad, excluded Muslims from those who had the right to enjoy tolerance according to his famous speech of 1762. He considered Turks a curse and called for their extermination. He confessed to Catherine the Great that the sacking of the Ottoman Empire would enable him to die content, adding as his one regret that he would die without having taken part in killing the Turks. This mode of thinking is by no means part of history. In his book *Le nouveau monde*, Pierre Lelouche, key adviser to Jacques Chirac, French majority leader and presidential candidate, warns against the growing dangers of fundamentalism and dictatorship in the Muslim world. Former Belgian interior minister and European Parliament member Joseph Michele played the same tune, saying: "We run the risk of becoming like the Roman people, invaded by barbarian peoples such as Arabs, Moroccans, Yugoslavs and Turks."[14]

Undoubtedly, the media found in the news of attacks against tourists, foreigners, and writers in Egypt and Algeria the daily material to nourish the western mind with the feelings of hatred and suspicion toward Islam, exaggerating events and portraying them as if they were the true expression of fundamentalism, or in other words Islam. Little is mentioned about the circumstances in which such acts are perpetrated or about the likelihood that they are perpetrated not by Islamists but by agents of intelligence services that defend existing dictatorships. Even if perpetrated by Islamists, the perpetrators usually belong to a marginal and limited minority within the broad Islamic movement.

Muslims' Perceptions

On the other hand, the West is increasingly perceived by practicing and nonpracticing Muslims as a conspirator against the interests of Arabs and Muslims — a monolithic black and white image, a simple fact that never changes. These are the same ones whose horses marched up to their knees in the blood of Muslims when Jerusalem was invaded. They are the ones who destroyed the Islamic caliphate, colonized our countries, imposed secularism and partition on us, and, through culture and intelligence, captured the hearts and minds of a generation of our children, instituted them as despotic rulers, and supplied them with material and moral support in order to embezzle our resources, sustain backwardness in our countries, and deny us the right to democracy. They are the ones who usurped our resources and implanted in the heart of our *umma* an entity, Israel, that is hostile to it so as to sustain division and fragmentation. They supported this entity with all available means and resources and stood watching in acquiescence the daily crimes committed by its troops. Bosnia is another Palestine in central Europe where, before the eyes of the European states and the United Nations, a people have been raped and annihilated by bloodthirsty bandits that enjoy overt and covert support and an encouragement of silence over the destruction of a state that would have been an international model of coexistence among religions and ethnicities and that would have been a meeting point between Islam and Christianity. The unarmed people of Bosnia have even been denied their legitimate right to defend themselves. Hundreds of conferences have been held, but they produced no more than maneuvers. Muslims ask this question: why have the fleets been deployed to protect Kuwait from Saddam Hussein and to restore democracy in Haiti while no move was made to rescue the people of Bosnia? They ask: why does the White House master warn and threaten the strugglers of Hamas as they defend their homeland, and why is he moved by the killing of a Zionist soldier who for years had no job other than repressing the uprising of the Palestinian men, women, and children, breaking their limbs in front of cameras while he remains silent toward the crimes perpetrated against the peoples of Bosnia, Kashmir, Tajikistan, and Azerbeijan? They ask: why are human rights in Iraq defended while those in Saudi Arabia, Egypt, Tunisia, and Algeria are not? Why is democracy in Haiti supported and fleets are rushed to its aid while dictatorships in Algeria and everywhere else in the countries of Muslims are aided? Muslims find no convincing logic for these scandalous western double standards except one simple explanation: namely, the fact that they are Muslims. Because they are Muslims, they have no right to live honorably—that is, if their right to life is recognized at all.

Limited and Hesitant Improvement

Despite this organized campaign to which strategic minds and apostles of politics in the West have been subjected—in the direction of incriminating the Islamic movement as a whole and even Islam itself, a matter that is exploited by arms merchants, Zionist lobbyists, and Arab states that reject the democratic option under the pretext of combating the fundamentalist threat—there remain a few courageous voices inside some western research centers and within political circles, especially in the United States, that resist the enormous pressures and blackmail. These persons insist on distinguishing between Islam and fundamentalism, considering Islam to be a religion that enriches civilization and culture, including the American culture, and that is embraced by millions of Americans. They resist the assumption that Islam is the new enemy that replaces communism and recognize that fundamentalists are not one thing or a simple reality but a broad spectrum of trends. They believe that the West, including the United States, is not an enemy of Islam or the Islamic movement, but an enemy of radicalism, whether Islamic or secular. The trend in this direction in U.S. official circles started with the 1992 Meridian speech by Edward Djerjian and was expressed later on by ambassador Robert H. Pellet and Anthony Lake in 1994. Similar remarks were expressed by President Clinton inside the Jordanian parliament, although he attacked those opposed to peace and threatened that he would resist them and not allow them to sabotage the peace.[15] The same trend was observed in Prince Charles's brilliant speech at Oxford University, which was indeed unprecedented by a western official.[16] These voices also include such great scholars and researchers as John Esposito, John Voll, Yvonne Hadad, John Intles, Graham Foller, Jennifer Noyon, Francois Burgat, and Garoudi. Their works have confirmed what is repeatedly stressed by the mainstream trend within the Islamic movement: (1) Islam, as a religion, is not entirely contradictory to the West. While not denying the existence of major differences, it is confirmed that the meeting points between the two civilizations are more significant than between any other two civilizations; (2) Islamic revivalism does not pose a threat to the West, but rather opens a window of opportunities; (3) the future bears the potential for normalization, cooperation, and the exchange of interests instead of alienation and conflict.

Compatibility

Islam, a religion and a civilization, is not entirely incompatible with the West. Coexistence is possible, and a common ground for both to stand on does exist.

If Islam to the Muslims means a religion and a way of life at the same time, and if in the life of Muslims Islam has a distinct experience and a special role in society and civilization, it can be argued that western civilization has not severed its relationship with Christianity since it embraced it. Although this relationship has witnessed some tense moments in history, Christianity remained a principal component of western conscience and culture, not only at the individual level but also at the social level: family ties, customs, and arts and literature. The influence of religion is seen even at the political level, evidently in the existence of major Christian political parties, either in government or in the opposition, in more than a western country. This is manifest also in the special status enjoyed by the Pope in international politics, the growth of religious trends in the United States, and the increasingly influential role they have been playing since the Reagan and Bush administrations — so much so that religion has become an important issue in election campaigns when certain issues such as abortion are discussed. Then came the unplanned agreement between Islamic and Christian representatives to the Cairo conference on population in the confrontation of the radical secularists from both the Muslim and western worlds. This was a vivid expression of the common religious roots shared jointly by the Islamic and Christian civilizations, roots that have occasionally been ignored by both sides, but more frequently by the West. These roots represent the belief in the oneness of God, in divine revelation, and in the hereafter; it comprises basic principles for distinguishing good from evil, for asserting family values and their sanctity, and for establishing social and political norms such as the existence of a unified law that governs people's lives and transcends their individual wills. Respecting the law is a value that is inseparable from religion, although it has been overwhelmed by a secular dimension in the West and by Shari'ah in Islam.

Sanctifying the law and believing in the unity of the universe and of God are all fundamental concepts in which these two neighboring civilizations were, in one way or another, founded. They both belong to one origin, the religion of Ibrahim. Any difficulty encountered pertains mostly to the Christian side, which has never recognized Islam as a religion, but continues to consider it a form of heresy, debasing its figures and honoring its abusers. On the other hand, Islam recognized Christianity, honored its scripture, praised its figures and prophets, and protected its churches and symbols. The Quran creates in the mind of every Muslim a most wonderful, a most bright, and a most sacred image of Christ and his mother, peace be upon them. It considers the Christians to be the closest in friendship to the Muslims. "Strongest among men in enmity to the believers wilt thou find the Jews and Pagans; and nearest among them in love to the believers wilt thou find those who say 'We are Christians': because amongst these are men devoted to learning and men who have renounced the world, and they are not arrogant." [17]

In addition to the religious womb wherein the Islamic and western civilizations evolved, there is the legacy of a common culture of rational knowledge, a legacy that was exchanged and interchanged. It emerged in the East, the cradle of religion and civilization, with the Babylonians, the

Assyrians, and the pharaohs, and later on moved to the Greeks and the Romans who enriched and developed it further. It returned to the East once more with the advent of Islam, which embraced it, preserved it, and brought very important developments to it. It would not have been possible to appreciate the modern western renaissance without taking into consideration Islam's significant contribution, which has been denied by the western renaissance, although the Muslims never denied the contribution of the Greeks. Discoveries and innovations of Muslims, such as blood circulation and numerous findings in mechanics, physics, mathematics, medicine, agriculture, engineering, music, and geography, have been denied. For more than a century now, Muslims have been sending their children to the West to learn the western wisdom just as the westerners used to send their children to Gordova, Baghdad, Shiraz, and Sarajevo. Rational knowledge, which emancipated the world from illusions and viewed it as a mere objective governed by norms and laws that can be discovered and utilized, is a relic of divine messages, of Unitarian religions, and is a mutual cultural womb for Islamic and western civilizations. No such relics can be traced in the civilizations such as those of East Asia, which are founded in manmade animistic religions that sanctify and worship nature and creatures.

What is really astonishing is that during the renaissance, Europe's religious reform developed a conception of Christianity and its relations with other religions that undermined Islam and denied it and its civilization all virtues. Ties were severed almost completely with Islam in favor of other religions, such as Judaism, in a process that led to the birth of the concept of a Judeo-Christian civilization. Although Judaism belongs to the same Abrahamic family of Unitarian religions, the Jews maintained their attitude toward other religions, denying them and debasing their cultures. They never recognized Christianity and maintained their disrespectful view of Christ and his mother, which is no less contemptible than their view of Muhammad, his book, or his followers. While in civilizational standards Judaism made no significant contribution to the European renaissance compared with that of the Islamic civilization, the Christian world, and particularly Protestants, went far beyond merely recognizing it as a religion to pronouncing it a civilizational partner. In fact, fair and objective studies have confirmed that it was the Islamic civilization that contributed effectively in the making of modern civilization. All the excavations undertaken by the Jews in Palestine to prove they had a civilization there have been in vain. If only the West could be fair and free from bigotry, what but Islam and its civilization would be recognized as the legitimate partners in this modern civilization?

In fact, the history of political conflict between Muslims and westerners was never void of interchange and complementarity. However, clash dominated the image of this relationship and obscured the attempts at rapprochement among scholars, traders, and craftsmen, not to mention the valuable cultural exchange across the Mediterranean, the Indian Ocean, and the Bosporus.

Religious fanaticism in the history of Europe did not permit Muslim minorities to live in western cities; even Christian sects did not tolerate one another, whereas in Muslim cities religious sects, whether Islamic or Christian, coexisted and enjoyed freedom. Thanks to the communications revolution and to a reduction in the levels of religious fanaticism as a result of the victory of secularism in the West, movement in both directions was encouraged and affiliates of both civilizations coexisted on both sides. Today, there are no less than fifty million Muslims living in the American and European continents and almost a similar number of Christians living in the Muslim world. Instead of perceiving religious minorities as a threat, they ought to be viewed as cultural bridges between the two civilizations. I was impressed by the response by the Reverend Father Antwan Dhaw to my call in Beirut last October for the initiation of an Islamic-western dialogue. He said: "We the Christians of the Orient are more capable of initiating this dialogue with the Westerners." Similarly, such Islamic institutions as the American Muslim Council in the United States and the Federation of Islamic Organizations in Europe and such western Muslims as Garudi, Bob Crane, Yusuf Islam, and Murad Hoffman can initiate communication between the West and the Muslim world so that the two sides can resolve problems through dialogue and cooperation.

The religious, cultural, and geographic proximity between the two civilizations has always compelled them to deal with one another. With the progress in transport and communications, and in view of the fact that the globe has become a small village, dealings and exchange of trade and other interests have increased enormously. Isolationism serves no purpose, and the exchange will have to continue unabated, even if Islamists assume power in the region. On the contrary, cooperation and coordination may increase and the problem of development may be resolved with the introduction of the Islamic factor, which will put an end to dictatorship and corruption. Then the direction of migration may be reversed back to the South, where stability will prevail; this is exactly what the North has been demanding as a condition for development and cooperation. The Islamic civilization has always been open and forward and has always encouraged trade, the exchange of commodities and ideas, and free movement of persons and goods.

As mentioned earlier, Islam is not only a faith; it is a way of life as well. Islam has put forward a comprehensive conception of the universe, of life, and of man, thus recognizing man's mental, spiritual, and physical needs. It eliminated the clash within society between religion and state, religion and ethics, religion and science, individual and community, and life and the hereafter.

Islam asserts the necessity of establishing an authority to organize and administer the affairs of the society. However, it stipulates that this authority be subject to the law, not to whims and desires, and that it should emanate from the will of the people in a form of a contract of allegiance: obedience in exchange for adherence to Shari'ah and Shura. The public should be guaranteed the freedom to object and comment. In fact, Shura is spoken of as one of the attributes of the believers and is mentioned concurrently with *salat* (prayer) and *zakat* (alms).

The democratic style of Western Europe has achieved a very important accomplishment by stripping power from a single person and turning it over to the public. It is the best mechanism ever invented by mankind thus far for resolving disputes without the use of force, for power sharing, and for a peaceful rotation of power. Perhaps the first experience of a peaceful rotation of power in the history of mankind was that of the early Muslims, when power was not separated from the public and when public affairs were discussed in the mosque in the presence of all men and women, who participated in decision making through freedom of expression and open criticism of the governor. Before long, however, the predominant imperial spirit of the time prevailed and styles of government that combined Islam and tribalism emerged. Today, the Islamists face governments very similar to those that prevailed in medieval Europe: autocracies wrapped in religious slogans (such as the Saudi regime) or in barren modernity slogans void of any element of genuine modernity where the law is above the ruler and not vice versa.

The Islamic movement has been called fundamentalist, a term borrowed by the western media from the West's own dictionary. It has nothing to do with fundamentalism, which means the literal adherence to the Bible, because Islam has allowed a spacious margin for *ijtihad* (human endeavor) to interpret the text, which is purposively meant to cover only a small area of the problems of the people. The human mind is left to cover the remaining areas, allowing it unlimited space for interpretation, deduction, and innovation. In the absence of an absolute religious authority for the interpretation of the text, the only authority left for resolving disputes is that of the public opinion. This too is not restricted to a specific form of organization. Hence, the Muslims have every reason to be happy with what democracy has provided in the form of tools and mechanisms, such as parliaments and supreme courts, for resolving disputes.

The Islamic movement is very much like the renaissance movement in medieval Europe — a movement of universal cultural revival that eventually seeks to translate its slogans into effective social reform in rigid societies that have become so backward. The term "fundamentalism" is, thus, misleading, and what we are witnessing is in fact a very liberal and a very progressive phenomenon.[18] The Islamic movement is the most democratic political movement in the Muslim world because it emanates from and addresses the people.[19] Politics, which has been isolated from the public by the ruling secularist elites, has now been communicated back to the public. Thanks to the efforts of the Islamic movement, average citizens are now actively engaged in public matters after having, for decades, been spoken to by the secularist elites in a language beyond their comprehension. By enforcing a separation between religion and politics, the groups of fake modernity in the Muslim world excluded the people from public affairs in a monopoly that resembles that of medieval priests and feudal lords. Excluding the Islamists from participation in government entails, as has been explained by impartial researchers, including many westerners, denying the overwhelming majority of the opposition the right to join the state's constitutional institutions. This consequently leads to dictatorship, which in turn leads to the "death of politics"[20] — as in Tunisia and in most of the Arab countries — or to the transformation of politics into some kind of a civil war, as in Algeria and to some extent in Egypt, and perhaps more will follow.

The conflict in the Muslim world, as explained by Professor Ernest Gellner, is between western values and the belief in the necessity of eventually turning to the *umma* for arbitration, considering it to be the source of guidance and inspiration.[21] Modernists in the Muslim world do not resemble their counterparts in the West, whose revolution was founded on the concept of regaining power from the priests and delivering it to the people, that is, bringing it down from the heavens to the earth. This is exactly the role the Islamic movement is performing, while modernists behave just like medieval priests: they have monopolized power, resources, and the press and have nationalized religion itself, whereas in the West secularists liberated religion from state influence. Most westerners, including some scholars, fall prey to the deceit of expressions. They think that Bourguiba, Ataturk, Saddam Hussein, and Nasser are pioneers of modernity who confront the symbols of medieval priesthood, Hasan Al-Banna, Turabi, Madani, and Anwar Ibrahim. In fact, it is the Islamic democrats, modernists, and revivalists who rise against the traditions of decline and who represent the second coming of the renaissance in confronting the feudal secularist priesthood represented by such symbols as Fahd and Hussein, who have, by wearing the ropes of religion, outdistanced Bourguiba, Gadhafi, BenAli, and Nasser. They all monopolized religion and acted as spokesmen for it. Bourguiba, like Ataturk, went as far as imposing a single uniform on men and women. He issued an edict nullifying the worship of fasting, and one of his judges sentenced a Muslim scholar to death for a set of charges including allowing himself to interpret the Quran in a manner that contradicted the understanding of his excellency the president.[22]

It has become obvious that the participation of the Islamists in any professional or political elections or in any intellectual function transforms these processes, giving them popular impetus and distinct vividness, rendering the conflict real and reviving the political, social, and intellectual dimensions of life. Conversely, the exclusion of the Islamists means the death of democracy and the replacement of ballot boxes by ammunition boxes.

If there are still some within the ranks of the Islamists who argue about the appropriateness of democracy and its compatibility with Islam, they do so mostly because of the ambiguities associated with democracy. It was brought to us on top of western tanks and has been associated in people's minds with corrupt elitist regimes, thus creating an environment of estrangement with the general public. Furthermore, western democratic systems have been perceived as oppressors of the Muslim world, especially in Palestine and in Bosnia. These factors have had an antagonizing effect on the efforts of the supporters of democracy within the Islamic movement.

The mainstream trend within the Islamic movement is earnestly searching for an opportunity to work from within the existing political order, presenting itself as a project seeking to compete peacefully with other projects. However, the problem today does not emanate from the need to convince the Islamic movement of the viability of democracy but rather in convincing the other side — that is, the ruling secularist theocracies. The problem is further augmented by the insistence of their western friends to provide them with certificates of good conduct and to reassert their friendship with corrupt dictatorships such as those in Tunisia, Egypt, and Saudi Arabia. U.S. officials have gone as far as inverting facts and fabricating stories to justify U.S. support for these antidemocracy, anti-Islam dictatorships.[23]

Hence, democracy constitutes no problem for the Islamic movement, which has been struggling for the restoration of legitimacy through democratization of the people's authority and for participation in administering public affairs, for political pluralism, for the equality of rights, for the rotation of power through the ballot box, and for securing the rights of minorities and women. As far as women are concerned, Islam clearly underlines the principle of equality between the sexes in freedom, dignity, and responsibility before Allah and the people. Those who know the Islamic movement would confirm that women are widely involved in its activities, whether social or political, and have a place in its high-ranking and leading positions. The Muslim Brotherhood has published an important document about the participation of women in political life at all levels.[24]

Within weeks, the Algerian ballot boxes explained matters pertaining to the Islamic trends that thousands of pages written about these trends have not been able to explain. In addition to decisively shattering the allegations that the Islamists were only minority groups that feared the holding of free elections lest they are marginalized, and that they find no means other than plotting to seize power by force, the 1991 Algerian elections clearly showed that the overwhelming majority of women voted for the Islamic Salvation Front. The elections also refuted the naive argument that there had been a mobilization against women.[25] The fact is that women had been more sensitive and more adversely affected by the process of secularization, which impoverished the country and shook its social edifice, placing it on the brink of collapse. Consequently, there had been a rush toward Islam in pursuit of protection and spiritual and social warmth. After all, Islam honors women, treating them as humans and not merely as objects for pleasure and business. This, perhaps, explains the phenomenon of the large number of women, compared with men, who embrace Islam in the West.[26] To women, Islam is not merely a *hijab* (veil); it is dignity. The *hijab* is only a symbol of this dignity, which mandates addressing women as humans to be judged in accordance with their thoughts and deeds and not merely as paintings or fashion shows or as a means for arousing desires.

Today the West is promoting the idea of the market economy and is almost turning it into a religion, which it seeks to impose on humanity, especially following the defeat of the socialist system. Undoubtedly, if the market economy were to be stripped of what capitalism injected into it of monopolies, protections, various forms of cheating and manipulation, and exploitation of the weak by the strong, it could become a natural and normal system subject to the law of supply and demand. If such were the case, Islam, the religion of natural instinct, could never be at odds with this system. Islam endorses the right of an individual to own and recognizes his or her right to dispose of what he or she possesses, linking it to work. Islam values the effort made by laborers and approves of trade-generated profits. The Prophet himself, peace be upon him, was a merchant; he married a prominent merchant lady, and some of his companions were well-known merchants as well. Islam encourages Muslims to search for knowledge, to discover the laws of nature, to locate natural resources, and to make use of all this for the benefit of humanity. Muslims are enjoined to walk through the earth, discover the secrets of the universe, and acquaint themselves with the cultures and habits of other peoples and exchange benefits and ideas with them.

It is only fitting for a global religion that calls for believing in the Lord of all worlds to eliminate the artificial restrictions imposed on humanity by religious and racial fanaticism, so humans can get acquainted, communicate, and cooperate. Which economic system is more appropriate and more compatible with the spirit of this Quranic teaching: "O mankind! We created you from a single (pair) of a male and a female, and made you into nations and tribes, that you may know each other (not that you may despise each other). Verily, the most honored of you in the sight of Allah is (he who is) the most righteous of you"?[27] Has the Quran left a single human group out of this address that calls on all to communicate and cooperate: "Help you one another in righteousness and piety, but help you not one another in sin and rancor"?[28]

However, Islam rejects the deification of the economy as Marxism and capitalism do, turning the human being into a mere productive creature that is assessed in term of its productivity. Both ideologies have caused an imbalance and have stripped values and faith of their meaning; they have led to the collapse of the family and have sacrificed social ties in favor of worshiping the god of economy. This god is so liberal that no traditional or moral values are treasured anymore. Production is the objective, profit making is the sole objective of production, and fulfilling material desires is the sole objective of profit making. Such a conception has been the source of great disasters for humanity; it has been the motive for colonialism and for the usurpation of other nations' resources. It has led to the destruction of the environment, the threatening of human lives, the destruction of the family, and the development of weapons of mass destruction instead of the means of food production.

As for Islam, it holds the balance right. It has a comprehensive conception of man and the universe, recognizing the rights of all; the body has a right, the mind has a right, the soul has a right, the family has a right, neighbors have rights, and each right should be recognized and served.[29]

Wealth, as viewed by Islam, belongs to God, and humans are entrusted with using it properly in accordance with the Islamic code of conduct. Islam forbids the dispensing of wealth in luxury or investing it in what could cause harm to others or freezing it and restricting its circulation. It prescribes a share for the community in this wealth so as to be spent on the poor and in serving the public interest. This is a worship whose performers are promised reward and whose neglecters are promised punishment.

Thus, we find ourselves before a market economy system that is bound by specific moral values that prevent the deification of wealth and prohibit its use in destroying the society or in inflicting wars on other nations.

Conclusion

Islam, as a religion and civilization, and the Islamic movement, as a reform and renaissance endeavor aimed at rebuilding a balanced human materially, mentally, spiritually, and socially and at rebuilding the civil society as a foundation for a legitimacy that was toppled by fake modernization, do not represent a threat to any religion or civilization. Islam is defending its existence in the face of an international alliance, a cartel of interests, disguised in the name of Judaism, or Christianity, or international legitimacy, or human rights, or civilization that alleges to confront a fabricated danger called fundamentalism. Muslim blood is being shed all over the world, blessed by those in charge of the cartel of sacred interests in the name of which they've been sucking the blood of nations in the East and the West. Mr. Clinton shed his tears for the killing of an Israeli soldier, who might have been raised like murderer Goldstein in the United States or in Poland, whence he came together with alien gangs to usurp a land whose owners are still alive and are witness to the crime of displacing them from their homes to make room for the invaders. Those original inhabitants who remained in their homes have been oppressed in their own land; more than a thousand of their men, women, and children have so far been murdered since the eruption of the Intifada. All these victims deserve no single word of lamentation from Mr. Clinton, not even the Ibrahimi Mosque worshippers who were sprayed with bullets while in an act of prostration. No one has protested the erection of a memorial monument for the murderer who butchered them, whom some considered to be insane, while the chief rabbi mourned him saying: "His nail is worth a million Arabs."

Experience from history has proven that a supporter of oppression will inevitably become its victim. The British and then the Americans and all the leaders of the West have, under financial and media influence of the Jews, granted them what does not belong to them. They have guaranteed them unlimited support to the extent that preserving Israel is the first and foremost priority in U.S. policy toward the Middle East. Wealth, weapons, advanced technology, and the global influence of the West have all been employed to serve the interest of four million Jews at the expense of one billion Muslims. Experience has proven the Israelis to be infinitely greedy, infinitely arrogant, and infinitely immoral. The British role in enabling the Zionists to establish the Jewish state in Palestine did not save them from the crimes of Zionist gangsters who killed their high commissioner and perpetrated a number of attacks on their subjects and interests. The day will come, if it has not already come, when the leaders in the West will feel captive in their own countries and find they have no say in their own affairs. They will be made to pay dearly at the hands of the arrogant Zionists as a reward for supporting them. This is God's justice; it is fair and unbiased. Whoever supports an aggressor will be made to suffer at his hands. As for the aggressor, it should be known that God, the omnipotent, the just and merciful, is not neglectful. It is only logical that justice will eventually win. As Jerusalem's archbishop Kapuchi said, it would be foolish to imagine that a few million could maintain their control over humanity and influence cultures and faiths forever.

We believe that the sinful alliance against Islam, in the name of Judaism, Christianity, and some other slogans and ideologies, will eventually collapse no matter how strong it becomes. Therefore, we call on the West to reconcile with Islam, which is closest to you as a civilization and in terms of interests.

If we disagree on the Palestinian issue or on other issues, let us not make these issues look as if they are insurmountable obstacles. Let us shelve the files we disagree upon, such as that of the Palestinian issue, and let us recognize the right to disagree. We should begin with the other mutual files, such as the economy, religion and culture, immigration, the environment, and human rights.

The prediction that conflict between Islam and the West is inevitable is a false one; it stands on no solid ground. The advances in technology, in the sciences, and in communications leave no option before the nations of the world, if they indeed are after a viable future, but to endeavor to know each other, communicate, and exchange interests. This should be based on a mutual recognition of the sovereignty of each nation on its soil, on a commitment to refrain from initiating aggression, and on a willingness to cooperate. Recognizing diversity and the right to be different is essential for defeating the conception of civilizational centralism. We are for the concept of pluralism in, diversification of, and cooperation among civilizational centers.

We appreciate that legitimate conflict will continue, but this conflict is not between Christianity and Islam, or between Islam and Judaism. We are not against a people because of their religion or because of their color. We alone have recognized everybody else and have been waiting for others to respond by recognizing us. The legitimate conflict according to our faith is the conflict against oppression and aggression, the conflict of truth against falsehood, against despotism and hegemony under whatever pretext, whether in the name of Islam or in the name of democracy. In fact, the worst form of despotism is that practiced in the name of noble slogans.

Events in the Muslim world send a message to those who hear and see: Islam is coming to restore dignity for its followers, to liberate them from despotism, to regain the lost popular legitimacy, to restrict the powers of the state, and to establish and reinforce the power of the people, the power of civil society. Islam is coming to liberate its land from local tyrants and from international tyrants. It is coming to set its community in a new civilizational cycle, where it will make a contribution to salvaging and developing the civilizational heritage of humanity. It is coming not as an alternative or a new page, but to complement, communicate, and cooperate. Muhammad, peace be upon him, had come to "perfect noble manners" and to endorse the missions of those messengers that preceded him, but not to discredit them or to disbelieve in them. In other words, his mission was to preserve and complement the legacy of those before him.

History has shown that Islam has had the experience of enduring in resisting those who encroach on its community or on its land. So none should be fooled by the present weakness of the Muslims, and none should take for granted the treaties and deals that are being concluded falsely and unjustly in its name or in the name of its people; these are but deals of capitulation and humiliation and not the deals of the peoples.

To westerners and to Americans we say: we want you to know that we Muslims harbor no ill feelings for you or for your superpower, but we want our right to freedom in our own countries, to choose the system we feel comfortable with. We want the relationship between you and us to be based on friendship, not subordination. We see a potential for an exchange of ideas, for a flow of information and for cultural exchange in a reality governed by rules of competition and cooperation rather than the rules of hegemony and subordination.

We call on you to halt your aggression against our people and against our religion. We invite you to a historic reconciliation, to rapprochement, and to cooperation. After all, you are the closest of all other humans to us, in terms of geography, religion, civilization, and interests.

"Say: O people of the Book! come to common terms as between us and you: that we worship none but Allah; that we associate no partners with Him; that we erect not, from among ourselves Lords and patrons other than Allah." [30]

— *Translated from Arabic by Azzam Tamimi*

Notes

1. Dr. Khorshid Ahmad, *International Affairs*, no. 209 (January 1994).
2. As remarked by the distinguished French orientalist François Burgat.
3. Robert Sole, *Le Monde* (Paris), October 13, 1994.
4. Dr. Yvonne Hadad, presentation at Islam and the West symposium,

Washington, D.C., October 1993, quoted in *Al-Mujtama'* (Kuwait), December 7, 1993.

5. Dr. Abdeen Jbarah, presentation at Islam and the West symposium, quoted in ibid.

6. See John L. Esposito, *The Islamic Threat: Myth or Reality?* (New York: Oxford University Press, 1992).

7. *Foreign Affairs* 72, no. 3.

8. Rachid Ghannouchi, "Israel's Strategy and the Fundamentalist Threat," *Ash-Sha'b* (Cairo), 1993.

9. *Al-Mujtama'* (Kuwait), December 7, 1993.

10. Ibid.

11. Ibid.

12. See Israeli ambassador Zalmal Shufal's statement published in *Al-Hayat* (London), April 7, 1992.

13. Daniel Pipes, ibid.

14. John Keane, "Power-Sharing Islam," in *Power-Sharing Islam?* ed. Azzam Tamimi (London: Liberty for Muslim World, 1993), pp. 16–18.

15. Press reports on President Clinton's visit to Jordan and his address before the Jordanian parliament.

16. Charles, Prince of Wales, "Islam and the West" (speech delivered at the Oxford Centre of Islamic Studies, October 1993).

17. Holy Quran 5:82.

18. Dr. Hasan Turabi, testimony before the U.S. Congressional Africa Committee in 1993.

19. François Burgat, "Bilateral Radicalisation," in *Power-Sharing Islam,* ed. Tamimi, pp. 43–48.

20. An expression used by Tunisian Socialist opposition leader Ibrahim Haider to explain his decision to withdraw from political life.

21. Ernest Gellner, "Marxism and Islam: Failure and Success," in *Power-Sharing Islam,* ed. Tamimi, pp. 33–42.

22. Rachid Ghannouchi, "What Modernity? Our Problem Is Not with Modernity" (paper presented at a symposium entitled "Islam and Democracy in the Arab Maghrib," London School of Economics, February 1992).

23. Refer to the press briefings given by U.S. Assistant Secretary of State Robert Pelletreau and his colleagues to define U.S. policies in the Middle East and North Africa. Concerning the U.S.

administration's reasons for denying Sheikh Rachid Ghannouchi an entry visa to the United States to participate in a seminar at the University of Florida, see, for instance, Mr. Pelletreau's reply to Professor John Esposito in *Middle East Policy*, no. 2 (1994).

24. See the 1994 issues of *Al-Daawah* and *Qadaya Dawliyah*.
25. Burgat, "Bilateral Radicalisation."
26. *Times* (London), 1994.
27. Holy Quran 49:13.
28. Holy Quran 5:2.
29. From a saying by the Prophet, peace be upon him.
30. Holy Quran 3:64.

Contributors

All biographical statements were supplied by the contributors.

Ali Alatas was born November 4, 1932, in Jakarta, Indonesia. He graduated from the Foreign Academy in Jakarta in 1954 and the School of Law, University of Indonesia, in 1956.

Mr. Alatas served in various diplomatic posts abroad, including first secretary in Bangkok, Thailand, and minister counselor in Washington, D.C. Later he served as Indonesia's ambassador and permanent representative to the United Nations in Geneva and then in New York.

Between his diplomatic assignments, he has also served as executive secretary to the vice president of Indonesia. He was appointed as minister of foreign affairs in March 1988 and remains in this position to the present.

Tariq Aziz was born in Mousel, Iraq, in 1936. He completed his elementary and high school education in Baghdad and graduated from the College of Art, English Department, in 1958, at which time he commenced a position as an editor at the newspaper *Al-Jumhuriya*. By 1963 he had risen to the position of editor-in-chief of the newspaper

Al-Jamahir; he was also editor-in-chief of the press for the Arab Ba'ath Socialist Party in Syria until February 1966. By 1967 he had also worked as editor-in-chief for the newspaper *Al-Thawra* for five years.

In April 1972 Mr. Aziz was appointed as a member of the General Affairs Office of the Revolutionary Command Council in addition to his work at *Al-Thawra.* In January 1974 he was elected candidate for the Regional Command of the Arab Ba'ath Socialist Party. Mr. Aziz was appointed minister of information in November 1974.

In January 1977 he was elected member of the Regional Command of the Arab Ba'ath Socialist Party. In September he was appointed member of the Revolutionary Command Council. In October 1977 he was elected member of the National Command of the Arab Ba'ath Socialist Party and excused from his position as minister of information. In November he was appointed executive director of the Board of Al-Thawra House of Publication.

In June 1982 Mr. Aziz was reelected member of the Revolutionary Command Council. In addition to his other duties, Mr. Aziz was appointed minister for foreign affairs in January 1983. In July 1986 he was reelected member in the Regional Command. Mr. Aziz was appointed deputy prime minister in March 1991.

James A. Baker has served in senior government positions under three presidents of the United States. He served in the Bush Administration as the nation's sixty-first secretary of state from January 1989 through August 1992. During his tenure at the State Department, Mr. Baker traveled to ninety foreign countries as the United States confronted the unprecedented challenges and opportunities of the post–Cold War era. Mr. Baker served from 1985 to 1988 as the sixty-seventh secretary of the treasury in the Reagan administration. As treasury secretary, he was also chairman of the President's Economic Policy Council.

Prior to his service as secretary of the treasury, Mr. Baker was President Reagan's White House chief of staff from 1981 to 1985. Mr. Baker's record of public service began in 1975 as President Ford's undersecretary of commerce. It concluded with his service once again as White House chief of staff, this time for President Bush from August 1992 to January 1993. He was, in addition, senior counselor to President Bush for this period.

Long active in U.S. presidential politics, Mr. Baker led presidential campaigns for Presidents Ford, Reagan, and Bush over the course of the last five presidential elections. Mr. Baker is presently a senior partner in the law firm of Baker & Botts. He is honorary chairman of the James A. Baker III Institute for Public Policy at Rice University and serves on the board of the Woodrow Wilson International Center for Scholars and a number of other nonprofit organizations. Mr. Baker was born in Houston, Texas, in 1930.

Benazir Bhutto is the second person to be twice elected, through popular mandate, to the office of prime minister of the Islamic Republic of Pakistan; her father, Zulfiqar Ali Bhutto, was the first. From 1977 to 1988, as leader of the Pakistan People's Party, she struggled for the restoration of democracy in her country, a struggle that symbolized a yearning for the rule of law after a long spell of martial law in the country.

After her party won the general elections of 1988, she formed a government that was dismissed in 1990. From then until 1993 she served as leader of the opposition. In 1993, following her party's victory in that year's general elections, she again became prime minister.

During the first tenure of her premiership, Benazir Bhutto initiated an aggressive program of economic liberalization, which she has successfully carried through her second term. The achievements of her government in the economic field have won praise from such institutions as the World Bank and the International Monetary Fund.

Boutros Boutros-Ghali became the sixth secretary-general of the United Nations on January 1, 1992, when he began a five-year term. At the time of his appointment by the General Assembly on December 3, 1991, he had been Egypt's deputy prime minister for foreign affairs since May 1991 and had served as minister of state for foreign affairs from October 1977 until 1991.

Mr. Boutros-Ghali became a member of the Egyptian Parliament in 1987 and was part of the secretariat of the National Democratic Party from 1980. Until assuming the office of U.N. secretary-general, he was also vice president of the Socialist International.

Fernando Henrique Cardoso was born in Rio de Janeiro on June 18, 1931. He took office as president of Brazil on January 1, 1995, for a four-year term. In the previous government he was finance minister (May 1993–March 1994) and minister of external relations (October 1992–May 1993). He is a founding member of Brazil's Social Democratic Party (PSDB). From 1983 to 1992, he was a senator for the state of São Paulo. During the military regime in Brazil, he lived abroad in exile for several years.

President Cardoso holds a Ph.D. in social sciences from the University of São Paulo. He has held the position of professor of social sciences at that university and at several other academic centers, including the University of California–Berkeley, Université de Paris, Cambridge University, Stanford University, Université de Paris–Nanterre, and Universidad de Chile. He has published numerous books, essays, and articles.

Osama El-Baz was born on July 6, 1931, in Egypt. He graduated in 1952 from Law School at Cairo University. From 1952 to 1956 he worked as an attorney at law. In 1956 he joined the Foreign Service. Consequently, Dr. El-Baz studied from 1961 through 1968 at Harvard Law School for the master's and Ph.D. degrees. In 1975 Dr. El-Baz was appointed director of the Office of the Minister of Foreign Affairs (Ismail Fahmy). In 1978 Dr. El-Baz became director of the Office of the Vice President (Hosni Mubarak). Since 1982 Dr. El-Baz has served as director for political affairs in the Office of the President and first undersecretary of the Foreign Ministry.

Eduardo Frei Ruiz-Tagle was elected president of the Republic of Chile on December 11, 1993, with 57.99 percent of the total vote.

His political career began in 1958, when Mr. Frei joined the Christian Democratic Party. He was a university student leader and actively accompanied his father in the political campaign that led the latter to become president of the republic in 1964.

During the military regime, he was one of the founders and promoters of the Committee for Free Elections, and traveled throughout the country in support of the vote for the "No" in the plebiscite of October 1988.

After his father's death in 1982, Mr. Frei participated in creating the Frei Foundation, a political and academic institution that he directed until April 1993. Meanwhile, he was elected senator for Santiago on December 14, 1989, with the largest majority in the national elections.

In 1991, he was elected president of the Christian Democratic Party, which made him its presidential precandidate in December of the following year. In May 1993, he received 64 percent of the votes in the primary elections of the Coalition of Parties for Democracy.

Mr. Frei graduated from the University of Chile with a degree in civil engineering with a special mention in hydraulics, and he completed a specialized course in administration and management technology in Milan, Italy. From 1969 to 1988, he practiced his profession privately at the firm Sigdo Koppers Engineering S.A. He was born on June 24, 1942.

Alberto Fujimori was born in Lima, Peru, on July 28, 1938. He graduated with honors and a mention of excellence from Lima's Alfonso Ugarte High School. He gained admission in first place to the National Agrarian University of La Molina in 1956 and also graduated in first place in 1961 as an agronomy engineer. He obtained a master's degree in mathematics at the University of Wisconsin in 1969 and holds Honoris Causa doctorates from the Universities of Glebloux, Belgium, and San Martin de Porres, Peru.

In 1962 he began a teaching career in the Mathematics Department of La Molina's Science Faculty, eventually becoming head of both the department and faculty. In 1984 he was chosen dean of La Molina University and he was elected chairman of the National Council of University Deans (1987–1989).

In 1988 he gathered a group of independent professionals and founded the political movement Cambio 90 (Change 90) to run for the 1990 presidential elections. After a first round of voting in April 1990, Alberto Fujimori was chosen president in a runoff between the two leading candidates by a margin of 65 percent to 35 percent. Mr. Fujimori was reelected for a second five-year term in April 1995.

Rachid Al-Ghannouchi is the leader of the Tunisian opposition party An-Nahdah (Renaissance). He was working on his Ph.D. thesis, entitled "Public Liberties in the Islamic State," when he was forced into exile. He was jailed for varying terms during President Bourguiba's era, and in 1987 he was sen-

tenced to life imprisonment, a sentence that
the authorities appealed; a retrial ended with
death sentences for him and three of his followers. He was forced into exile by the present regime after his party was outlawed and
thousands of his followers killed, jailed, or
banished.

Mr. Ghannouchi is considered to be
among the most prominent contemporary
Islamic political thinkers and has published
a number of books (all in Arabic): *We and
the West, Our Way to Civilization, The Islamic Movement and Modernization, The
Woman between the Quran and Society, The
Basic Principles of Democracy and Islamic
Government, The Rights of Citizens in the
Islamic State, Destiny and Man in Ibn
Taymiya's Thought,* and *The Rights of Non-
Muslims in the Islamic State.* His book *Public Liberties in the Islamic Political System*
(the proposed theme of his Ph.D.) has been
published in Arabic, and the English edition
is forthcoming.

Mikhail Sergeyevich Gorbachev was born in
Privolnoye, a village in the Stravropol region
of Russia, on March 2, 1931. He graduated
from Moscow University in 1955 and returned to Stravropol, where he worked until
1979 in Komsomol and Communist Party
organizations.

In 1978 he was elected secretary of the
Central Committee of the Communist Party
of the Soviet Union and in 1985, general secretary. Following the first free elections in
the history of the Soviet Union in 1989, he
was elected chairman of the USSR Supreme Soviet and later president of the So-

viet Union. He resigned that post in December 1991.

He is now president of the International Foundation for Socioeconomic and Political Studies, a research organization based in Moscow, and of Green Cross International, dedicated to environmental concerns.

Kamal Kharrazi is the permanent representative of the Islamic Republic of Iran to the United Nations, a position he has held since 1989.

Mr. Kharrazi has also held a number of other governmental, diplomatic, and academic posts. From July 1980 to September 1989 he was president of the Islamic Republic News Agency. In the meantime he served as a member of the Supreme Defense Council of Iran and the head of the War Information Headquarters from September 1980 to September 1988. He was also a professor of management and educational psychology at Tehran University from 1983 to 1989.

Prior to his service in those posts he served as deputy foreign minister for political affairs from August 1979 to March 1980. From August 1979 to July 1981, Mr. Kharrazi was managing director of the Center for Intellectual Development of Children and Young Adults. He was the vice president for planning and programming of Iranian National Television from March to August 1979. He was also a teaching fellow at the University of Houston in the United States from 1975 to 1976, when he returned to Iran.

Mr. Kharrazi was a founding member of the Islamic Research Institute in London and a member of the American Association of University Professors. He is also a member of the New York Academy of Sciences. He earned a doctorate in education from the University of Houston in 1976. He also holds a master's degree in education from Tehran University, where he received his undergraduate education. He has written and translated a number of textbooks and articles on education and management. Mr. Kharrazi was born in Tehran on December 1, 1944.

Andrei Vladimirovich Kozyrev was born in Brussels on March 27, 1951. His father, an engineer by education, worked at the Foreign Trade Ministry. His mother was an evening-school teacher. Prior to his academic career, Kozyrev worked at Kommunar, a machinery manufacturing plant. In 1974 he graduated from the Moscow Institute of International Relations of the USSR Foreign Ministry.

In diplomatic service he rose from a position as Soviet Foreign Ministry aide to head of the Department of International Organizations. As a member of Soviet delegations, he attended U.N. General Assembly sessions and other international forums. In October 1990 he was appointed foreign minister of the Russian Federation. He is a candidate of history and speaks English, Spanish, and French. In 1991 his book *The World and This Country Mirrored by the UN*, was published. He is also the author of other books on disarmament and the work of international organizations.

Leonid Danylovich Kuchma was born on August 9, 1938, into a farmer's family in the village of Chaikine in the Chernihiv region. In 1960 Mr. Kuchma graduated from Dniepropetrivsk University with a degree in mechanical engineering. Later he obtained his Ph.D. degree in technical sciences.

From 1960 through 1975, Mr. Kuchma worked as an engineer, senior engineer, leading designer, and assistant chief designer at the highly classified Pivdenne design bureau in the city of Dniepropetrivsk and as a technical manager of Baikonur, the main Soviet space launching facility in Kazakhstan. From 1975 to 1982, Mr. Kuchma was secretary of the party organization at Pivdenne, and from 1982 to 1986 he served as the first deputy general designer of the bureau. From 1986 through 1992 he worked as the general director of the world's largest missile factory, Pivdenniy, in Dniepropetrivsk.

Mr. Kuchma was prime minister of Ukraine from October 1992 until September 1993. He has been the president of the Ukrainian Union of Industrialists and Entrepreneurs since December 1993. Mr. Kuchma was elected president of Ukraine in July 1994.

He is also a professor at the Dniepropetrivsk University and a member of the Engineering Academy of Ukraine.

Nelson Rolihlahla Mandela was born in Transkei, South Africa, on July 25, 1918. His father was Chief Henry Mandela of the Tembu tribe. Mr. Mandela himself was educated at University College of Fort Hare and the University of Witwatersrand and qualified in law in 1942. He joined the African National Congress in 1944 and was engaged in resistance against the ruling National

Party's apartheid policies after 1948. He went on trial for treason in 1956–1961 and was acquitted in 1961.

After the banning of the ANC in 1960, Mr. Mandela argued for the setting up of a military wing within the ANC. In 1961 the ANC executive considered his proposal, and this led to the formation of Umkhonto we Sizwe. Mr. Mandela was arrested in 1962 and sentenced to five years' imprisonment with hard labor. In 1963, when many fellow leaders of the ANC and the Umkhonto we Sizwe were arrested, Mr. Mandela was brought to stand trial with them for plotting to overthrow the government by violence. His statement from the dock received considerable international publicity. On June 12, 1964, eight of the accused, including Mr. Mandela, were sentenced to life imprisonment. From 1964 to 1982 he was incarcerated at Robben Island Prison off Cape Town; thereafter he was at Pollsmoor Prison as well as Victor Verster on the mainland.

During his years in prison Nelson Mandela's reputation grew steadily. He was widely accepted as the most significant black leader in South Africa and became a potent symbol of resistance as the anti-apartheid movement gathered strength. He consistently refused to compromise his political position to obtain his freedom.

Mr. Mandela was released on February 18, 1990. After his release he plunged himself wholeheartedly into his life's work, striving to attain the goals he and others had set out almost four decades earlier. In 1991, at the first national conference of the ANC held inside South Africa after the organization had been banned in 1960, he was elected president of the ANC while his lifelong friend and colleague, Oliver Tambo, became the organization's national chairperson. On May 10, 1994, Nelson R. Mandela became the first democratically elected president of South Africa.

Nursultan Abishevich Nazarbayev was elected president of the newly independent state of the Republic of Kazakhstan by popular vote in December 1991, shortly after the Kazakhstan Soviet Socialist Republic declared its sovereignty.

In 1990 Mr. Nazarbayev's government positions in the Kazakhstan Soviet Socialist Republic included the following: president of the Kazakhstan Soviet Socialist Republic; chairman of the Supreme Soviet of Kazakhstan; member of the Supreme Soviet of the USSR; and member of the Federation Council of the USSR. From 1984 to 1989, he was chairman of the Council of Ministers of the Kazakhstan Soviet Socialist Republic of the former USSR.

From 1969 to 1984, Mr. Nazarbayev devoted his efforts to economic development in the Karaganda Oblast. He has a Ph.D. degree in economic science and a B.S. degree in metallurgy. Mr. Nazarbayev was born in June 1940.

Olusegun Obasanjo was born on May 5, 1937 at Abeokuta, Ogun State, in a Yoruba family. He was educated at the Baptist High School, Abeokuta. He joined the army in 1958 and was commissioned as an officer in 1959. He was promoted to lieutenant in 1960 and served with the U.N. force in the Congo. He later joined the engineering unit of the Nigerian army. He was promoted to captain in 1963 and became its commander. He was promoted to lieutenant-colonel in 1967 and served as commander of the Ibadan Garrison from October 1967 to May 1969. After a promotion to colonel, he commanded the Third Infantry Division, then the Third Marine Commando Division, operating on the southeastern front of Biafra during the Nigerian civil war. He accepted the surrender of the Biafran forces in January 1970.

After the war he resumed command of the Engineering Corps. He was promoted to brigadier in October 1972. He was appointed federal commissioner for works by General Gowon and served in that capacity from January to July of 1975. He served as Supreme Headquarters chief of staff from July 1975 to February 1976 and was promoted to lieutenant-general in January 1976.

On February 13, 1976, after the assassination of Murtala Muhammed, he took over, somewhat reluctantly, as head of state of Africa's most populous state, as he was the most senior military officer. His task was to return the country to civilian rule by 1979 and to use its burgeoning oil wealth to the best effect. He followed the policy already established by Muhammed of returning the country to civilian rule by October 1979, when he handed over power to the new civilian government under Shehu Shagari after thirteen years of military government.

He subsequently retired from the army, returned to his farm at Abeokuta, and took up academic work at the University of Ibadan. He remains one of his country's most senior statesmen in international forums. On March 13, 1995, General Obasanjo was arrested by the military and accused of plotting against the regime under the current general-in-charge, Sani Abacha, because of his support for a return to civilian rule. General Obasanjo has since been sentenced to life imprisonment.

Muammar Abu Minyar El-Qadhafi was born in the Sirt Desert in 1942. He attended elementary school in the town of Sirt, then moved to the city of Sabha, the capital of the province of Fazzan in the south of Libya where he attended high school. It was there that his revolutionary spirit began to show. Conditions then prevailing in Libya as well as in the rest of the Arab world were a source of discontent and resentment for the young Qadhafi. He was an ardent admirer of the late Egyptian president Gamal Abdel Nasser, in whom he found his role model.

He soon found out that other southern Libyan students harbored the same revolutionary spirit as his, and with them he formed a secret revolutionary movement called the Free Unionists Movement, devoted to the Nasserite concepts of freedom, socialism, and unity and working toward a revolution in Libya that would free it from the rule of King Idriss Alsanoussi, who was attached to the West; from all the foreign military bases — namely, the U.S. Wheelus base in Tripoli and the British base of Aladam in Tobruk; and from the last vestiges of the fascist Italian community, which was in control of the whole Libyan economy.

Muammar El-Qadhafi's revolutionary ideas and activity led to his expulsion from high school, and they also earned him the ire of the local government, which grew impatient with that young rebel. He then went to the Libyan coastal city of Misrata, where he graduated from high school. In 1963 he joined the military academy at Benghazi, graduating in 1965 with the rank of first lieutenant, and was assigned to the signal battalion. In 1966 he was sent to England to attend a training course.

Upon his return to Libya, he continued exerting extraordinary efforts in recruiting students of the military academy. When he found that he had enough numbers to carry out the revolution, he ordered the free officers to start moving by the dawn of September 1, 1969. Colonel Qadhafi broadcast from Radio Benghazi the first communiqué of the revolution, in which he declared the fall of the monarchic regime and the establishment of a republic. He then formed the revolution command council under his leadership and another eleven members of the Free Unionist Officers Movement.

Fidel V. Ramos was inaugurated as the twelfth president of the Republic of the Philippines on June 30, 1992, following his victory in the May 1992 elections.

Before his election, he served for some forty years in the military and government. While Armed Forces of the Philippines chief of staff (1986–1988) and defense secretary (1988–1991) under the Aquino government, he successfully led the defense of the country's newly regained democracy from seven coup attempts. Upon inauguration in June 1992, President Ramos launched a wide-ranging program of reform that seeks to end various internal conflicts in the country, establish honest and effective government, and retain double-digit economic growth.

Mr. Ramos graduated from the U.S. Military Academy at West Point in 1950. He also holds three master's degrees — in business administration from the Ateneo de Manila University in 1980, in civil engineering from the University of Illinois in 1951, and in national security administration from the National Defense College of the Philippines in 1969.

Mr. Ramos was born on March 18, 1928, in Lingayen, Pangasinan.

Pamulaparti Venkata Narasimha Rao was

sworn in as the ninth prime minister of India on June 21, 1991. He was born on June 28, 1921, in Vangara in the Karimnagar district of Andhra Pradesh. He was educated at Osmania University, Hyderabad, Bombay University, and Nagpur University, and holds bachelor's degrees in science and law.

Mr. Rao entered into public life as a student at the impressionable age of fifteen, like many others during the freedom struggle. He started in the Vande Mataram movement, launched by students at Osamania University against the discriminatory attitude of the then Nizam's government. He also became a part of the agitation launched by the Hyderabad State Congress under the leadership of Swami Ramananda Tirtha. He continued his studies, however, with short breaks and obtained his law degree from

Nagpur University. After a short spell of practice in Hyderabad High Court, he was drawn into the lawyers' agitation and later became a full-fledged Congress worker. He rose quickly in the Congress ranks and eventually became the general secretary of the All India Congress Committee.

He was a member of the Andhra Pradesh Legislative Assembly for twenty years (1957–1977) and a minister in the Andhra Pradesh government from 1962 to 1971. He served as the chief minister of the state during 1971 and 1973. He was elected to the parliament in March 1977. In the 1980 general elections he was reelected from Hanamkonda (Andhra Pradesh) and in December 1984 and November 1989 he returned to the Lok Sabha from the Ramtek constituency in Maharashtra.

He has served as minister of external affairs (January 1980–July 1984, June 1988–December 1989); home affairs (July 1984–December 1984); defense (December 1984–September 1985); human resource development (September 1985–June 1988); and health and family welfare (July 1986–February 1988).